ProfScam

ProfScam:

PROFESSORS AND THE DEMISE OF HIGHER EDUCATION

Charles J. Sykes

Regnery Gateway
Washington, D.C.

Library of Congress Cataloging-in-Publication Data

Sykes, Charles J., 1954–
    ProfScam : professors and the demise of higher education / by
Charles J. Sykes.
        p.   cm.
    Bibliography: p.
    Includes index.
    ISBN 0-89526-559-1 : $18.95
    1. Education, Higher—United States.   2. College teachers—United
States—Attitudes.   I. Title.
LA227.3.S94 1988   88-21942
378.73—dc19   CIP

Published in the United States by Regnery Gateway
1130 17th Street, NW, Washington, DC 20036

and by Reardon & Walsh (a division of Summit Press Syndicate)
4028 N. Richland, Milwaukee, WI 53211

Distributed to the trade by Kampmann & Company, Inc.
9 E 40th Street, New York, NY 10016

10   9   8   7   6   5   4   3   2   1

Dedicated to Professor Jay G. Sykes (1922–1985), author, curmudgeon, journalist, lawyer, politician, anti-hero, father, mentor, friend—and teacher extraordinaire.

Acknowledgments

I am deeply indebted to the many individuals, both inside and outside of academe, who offered me their counsel, encouragement, and wisdom. I am especially grateful to Professors Phillip Anderson, Fred Gottheil, David Berkman, William Rau, Paul Baker, Stanislav Andreski, and Serge Lang; as well as to Walter Stewart, Lawrence Mann, and the many others who gave me the benefit of their time and experience. Some were kind enough to provide me with their unpublished manuscripts, which often proved invaluable.

This project arose out of an article that my late father, Jay G. Sykes, wrote in 1985 for a magazine that I then edited. Titled "The Sorcerers and the 7½ Hour Week," it drew upon his experiences over nearly two decades in academia. It presented a devastating indictment of his professional colleagues. So devastating, in fact, that the official spokesman for the university at which he taught later publicly criticized the magazine for daring to publish the article at all. Outside of university circles, however, the reaction was far different, and far more enthusiastic. In that piece, my father said what many others, apparently, had been thinking for a long time. His article was the inspiration and the foundation of this book, and—I should acknowledge here—some passages in the following pages are drawn in whole or in part from that article (all are identified in the endnotes). My father was never one to suffer fools; and the culture of the American professor was custom-made for his pen. I am deeply indebted to his sharp-eyed and sardonic analysis of academia in all of its absurdity. I would like to think that this book is a reasonably close approximation of the book he would have written had he lived.

Even so, this project would never have been possible without the encouragement of my editor, Pat Reardon, who never wavered in his conviction that the American professor was fertile ground for muckraking. It was he who suggested the idea of a book in the first place; and it was his constant nagging that made it a reality. I would also like to express special appreciation to Harry Crocker, Editor at Regnery Gateway, for excellent advice, extremely helpful suggestions, and encouraging support.

But my deepest thanks go to my wife, Diane, and daughter, Sandy, who provided me with their support, their faith, and their love; and to my mother Katherine, who worked tirelessly searching through the darkest corners of university libraries for academic outrages. For the tedious months she spent wading through literally hundreds of thousands of words of profspeak, I can make no recompense except my gratitude.

Contents

PROFSCAM

1 *The Indictment*

H. L. MENCKEN had a simple plan for reforming American higher education. He suggested that anyone who really wanted to improve the universities should start by burning the buildings and hanging the professors. [1]

It's easy, of course, to dismiss Mencken's prescription as frivolous, lacking the ponderous gravity that afflicts debates about higher education. And surely stringing up a few professors of sociology, chemistry, and French, along with the stray expert in Chaucerian verse, is hardly a serious or humane reform program, entertaining as it might be for the undergraduates.

But Mencken's plan did something the hosts of critics and would-be reformers before and after him have failed to do: It went directly to the rot at the heart of the university. In recent years, dozens of commissions, foundations, and free-lance pathologists have conducted endless post-mortems on higher education: the decline of humanities, the fragmentation of the curriculum, the pathetic state of teaching, and the boggling price tag on the universities' tapestry of failure.

And predictably, they have rounded up the usual suspects: the students themselves, television, the federal government, capitalism, public grade schools and high schools, teenage sex, German philosophers Nietzsche and Heidegger, and, for good measure, the Walkman radio. So far they all have missed the mark.

3

Mencken, writing more than 80 years ago, with his usual directness, identified the real villain of the piece: the American university professor.

Mencken caught the flavor of the New Academic when he wrote: "The professor must be an obscurantist or he is nothing. He has a special unmatchable talent for dullness; his central aim is not to expose the truth clearly but to exhibit his profundity—in brief, to stagger the sophomores and other professors."[2]

With only minor updating (the modern professors would rather have root-canal work than spend time with any undergraduates), Mencken's analysis remains on target. The professoriate has multiplied in the years since Mencken's analysis even beyond his grimmest nightmares. The result is a modern university distinguished by costs that are zooming out of control; curriculums that look like they were designed by a game show host; nonexistent advising programs; lectures of droning, mind-numbing dullness often to 1,000 or more semi-anonymous undergraduates herded into dilapidated, ill-lighted lecture halls; teaching assistants who can't speak understandable English; and the product of this all, a generation of expensively credentialed college graduates who might not be able to locate England on a map.

In the midst of this wasteland stands the professor.

Almost single-handedly, the professors—working steadily and systematically—have destroyed the university as a center of learning and have desolated higher education, which no longer is higher or much of an education.

The story of the collapse of American higher education is the story of the rise of the professoriate. No understanding of the academic disease is possible without an understanding of the Academic Man, this strange mutation of 20th-century academia who has the pretensions of an ecclesiastic, the artfulness of a witch doctor, and the soul of a bureaucrat.

His greatest triumph has been the creation of an academic culture that is one of society's most outrageous and elaborate frauds. It is replete with the pieties, arcane rituals, rites of passage, and dogmas of a secular faith. It also has an intimidating and mysterious argot (best described as "profspeak") and a system of perks and privileges that would put the most hidebound bureaucrat to shame. Ultimately, the academic culture represents a sort of modern-day alchemy in which mumbo-jumbo is transformed into gold, or, in this case, into research grants, consulting contracts, sabbaticals, and inflated salaries.

Professors have convinced society that this culture is essential for higher learning, and have thus been able to protect their own status and independence while cheating students, parents, tax payers, and employers, and polluting the intellectual inheritance of society. Over the last 50 years, this academic culture has secured professors almost ironclad job security and the freedom to do whatever they like—and to do it well or poorly—or to do nothing at all.

A bill of indictment for the professors' crimes against higher education would be lengthy. Here is a partial one:

- They are overpaid, grotesquely underworked, and the architects of academia's vast empires of waste.
- They have abandoned their teaching responsibilities and their students. To the average undergraduate, the professoriate is unapproachable, uncommunicative, and unavailable.
- In pursuit of their own interests—research, academic politicking, cushier grants—they have left the nation's students in the care of an ill-trained, ill-paid, and bitter academic underclass.
- They have distorted university curriculums to accommodate their own narrow and selfish interests rather than the interests of their students.
- They have created a culture in which bad teaching goes unnoticed and unsanctioned and good teaching is penalized.
- They insist that their obligations to research justify their flight from the college classroom despite the fact that fewer than one in ten ever makes any significant contribution to their field. Too many—maybe even a vast majority—spend

their time belaboring tiny slivers of knowledge, utterly without redeeming social value except as items on their resumes.

- They have cloaked their scholarship in stupefying, inscrutable jargon. This conceals the fact that much of what passes for research is trivial and inane.

- In tens of thousands of books and hundreds of thousands of journal articles, they have perverted the system of academic publishing into a scheme that serves only to advance academic careers and bloat libraries with masses of unread, unreadable, and worthless pablum.

- They have twisted the ideals of academic freedom into a system in which they are accountable to no one, while they employ their own rigid methods of thought control to stamp out original thinkers and dissenters.

- In the liberal arts, the professors' obsession with trendy theory—which is financially rewarding—has transformed the humanities into models of inhumanity and literature departments into departments of illiteracy.

- In the social sciences, professors have created cults of pseudo-science packed with what one critic calls "sorcerers clad in the paraphernalia of science . . . wooly-minded lost souls yearning for gurus,"[3] more concerned with methodology and mindless quantification than with addressing any significant social questions.

- In the sciences, professors have mortgaged the nation's scientific future and its economic competitiveness to their own self-interest by ignoring undergraduates and an epidemic of academic fraud.

- In schools of education, their disdain for teaching and the arrogance with which they treat their students has turned the universities into the home office of educational mediocrity, poisoning the entire educational system from top to bottom.

- They have constructed machinery that so far has frustrated or sabotaged every effort at meaningful reform that might interfere with their boondoggle.
- Finally, it has been the professors' relentless drive for advancement that has turned American universities into vast factories of junkthink, the byproduct of academe's endless capacity to take even the richest elements of civilization and disfigure them into an image of itself.

The extent of the professors' success in imposing their culture on the university should really not be surprising. Professors, after all, control everything that matters in the universities.

"Their authority in academic matters is absolute," declared the U.S. Supreme Court in a 1980 case.[4] "They decide what courses will be offered, when they will be scheduled, and to whom they will be taught. They debate and determine teaching methods, grading policies, and matriculation standards. They effectively decide which students will be admitted, retained, and graduated. On occasion their views have determined the size of the student body, the tuition to be charged, and the location of a school. . . . To the extent the industrial analogy applies, *the faculty determines within each school the product to be produced, the terms upon which it will be offered, and the customers who will be served.*"

The modern university—insatiable, opportunistic, and implacably anti-intellectual—is created in the image of the *Professorus Americanus.* Today, the professor is the university.

The modern professoriate bears little resemblance to the rumpled, forgetful, impractical academics of popular imagination. In the years since World War II, the profession has changed radically. The modern academic is mobile, self-interested, and without loyalty to institutions or the values of liberal education. The rogue professors of today are not merely obscurantists. They are politicians and entrepreneurs who fiercely protect their turf and shrewdly hustle research cash while they peddle their talents to rival universities, businesses, foundations, or government.

But when it comes to the decline of American higher education, they have been remarkably successful in diverting attention from themselves and assigning blame elsewhere. Yet the impact of their scam on their customers has been devastating.

- For students, it has meant watered–down courses; unqual- ified instructors; a bachelor's degree of dubious value; and an outrageous bill for spending four or five years in a ghetto of appalling intellectual squalor and mediocrity.

- For parents who pay college costs (especially those who chose a school because they thought their children would actually study at the feet of its highly touted faculty), it has meant one of the biggest cons in history.

- For American business, it has meant hiring a generation of college graduates who are often unable to write a coherent sentence, analyze even simple problems, or understand why their elders keep talking about a *Second* World War (was there a First?).

- And for American society—which has picked up the tab for hundreds of thousands of literary scholars, social workers, sociologists, economists, political scientists, psychologists, anthropologists, and educationists—it has meant the re- alization that we are not discernibly more literate, more competent, more economically secure, safer, wiser, or saner than we were before spending untold billions on this embarrassment of academic riches.

The following chapters will detail this bill of indictment. They will trace the process by which the professors seized control of higher learning; what they have done with that power; the cruci- fixion of teaching within the academy; the sabotage of the curricu- lum and efforts to reform higher education; the bizarre world of academic research and publishing; the professoriate's self-serving distortion of academic freedom; and the corruption of the social sciences, humanities, and sciences by the professoriate's crass academic careerism. Finally, this book will describe what might be the last option available to break the tyranny of the academic culture—and the professors—over the nation's universities, intel- lectual life, and ultimately, its future.

2 *The Rise of the Professor*

What rough beast. . . .

WERE William Shakespeare somehow to materialize now and apply for a job at one of our leading universities, he would probably get a letter along the lines of:

"Dear Mr. Shakespeare:
   "We are indeed pleased to have your application to teach Beginning Drama in our English Department, but unfortunately we find serious gaps in your credentials. Your letter does not indicate that you have received either a master's or doctoral degree from any accredited institution of higher learning.
   "Although you have submitted copies of several of your publications, including *King Lear* and *Macbeth*, you have failed to offer evidence that any of them has ever been published in any scholarly journal, and you have not submitted any source notes. . . ."

Shakespeare, quite simply, would lack the credentials to win entry to the closed guild of the modern university. Talent, imagination, and creativity simply won't cut it. But those qualities can be cured. The success of academia in beating young and callow minds into the plowshares of scholarship remains the wonder of the American university. Every year, through rites of initiation that have grown from their early simplicity into models of baroque ritual, the universities succeed in taking young men and women of

9

broad and catholic tastes, still brimming with intellectual curiosity, and molding them into people who write:

- "Effects of a Signal of Timeout From One Reinforcer on
  Human Operant Behavior Maintained by Another Rein-
  forcer."
- "The Facilitation of Preschoolers' Verbal Responding by
  Attachment Objects: The Influence of Mothers, Fathers,
  and Security Blankets Upon Projective Testing."
- "The Effects of Operant Control on Disruptive Behavior
  During Swimming Instruction."
- "Evaluating Judgments of Aspects of Life as a Function of
  Vicarious Exposure to the Hedonically Negative."[1]

A few skeptics may doubt the value to college students of their
professor's analysis of disruptive swimming or the danger of negative hedonism. But such knowledge is the key to entering academia. Simon O'Toole, the pseudonymous author of *Confessions
of an American Scholar*, describes the gradual process of academ-
ization in his own field: "The adolescent begins by liking literature, by thinking he will write novels and poetry, by lacking an
appetite for science, by having an urge to make the world better
. . . by wanting to avoid work. Graduate school happens to him;
then teaching; then scholarship."[2]

The story of how Academic Man secured this throttlehold over
the universities is a remarkable tale that begins well before the
turn of the century. It goes a long way toward explaining many of
the more troubling paradoxes of academic life: why professors
who are ostensibly paid to teach are instead trained to research,
why professors who publish are rewarded with tenure while those
who star in the classroom often find themselves unemployed, why
the modern university president seems so impotent and pathetic
in his dealings with his underlings, and why universities seem so
immune from reform.

Part of the explanation lies in the structure of the university.
Depending on your point of view, the university is either like a
vast medieval-style corporation or . . . Woodstock. On paper, its

lines of authority seem clear enough. The university is gilded with the full panoply of power associated with more traditional organizations: On top sits a president, with a salary and perquisites that normally accompany great power; below the president are chancellors, vice chancellors, a pride of vice presidents of various denominations and suitably vague responsibilities, a whole assortment of provosts, deans, and department chairs and, at the very bottom, a fractious and improvident faculty.

But despite the elaborate pyramid, universities are notoriously unruly. The organizational charts are for outside consumption only. Internally, the real distribution of power is an inverted pyramid, with all the most important powers concentrated not at the top, but at the bottom, tightly held and jealously guarded by the professors themselves.

This is a fact of life well understood by university presidents, if by no one else. In fact, the modern university can be defined in part by the type of person at the top. The most trenchant portrait of the academic personality remains Randall Jarrell's 1952 novel, *Pictures from an Institution,* in which the new breed of academic administrator is embodied in the person of Dwight Robbins, the president of fictional Benton College. On any conceivable subject, Jarrell wrote, Robbins "believed what it was expedient for the president of Benton College to believe. You looked at the two beliefs, and lo! the two were one." Robbins "loved to say to you, putting himself in your hands: 'I know I'm sticking my neck out, but . . .' How ridiculous! President Robbins had no neck."[3]

The modern neckless successors to Dwight Robbins are, above all, men and women who never, ever, no matter how inflammatory their rhetoric might sound to untrained ears, challenge the core values of academia. When a vacancy occurs, the search for a modern university president is a laborious process, involving an exhaustive, in-depth national hunt for candidates with genuine leadership skills, strong convictions, and commitment to reform—and then eliminating them.

University presidents are often accused, unfairly, of being unable to make decisions. But the reality is much simpler: Fundamentally, they are impotent figureheads; they sit atop a structure that is girded about with the privileges and prerogatives of the professoriate. Faculty members are locked in place through tenure, and they wield the moral authority of "academic freedom" like a mighty engine of destruction. No reform can be implemented without the consent of the faculty, because the professors can simply refuse to do anything they don't like. No administrator would dare venture the slightest intervention into the classrooms of the professors.

One study, based on interviews with more than 700 college and university presidents, concluded that *only 2 percent* were "fully involved and play a central role in academic life." Fewer than one in five played even a substantial role.[4]

But academia is not an anarchic free-for-all. The administration might be largely impotent, but there are centers of power and authority, focused not in the administrative hierarchies but in the disciplines themselves. In effect, they make up a shadow university. Unlike the formal university, they are neither formal in structure nor geographically limited to any single campus. Although the university's formal structure is vertical, the real structure of academia is horizontal. Simply put, a professor of economics at University A is more tightly bound to a fellow economist at University B than to the deans and chancellors at his own school.

The disciplines can be thought of as academic villages, complete with elders, wise men, and elaborate rituals of initiation and ostracism. They communicate through journals, conferences, books, papers, monographs, as well as through peer review committees, professional organizations, and the formal reviews of grant applications. And although they have no official hierarchy, they control the informal hierarchy of status, reputation, and prestige.

To understand the nature of this power, it is important to understand the intensity of the professoriate's longing for recognition, acceptance, and honor. No 12-year-old is more caste-haunted or tortured by the desire for the approval of peers than the average American academic.*

* "The psychological damage wrought by this incessant struggle for status is enormous just because of the extraordinary power of these institutions to confer

No matter what image they might present to the outside world, an ingrained sycophancy is at the heart of the professors' culture. No peasant furiously tugging on his forelock as his seignior passes reflects the soul of feudalism as enthusiastically as a junior professor in the presence of his betters. If absolute power corrupts absolutely, academic power tends to corrupt absurdly. One of the inevitable signs of academic prosperity is an invitation to deliver papers to conventions of one's peers, a ritual in which professors bore other professors by reading aloud obscure products of their research.

Whenever the sociologists, or political scientists, or the members of the Modern Language Association gather, the lobbies of convention hotels are filled with various versions of the academic cluster: a senior, tenured professor, surrounded by eager, fawning junior profs and graduate students, vying with one another in ingratiating themselves and showing off their trendy terminology. In bars and elevators, eyes flit furtively to name tags, and reactions are carefully calibrated to the ranking of the bearer's school in the discipline.

Local deans or university presidents have no power to dispense the easing balm to the professor in the grips of prestige envy; only peers within the disciplines control the taps of publication, which lead to tenure and promotion. Those peers have the power to send recalcitrant academics into exile and oblivion. Despite the average professor's tendency to liberalism and broad-mindedness and his or her eager egalitarianism in political and social matters, the realities and taboos of the academic hierarchy are burned into the heart of every academic. No matter how often academics talk

---

prestige," writes author Paul Fussell. "The number of hopes blasted and hearts broken for status reasons is probably greater in the world of colleges and universities than anywhere else. . . . I've never actually known a college teacher who killed himself or others because he lost status by not being retained at a 'most selective' institution and had to move to a 'highly selective' or merely 'very selective' one. But I've known many college teachers thus ruined by shame and convictions of inadequacy, who thenceforth devoted their lives to social envy and bitterness rather than wit and scholarship. . . ." (*The New Republic*, October 4, 1982)

about democratization, pluralism, and diversity, none would be so foolish as to think that a doctorate from Northern Iowa State is equivalent to one from Stanford, or that a professor from Memphis State is the equal of a professor from Harvard. Ultimately, it is the villages that decide who will practice scholarship at the pinnacles of prestige—Berkeley or Yale or Michigan—and who will nurse their disgrace in the teachers' colleges of western Colorado. From the perspective of a single campus, the influence of the villages is nearly invisible, but their control over the universities is absolute, unchallenged, and often ruthlessly enforced.

The German Invasion

The rise of the academic villages at the expense of the universities began in the middle of the 19th century. Indeed, the fight for the soul of academia really was lost even before the turn of the century. The first stirring of change in the breast of the American professor was inspired by the example of the new German university. While the American and English universities emphasized a traditional approach to the passing on of knowledge—characterized by John Henry Cardinal Newman as the development of the "real cultivation of mind"—the German universities seemed to be daring pioneers on the frontiers of knowledge. The Germans were building universities not centered on educating callow undergraduates but on the creation of knowledge through research. The father of the German academy, Wilhelm von Humboldt, had declared: "The teacher no longer serves the purposes of the student. Instead, they both serve learning itself."[5] In the musty halls of 19th-century academia, where the new scientific spirit was beginning to burn, Humboldt's creed rang like a thrilling call to independence.

The German ideal made its first landing in force with the founding of Johns Hopkins University in Baltimore as an institution that specifically gave pride of place to research rather than teaching. From the very beginning, the image of the professor as "teacher" was overshadowed by the professor as creator of knowledge or "scientist." In the early days, the model of the professor as scholar-teacher was merely lacking in tone; later it would be swept aside by the avalanche of emoluments, honors, and money held out for the scholar-researcher.*

The new model of the academic as knowledge creator spread rapidly through the universities. By 1909, even athletic directors and coaches took their new academic respectability so seriously that they began to gather to read "research" reports to one another.[6] It also changed the way professors taught. The focus was now on teaching not the unwashed generalist but only the elect, the new breed of academic specialist. Elijah P. Harris, a German-trained chemist at Amherst, ushered in the new era by intentionally making his lectures incomprehensible to undergraduates. His argument was that the gifted students who had a genuine vocation for chemistry would approach him after class.[7]

The doctor of philosophy degree, with its narrow focus on research skills and hyperspecialization, was both the symbol of the change and its instrument. The traditional goal of the university had been the well-rounded graduate. But the new academy's mission was the creation of specialists—the more technical the better. The academy had rejected the Renaissance Man and replaced him with the specialist, whose glory was to have tightly grasped in his fists his very own sliver of knowledge.

The doctoral dissertation was the perfect vehicle for the shaping of this new breed of professor. Instead of insisting that would-be professors extend the range and breadth of their learning, the new academy insisted that the Ph.D. candidate choose a subject of exquisite narrowness and produce 100 or 200 pages of detailed research. No matter how tiny or insignificant it might be, it was now his admission ticket.

But most important of all, the requirement of the Ph.D. dissertation represented a subtle but crucial shift in emphasis. Where doing research had once been considered valuable because it helped a professor teach a subject better, research was now an end

* In 1987, Johns Hopkins got more than $465 million in federal research aid, more than any other American university and more than twice the second leading recipient, the Massachusetts Institute of Technology.

in itself. And only the dimmest of Ph.D. candidates could fail to get the message.

Philosopher William James fought a gallant, rear-guard action, warning that the Ph.D. was an octopus that would strangle the academy. In 1884, only 19 of Harvard's 189 professors possessed the doctor of philosophy degree. But within a decade the rise of the Ph.D. was almost complete. By 1905, the degree that James had labelled "the Mandarin disease" and "a sham, a bauble, a dodge whereby to decorate the catalogues of schools and colleges," was declared mandatory even by the University of Illinois (which was then both academically and geographically far in the outback) for anyone aspiring to the rank of professor.[8] Henceforth anyone who wanted to teach would be trained to research. This *non sequitur* at the heart of academia's fascination with the Ph.D. did not go unnoticed.

"There are persons at present," said Irving Babbitt in 1908, "who do not believe that a man is fitted to fill a chair of French literature in an American college simply because he has made a critical study of the text of a dozen medieval beast fables and written a thesis on the Picard dialect, and who deny that a man is necessarily qualified to interpret the humanities to American undergraduates because he has composed a dissertation on the use of the present participle in Ammianus Marcellinus."[9] But he was in a distinct minority.

By 1918, Thorstein Veblen could complain in *The Higher Learning in America* that the universities had fallen into "scholastic accountancy," an earlier version of what was to become known as "publish or perish." And in 1923, Upton Sinclair derided universities for devoting their resources to preparing "for mankind full data on 'The Strong Verb in Chaucer' " and "making it possible for mankind to acquire exact knowledge concerning 'The Beginnings of the Epistolary Novel in the Romance Languages. . . .' "[10]

By the turn of the century, professors at the better schools were already being judged by their scholarly "productivity" rather than their teaching ability. Inevitably, competition between schools became a matter of comparing the publication records of their faculties. As publications became more important, influence inevitably shifted from the formal hierarchies of the universities to the disciplines themselves. After all, only professors of economics were qualified to really judge the scholarship of a fellow specialist. As specialization begot subspecialization and grandfathered microspecialization, the ability of outsiders to venture any judgment eroded to the point where the prestige mechanisms of academia rested solely with the specialists themselves. When professors declared that So and So's department was a good one or that Professor X was doing good work, they were not, of course, talking about his methods in the classroom. They were judging him solely on his published work.

In issuing his call for the new research academy, Humboldt had insisted that the new emphasis on research would in no way detract from the teaching mission of the universities. University teaching, he wrote, "is not so irksome that it need interrupt— indeed it may rather benefit scholarly leisure."[11] Humboldt thus joined the long line of educational theorists who never had a chance to see the damage their fallacies wrought upon the world.

By 1930, the new vogue of specialization had penetrated into every conceivable discipline. Abraham Flexner, an early reformer, found innumerable tracks of the new Academic Man across the blighted landscape of academia. Proto-Educationists (who would become familiar figures to later generations) were already turning out doctoral theses on subjects like: "The Equipment of the School Theater," ". . . Janitor Service in Elementary Schools," and "The Experience Variables: A Study of the Variable Factors in Experience Contributing to the Formation of Personality." The last one was a study of the social background and activities of education students. It applied painstaking scientific methodology in determining whether the teacher-trainee came from a home with a lawn mower, a desk set, a rag carpet, a built-in bookcase, potted plants, or company dishes. Among the leisure activities investigated were shopping, "heart-to-heart talks," sitting alone, going to picnics, "idle conversation," dates, "telling jokes," "teasing somebody," and "doing almost anything so you are one with the gang." At the University of Chicago, Flexner found a master's thesis on "A Time and Motion Comparison of Four Methods of Dishwashing."[12]

Flexner had won international fame for his 1910 study that led to the wholesale reform of medical education in the United States. But by 1930, the trends in the universities themselves were already flaming out of control. By 1936, Robert Maynard Hutchins, the young president of the University of Chicago, said the American university had come to "approximate a kindergarten at one end and a clutter of specialists at the other . . . and the process has carried with it surprising losses in general intelligibility."[13]

The Post-War Boom

Before World War II, despite the changes in the academy, traditional values and public expectations still weighed heavily on the shoulders of the professoriate yearning to breathe the bracing winds of freedom long enjoyed by their European brethren. (The fact that the German universities had cravenly capitulated to the Nazis seemed to dissuade no one from following their blueprint for the new university.)

In 1940, mass higher education would have been regarded as little more than an absurd contradiction in terms. College was for an intellectual and economic elite, and that assumption was seldom challenged. Universities with 10,000 or more students were unusual and considered unwieldy academic behemoths, more to be deplored than emulated. There were only 110,000 faculty members nationwide, and the total bill for higher education came to only about $700 million.[14] The changes that were about to burst upon the universities were generally unplanned, unforeseen, and often unwanted. But they were also irresistible.

The G.I. Bill brought the biggest surprise of all. One administrator predicted that no more than 150,000 veterans would attend college in any year. But by the fall of 1946, one million veterans were enrolled, and they represented less than half the total that would take advantage of the free tuition, monthly allowances, and fees the federal government had promised in the naive expectation that only a small percentage of vets would take them up on it.

"Almost overnight," one historian comments, "the GI Bill changed our ideas about who should go to college."[15]

The flood of veterans into the universities had a ripple effect, influencing friends, relatives, even acquaintances, and raising expectations throughout society. By the end of the 1960s, the number of graduate students alone would exceed the total number of undergraduates in 1940. By the late 1980s, the number of institutions of higher education would almost double, the number of students would increase eightfold, and the cost would exceed $120 billion.[16]

In an age of optimism and growth, American society seized on higher education as a potent instrument of social change and economic transformation. In 1947, a commission appointed by President Truman captured the mood of the moment with this declaration: "Every citizen, youth, and adult should be enabled to and encouraged to carry his education, formal and informal, as far as his native capacities permit." It set the goal of doubling enrollments by 1960.[17]

When the Soviets shocked Americans in 1957 with the launch of Sputnik, the federal government turned again to the universities, just as President Franklin Roosevelt had in World War II for the development of the atomic bomb.

Instead of creating separate new labs, the government created vast new research capabilities in the heart of higher education. By 1947, government spending for research at colleges and universities was *three times* the combined income of all institutions of higher education in 1941. "With no official policy toward higher education," notes one chronicler, "the federal government had become the largest single supporter of the nation's higher education system."[18]

In 1958, the National Defense Education Act was passed, and the government for the first time began giving direct aid to students who were not veterans. Federal support for science and math grew exponentially. When the Kennedy administration took office in 1961, it was also eager to tap the resources of the universities. It quickly pushed through a flood of new legislation providing grants, loans, and aids in unheard of variety and scope to the universities, bankrolling the expansion of academic programs, ambitious building projects, and the creation of impressive new research facilities.

The federal money that flowed into academia was like radical shock therapy, jump-starting the academic enterprise from its dormancy. The prestige that accompanied the traditional sciences now not only meant money, it meant advancement, security, and a kind of celebrity never before dreamed of by the cloistered academic. Humanists watched longingly as the resources of the federal government turned drowsy departments into vast bustling empires. Professors who once had been content to preside over sleepy seminars now found themselves at the head of research institutes with dozens of younger scientists and graduate students on bended knee. The new cash meant laboratories, assistants, sabbaticals, research grants, leaves of absence. Compared with this jackpot, traditional academia seemed hopelessly dreary.

But it also set the scene for one of history's more poignant and tragic ironies. The nation thought that the changes in universities were democratizing higher education, but it did not understand the opportunism of the professoriate. Under cover of the federal dollars and the massive surge of new undergraduates, another revolution was taking shape.

The Rise of the Academic Villages

The result of this new flood of federal cash, Jacques Barzun would later write, was "interlocking of university prestige specifically with contract money: Without contracts you cannot 'buy' the best graduate students, because the best want to do only research and none of the teaching they did before. Nor can you attract the best scientists, because they want the best students and the most expensive equipment plus the summer bonus of two-ninths or three-ninths chargeable to the contract. Note in passing that this closed circuit takes away from teaching half the senior men and the best juniors."[19]

The formal powers and perquisites of university administrators often remained intact. But the real authority of academia had slipped away from them. The administrators did not become completely irrelevant in the new regime in the academy; they still held some reins, but not the ones that controlled the horses. In the years before World War II, the two parallel university communities had existed more or less in balance. The formal university administration had handled undergraduate education and curricular matters while the villages—the disciplines themselves—had controlled graduate education.*

Suddenly, with the windfall of federal aid and with society's blank check to educate untold millions, the academic villages had access to incontrovertible power. Who else could evaluate the various research proposals? Who else could judge the worthiness of applicants? Of programs? More than academic egos were at stake. The universities, once considered temples of knowledge, were fast becoming vast industries.

University of California President Clark Kerr enthused in the 1960s that the "production, distribution, and consumption of 'knowledge' in all its forms is said to account for 29 percent of the gross national product, and knowledge production is growing at about twice the rate of the rest of the economy. . . ." Kerr's vision of the future of this new industry was stirring: "What the railroads did for the second half of the last century and the automobile for the first half of this century," Kerr predicted, "may be done in the second half of this century by the knowledge industry. . . ."

At the heart of Kerr's vision of the university as a vast mill churning out brightly polished new bits of knowledge was a new sort of professor. As universities became more like businesses, he wrote, "the professor—at least in the natural and some of the social sciences—takes on the characteristics of an entrepreneur."[20]

---

* I am using the term academic villages to describe in a general way, the parallel, shadow universities that dominate the academic culture. While they are basically synonymous with the disciplines themselves, they are also found in clusters, such as the Modern Language Association, a sort of super-village that acts as a kind of umbrella for the smaller villages of English, Comparative Literature, etc. The National Academy of Sciences also has many of the markings of a super-village, as we will see in Chapter 12.

Indeed, professors who succeeded in tapping the system of private and public grants for research quickly became powers in their own right in academia. Because they brought in money, they were considered virtually self-employed. And this fundamentally changed the politics of university power and funding.*

"Deans and presidents and college opinion are now merely minor local deities," classicist William Arrowsmith wrote in the sixties, "almost powerless to touch a man who is honored by his profession, whether rightly or wrongly."[21]

The key was the academic prestige hierarchy. "Academic rank is conferred by the university," wrote Reece McGee and Theodore Caplow in their classic *The Academic Marketplace*, "but disciplinary prestige is awarded by outsiders, and its attainment is not subject to the local institution's control. Everyone in the university recognizes and almost everyone lives by disciplinary prestige."**[22]

The importance of the villages in controlling the prestige hierarchy is reflected in the way federal aid goes to the same schools year after year. The money is handed out under a system referred to as merit review, which is a euphemism for the academic villages' control over distributing grants. Sixteen of the top 20

---

* "Other things being equal," wrote Professors William Rau and Paul Baker in a recent study of the university culture, "departments with nationally prominent faculty and/or success in attracting grants are most likely to escape the ax. . . . Unless addled, deans do not hassle high status departments, particularly those with a large contingent of self-employed faculty." ("The Organized Contradictions of Academic Sociology: An Agenda for the 21st Century," unpublished manuscript)

** In the university, argue researchers Rau and Baker, prestige has taken the place of profit. "If they wish to play the game, university administrators must grant substantial autonomy to departments and faculty and allocate considerable resources and rewards to research activity. They must do so because the disciplinary communities control the prestige economy of the university system. It is these communities that control the journals, the peer review system and, by way of peer review, publications and the allocation of research grants. Ultimately then, the disciplinary communities preside over the prestige rankings of departments and universities. They therefore control the key factor of production." (Rau and Baker, *op. cit.*)

schools that received federal largess in 1967 were still in the top 20 in 1984.*

University administrators could hope to exert influence over the faculty as long as the professors felt some sense of loyalty or identity with their school. With such an identification came a sense of responsibility and a certain degree of reliance on the good will of university administrators. But the rise of the villages meant a radical shift in loyalties. The new Academic Man regarded his institution, McGee and Caplow said, "as a temporary shelter where he can pursue his career as a member of the discipline." In some fields, they said, "for the successful professor the institutional orientation has entirely disappeared."[23]

This was at the heart of the Academic Revolution. "The result," wrote sociologists David Riesman and Christopher Jencks in 1968, "is that large numbers of Ph.D.s regard themselves as independent professionals like doctors or lawyers, responsible primarily to themselves and their colleagues rather than their employers. . . ."[24]

With his emphasis on specialization, the new breed of professor exerted an almost irresistible pull away from general education and toward a curriculum devoted to training other specialists. "You can have a man studying the herring industry from 1590 to 1600 in Scandinavia," Vassar President Alan Simpson said, "and

---

* They are: Johns Hopkins University, MIT, Stanford, the University of Washington, Columbia, UCLA, Cornell, the University of Wisconsin, Harvard, Yale, the University of Michigan, the University of Pennsylvania, the University of California at Berkeley, the University of Minnesota, the University of Illinois, and the University of Chicago.

The bias of the villages' old boy network in favor of established institutions is an unshakable given in the academic world. One study found that the top 20 institutions supplied fully 25 percent of the peer reviewers on grants, and not surprisingly in the competition with literally hundreds of other institutions these same 20 schools ended with 24 percent of the awards and 46 percent of all the science foundation university research money. The operation of the network is even more pronounced with money handed out by the federal government's National Institutes of Health. The top 20 schools provided almost one-third of the reviewers and received 44 percent of all the NIH research money for universities. (*The New York Times*, February 28, 1987)

when that young man gets his Ph. D. and is employed by a university, the first request he makes to them is, 'May I teach the herring industry from 1590 to 1600 in Scandinavia?' "[25]

"Each professor," Clark Kerr wrote in 1963, "wanted the status of having his own special course, each professor got his own course—a university catalogue came to include three thousand or more of them."[26]

The drive for prestige was reflected in a dramatic shift in priorities. At Harvard, the number of departments and degree-granting committees in the College of Arts and Sciences rose by almost one-third; between 1952 and 1974, the size of the faculty more than doubled, and the graduate student population jumped by 45 percent. But the number of undergraduates rose by only 14 percent. Most dramatic of all was the fact that during this period of rapid and incessant growth, the number of courses in which undergraduates were enrolled *actually fell by 28 percent.* Over a period of 22 years, the number of Harvard professors had risen from 300 to 608 but, one critic noted with massive understatement, "the indication was that contact between undergraduates and professors had not increased proportionately."[27] The needs of Harvard's students had obviously not driven the growth in the professorial ranks.

"What counted in recruiting faculty," Phyllis Keller, an administrator at Harvard, wrote, "was the acquisition of scientists and scholars who could staff the burgeoning graduate training programs, attract federal research dollars, and establish a school's reputation as a center of knowledge production."[28]

The pattern was repeated throughout the upper tier of the nation's most distinguished schools. In their 1987 study, Professors William Rau and Paul Baker found that while the top schools spent three times more per student than their less selective counterparts, their research budgets were *fifty times* greater. "In the prestige-maximizing equation," they concluded, "the quality of incoming undergraduates counts, but the quality of their instruction does not."[29]

A chasm had opened between academia's purported goals and its actual practices. In fact, while professors were still hired ostensibly to teach, they were now increasingly judged only by their research activities. Those professors so naive as to believe that their teaching duties were more important discovered their error when they were denied tenure by their peers.

"It is only a slight exaggeration," wrote McGee and Caplow, "to say that academic success is likely to come to the man who has learned to neglect his assigned duties in order to have more time and energy to pursue his private professional interests."[30] Indifference to teaching seemed built into the system, virtually institutionalized in the way that graduate students were trained and credentialed as professors. Jencks and Riesman wrote in 1968 that even if faculty members know a student to be an incompetent teacher, "they would never refuse him a Ph.D. on that ground alone."[31]

The new patterns inevitably shaped the "democratization" of higher education. Since 1940, the number of institutions of higher education has doubled. But even that number does not capture the larger surge toward academic respectability. As critic Paul Fussell noted, one of the great instruments of expanding educational opportunity was simply, "the process of verbal inflation." Normal schools, teachers' colleges, theological seminaries, trade schools, business schools, and secretarial institutes were all promoted to "universities," Fussell noted, "thus conferring on them an identity they were by no means equipped to bear or even understand."[32]

Thus, schools like Ball State, Kent State, and Southern Illinois at Carbondale have now made themselves into full-fledged universities, with Southern Illinois even boasting its own university press.

It is one the ironies of this process of democratization that its primary result was to sharpen the edges of the prestige system: Where once all Ph.D.s were roughly equal, distinctions now needed to be drawn. Departments now were ranked numerically; while Harvard, Stanford, the University of Michigan, and Berkeley often vied for the top spots, competition for the top 20 or 30 became the equivalent of academic trench warfare.

The Rise of the Multiversity

The new power of the academic villages inevitably loosened the ties that had once bound together the various disciplines and faculties in the university. Whatever this new institution was, it hardly lived up to the traditional understanding of the university. Universities had been distinguished by their overall concern with knowledge, a fellowship of scholars. If they did not always work together in mutual amity, they nevertheless felt a shared bond of concern and responsibility for the university. But what had once been an institution devoted to the sharing of universal knowledge was now a vast plain of competing fiefdoms, rent with turf warfare, alarums, and feints. "The close-knit community of scholars dissolved into a Babel of conflicting groups," recounted writer and former academic Alston Chase, "each using the campus as an arena in which to pursue its interests and ideas . . . each fighting for its slice of the pie. . . . Somewhere in the profusion of competing interests the goal of the pursuit of knowledge was submerged."[33] One observer at a midwestern university in 1965 reported that "the faculty and lower administration have been divided into all sorts of distinct interest or professional groups which have little or no intellectual or social unity . . . no department or division has responsibility for the total intellectual life of the student."[34]

But academics are nothing if not flexible on matters of image. As a sort of benediction on the new confusion, Clark Kerr, the president of the University of California, dubbed the new academy the "multiversity." In his 1963 book, *The Uses of the University*, Kerr defined the multiversity as "not one community, but several—the community of the undergraduate and the community of the graduate; the community of the humanist, the community of the social scientist, and the community of the scientist; the communities of the professional schools; the community of non-academic personnel; the community of the administrators."[35]

"Its edges," Kerr concluded somewhat lamely, "are fuzzy. . . ." In other words, the multiversity was nothing more than a series of academic villages vaguely strung together under a single institutional name.

The multiversity had several marks, but primarily it was distinguished by an overriding and omnipresent impersonalization. Kerr's great contribution was to provide an ideological and educational justification for the beast. Part of it was in the form of a new vocabulary. What others saw as confusion, fragmentation, and indifference were blessed by Kerr under the rubric of diversity, pluralism, and democratization.

He also acknowledged the decline of undergraduate education, going so far as to say that "there seems to be a 'point of no return' after which research, consulting, graduate instruction become so absorbing that faculty can no longer be concentrated on undergraduate education as they once were. This process has been going on a for a long time; federal research funds have intensified it. As a consequence, undergraduate education in the large university is more likely to be acceptable than outstanding. . . ."[36]

But Kerr prided himself on his hard-headed realism. He regarded the changes taking place in the universities as inexorable. Opposition to the professors was futile. The multiversity, he wrote in the 1960s, "is an imperative rather than a reasoned choice."[37]

Author Ronnie Dugger, who chronicled the rise of the multiversity at the University of Texas, was struck by the "toneless defeatism" with which Kerr took note of these distortions, dislocations, and failures. It amounted to "surrender with a shrug," Dugger wrote.[38]

What Dugger was seeing was the prototype of the modern university president with his nearly infinite capacity to deplore the university's shortcomings while doing nothing whatsoever about them. Part of that stemmed from Kerr's new vision of the role of the university president. "Instead of the not always so agreeable autocracy," Kerr wrote, "there is now the usually benevolent bureaucracy. . . . Instead of the Captain of Erudition . . . there is the Captain of the Bureaucracy who is sometimes a galley slave on his own ship. . . ."[39]

It was, all told, a rather elegant way of washing his hands of responsibility for the monster he had helped the professors create.

The Sixties

The student revolution of the 1960s took the new professoriate by surprise. This was, after all, their golden age; more jobs, more money, more opportunities than ever before. The future appeared limitless, the work conditions almost beyond belief. If their institutions had become cold and impersonal and if undergraduate education had been largely turned over to T.A.s, well, that was a small price to pay for the rise of a new sovereign profession committed to the search for truth.

In the wake of the student uprisings, the public image was of the university as prostrate before the triumphant student. But both winners and losers were preordained. The student revolt was destined for defeat by the simple logic of higher education: The students would eventually graduate and pass on; the professors would remain.

Until the 1960s, the greatest barrier for the new breed of professor was the tattered but still lingering obligation of the university to teach undergraduates a generally defined body of information. As long as universities felt the responsibility to offer up courses that would at least expose students to the broad expanse of Western civilization, its literature, arts, history, political ideas, and institutions—and as long as universities continued to define themselves by the knowledge they hoped to impart to students—there were built-in limits on just how far the professoriate could go in its flight from teaching. The 1960s resolved that problem, spectacularly.

The young revolutionaries thought they had unshackled themselves from a rigidly authoritarian curriculum. They had really unshackled the professoriate from the students themselves.

The professors were not slow in exploiting the opening.

Sidebar:
WHAT IS A UNIVERSITY FOR?

Most parents, legislators, and perhaps even college trustees, still have a mental picture of a university mainly as a place where young people go to be educated. The very phrase "higher education" encourages such speculation. Professors are still called college "teachers," as if their primary mission were the nurturing of young minds and the passing on of the accumulated wisdom of the academy to their students. And even though spending for instruction is less than one-third of university budgets (down to 32.2 percent in 1983-84),[1] the average American persists in thinking that the classroom is the center of activity of a university.

Because it makes for good relations with the public (as well as with the legislature), university administrators encourage such fanciful notions. But among themselves, they know how anachronistic and downright inaccurate they are.

Asked to describe the mission of his school, a vice chancellor of a Big Ten university listed five separate areas of responsibility:[2]

- Economic development.
- Service to the state.
- The creation of new knowledge.
- Training graduate students.

And, finally, dead last:

- Teaching.

Teaching

3 *The Flight from Teaching*

IN 1965, the Wisconsin legislature's discussion of the state's budget for higher education was dominated by the imposing figure of State Senator Gordon Roseleip. A Republican of the unreconstructed sort, Roseleip had been sent to the state capitol by his constituents to weed out waste and communism, and, since the university budget seemed an especially ripe opportunity to do both, he was an active and voluble irritant throughout the proceedings.

At one point, zeroing in on a witness, he asked: "Professor, exactly how many hours do you and your colleagues teach in the classroom?"

"Nine," the witness answered gravely.

Even to Senator Roseleip that sounded reasonable, perhaps more than reasonable, and he settled back in his chair, satisfied for the moment. But something in the professor's manner prompted him to seek reassurance a few minutes later.

"When you testified earlier that you taught nine hours, you meant nine hours a *day,* of course, didn't you?" In the audience, the assembled academics, on hand to protect their patch from the Neanderthals and bullies of the legislature, shifted uneasily. Some rolled their eyes. No, the witness answered with a touch of pro-

fessorial indignation, he had meant nine hours a week. The senator did not audibly respond.*[1]

It remains one of history's great ironies that as millions of new
students poured into college classrooms after World War II the
professors were pouring out of those same classrooms. By 1963,
John Gardner could write that "extremely small teaching loads are
an attribute of the leading institutions."[2] Even so, a survey by the
Brookings Institution of more than 3,000 faculty members in the
early 1960s found that professors of every rank "regardless of how
little time they devoted to undergraduate teaching, wished to
reduce that time still further. . . ."[3] By 1965, two-thirds of the
courses with 30 or fewer students at the University of California at
Berkeley were taught by teaching assistants rather than regular
faculty members.[4]

The rise of the academic villages had radically inverted the
values of higher education. It had become obvious that the higher
one rose in academia, the less one had to teach. Big teaching loads
were a sign of small rank; avoidance of teaching a perquisite of
eminence. The new academics, remarked the Carnegie Foundation more than 20 years ago, had come to view students as "imped-
iments in the headlong search for more and better grants, fatter
fees, higher salaries, higher rank."

"Needless to say," the foundation remarked with deadpan
understatement, "such faculty members do not provide the
healthiest models for graduate students thinking of teaching as a
career."[5]

The student revolution of the 1960s was the decisive event. The
flight became a stampede as professors vied with one another in a
mad scramble to put as much distance as possible between themselves and undergraduates. In 1967, 41 percent of the faculty at
the University of Texas taught more than two courses a semester.

---

* Of course, only a boor would point out that even in 1965, nine hours a week
really didn't mean nine hours as the world knows it. The professor was talking
about academic hours, which are only 50 minutes long; thus, nine hours is really
only seven and a half hours; and a six hour academic week translates into five
hours in the real world.

The next year, that dropped to only 29 percent. In language courses, 70 percent of the freshmen and sophomores at Texas were now taught by graduate students. Class sizes swelled. Freshmen chemistry students could expect 500-person classes; geology students, 700-person lectures. Meanwhile, the professors had arranged for their own teaching loads to consist largely of tiny seminars that require little, if any, preparation. The average botany professor had only five and one-half students per class; the physics professor only 12. Even at the junior and senior levels, 47 percent of the economics classes at the university were taught by T.A.s rather than by professors.[6]

"By the end of the 1960s," recounted author Ronnie Dugger in his history of the University of Texas, "it had become literally possible for a student to obtain a B.A. degree in economics [at Texas] without having been taught by a member of the faculty."*[7]

The pressures that drew university professors from the classroom were many, including the obligation to serve on some of the many university and department committees (does the department need a new logo for its stationery?) and the interminable demands of internal politicking that burn up so much of the university's energy. But the most powerful lure was research and the cause of advancing knowledge.

Throughout their flight from the classroom, the professors insisted they were not so much fleeing their teaching responsibilities as answering the urgent call of science. But if there were a call, it must have been of such a high pitch that it could be heard by the professors alone. In 1965, at the height of the exodus from teaching, *Science,* the official publication of the American Association for the Advancement of Science, addressed itself to the question "What Are Professors For?"[8] *Science's* answer was unambiguous:

* Twenty years later, Secretary of Education William Bennett proposed his own axiom to describe the peculiar interplay of cash and academe: "x dollars buys the student one professor, $2x$ dollars buys them two, but $3x$ and $4x$ and $5x$ dollars gradually remove the professor from the student and $6x$ dollars may replace all the classroom professors with graduate students."

"The professor's primary activities should be teaching and research," *Science* editorialized, "with the priority in that order. . . ."

It was already too late.

The Absentee Professor

The University of Wisconsin campus is dominated by Bascom Hill, which in turn is dominated by a massive statue of Abraham Lincoln seated in a state of contemplative repose. Generations of students have heard the legend surrounding it: Abe will stand up whenever a virgin walks past. The story has undergone a slight revision. Lincoln now stands whenever a virgin or a senior professor who teaches more than two undergraduate courses a semester passes by.

According to the administration, the average professor at the University of Wisconsin now teaches not nine, but six hours a week.[9] Even that is questionable. After two decades of The Historic Escape From Teaching (which has the fitting acronym of THEFT), university administrators have grown remarkably imaginative in concealing the reality of the professorial workload.* In fact, as auditors for the State of Wisconsin discovered, the six-hour average includes only the fall semester, when teaching loads tend to be higher.[10] Many professors teach two courses in fall and one in the spring. But most outrageous of all, the 1986 audit covers only those 1,318 professors who actually were teaching at all, which represent fewer than two-thirds of the professors actually on the payroll (2,027).[11] The rest were assigned to administrative duties, on leave or sabbaticals, or on research projects. Moreover, the auditors found that despite the legislature's increased funding for classroom instruction in recent years, fewer actual classes were being taught. The auditors concluded that the money had merely gone to further *reduce* teaching loads.[12]

* One popular gambit is to publish numbers claiming to reflect "student contact hours," in which professors are credited with the classroom time that is actually handled by teaching assistants. (Wisconsin Legislative Audit Bureau, April 8, 1986)

By the late 1980s, the flight of the professoriate had affected nearly every aspect of life on the Wisconsin campus. Many classes (outside of tiny graduate seminars) were huge. Freshmen and sophomores were often consigned to auditoriums with 500 or more students. Upperclassmen were not immune. According to one administrator, it became possible to get a bachelor's degree from Wisconsin in a field like international relations without ever taking a class with fewer than 100 students in it.[13]

The pressure of too many students chasing too few professors has turned registration times into nightmares as students scramble for courses that are too often filled. In 1987, freshmen trying to enroll in Communication Arts 101 were confronted with huge signs in English, Japanese, and a half-dozen other languages: "NO! All courses are closed. This is no joke."[14] Because professors customarily get to choose their own teaching times and tend to pick times between 10 a.m. and 2 p.m., many of the courses conflict. That makes it difficult or impossible for students to schedule required courses. UW officials admit that in 1987 they closed seniors out of courses *in their own majors* in the first hour of registration.[15] By the mid-1980s, it took five and one-half years for the average student to get a bachelor's degree from the University of Wisconsin.[16]

Typically, however, Wisconsin administrators took out their wrath not on the faculty, but on the students, the taxpayers, and the legislature. The solutions were by then familiar: Tuition was raised,* the number of students cut back, and the programs for undergraduate classrooms eviscerated.

Frogs were a symbol of what was happening. In the beginning, every biology student got to disembowel a frog of his own. But, former UW Chancellor Irving Shain complained, because of insufficient generosity from the legislature, the university had to cut back to one frog per class. "Now we show a movie of someone dissecting a frog and we show it over and over," Shain bemoaned with the gravity that university administrators assume when they

* Wisconsin was hardly alone in this. Between 1975 and 1986, college costs jumped 150 percent, or 25 percent faster than family income. For families with only one parent working, college costs rose 50 percent faster than family income.

are asking for more money. [17] What was once a profound anatomical experience had been turned into a spectator sport. Shain said UW's problems could be fixed if the legislature came up with $68 million. *

But when a state legislator suggested that the problems could also be solved by actually putting professors back into the classroom and introduced a bill requiring a teaching load of 15 hours a week, the university exploded in indignant rage.** Not only would most of the professors leave if forced back into the classroom, administrators warned, but the school would become a laughingstock among its peers. If Wisconsin were turned into a mere "teaching college," they proclaimed, UW degrees would be worthless; graduate schools around the country would scorn UW graduates seeking admission; UW doctoral recipients would be unemployable and, worst of all, research money would dry up. "If this bill [requiring a teaching load of 15 hours a week] passes, every professor who can leave UW will do so—fast," one critic barked in a letter to a student newspaper. The requirement would "make research impossible," and the only faculty who would stay at such an institution "would be those who are duds." And, because "a university's reputation is mainly a matter of the faculty's scholarly reputation," the 15-hour requirement would mean

* To his credit, Shain later said that the university's undergraduate program was a disaster. When he left UW for a job in the private sector in 1986, he said that undergraduate education at UW would probably rate only a "4" on a scale of 1 to 10. "Ten or 15 years ago," he said at a farewell press conference, "we would have a professor in a class with 30 students and the exam was usually a blue-book essay-type examination and the professor would grade not only the substance of the examination but also the spelling, grammar and composition. Now that same professor has 300 kids in the same class and so . . . he gives a multiple-choice, machine-graded examination. There's no feedback . . . and the student does not have as high a quality of education." (*Milwaukee Sentinel,* December 12, 1986) The current slogan of the University of Wisconsin, by the way, is "Quality is the Key."

** When he introduced the bill, State Representative Robert Larson said: "I have had students tell me they would have difficulty picking their professors from a police line-up because they see so little of them." (Press release, March 9, 1987)

that "UW degrees would immediately—and retroactively—lose much of their value. . . . No one would hire UW Ph.D.'s, whose professors would be unknowns and whose university would be an object of pity and mockery among academicians (who, after all, do all that hiring)."[18]

The doomsday bill never got to the floor of either house of the legislature.

Throughout the flight from teaching, the salaries of professors continued to rise in inverse proportion to their teaching loads. By mid-1987, the average full professor at UW made more than $51,000 a year.*[19] But salaries at other top research universities, where teaching loads are the slightest, were much higher—especially for professors in hot fields where they could bargain not only for more money, perks, research assistance, and low or no-interest housing loans, but also for guarantees of small or no teaching responsibilities.

The upward pressure of smaller schools struggling toward the light of academic prestige meant that even in schools like the University of Wisconsin's poor relation, the University of Wisconsin-Milwaukee, one professor in the business school taught only four hours a week in a recent semester—all on Monday. That freed him for lucrative consulting work to supplement his $66,300 university salary.[20] A professor of comparative literature who was paid more than $70,000 had a teaching load of two and one-half hours—for his "Background in Modernism" course.[21] At the Madison campus of the University of Wisconsin, a professor in the Economics Department making $91,608 taught only a single course in the spring of 1987, as did professors making $81,609, $75,700, and $75,700.[22] Of course, these salaries are for an "academic year," which is to say for nine months a year. So for those who teach 10 months (which many do), add one-ninth to their salaries; for an 11-month teacher "year," add two-ninths. Although university professors frequently complain that they are underpaid, the fact is

* Nationally, the average full professor made well in excess of $40,000 a year. (*The Chronicle of Higher Education*, July 15, 1987, source American Association of University Professors)

that their classroom teaching is a precious commodity on university campuses. Out of about 40 professors in the Economics Department, only two taught three courses in a recent semester, and only about one-quarter taught two.*[23]

At the University of Illinois, only slightly more than half of the more than 50 faculty members in the Economics Department taught even two courses in the fall of 1987. And in the Political Science Department fewer than one-third of the professors taught two courses.[24] At the highly ranked University of Michigan, some top-salaried professors teach so few classes that—figuring in university breaks and frequent holidays—they are paid nearly $1,000 an hour for their contact with students.[25]

Not surprisingly, the flight has had dramatic ramifications for the way undergraduates are taught. Because of steadily increasing class sizes, students are seldom asked to write papers, and their exams are often merely multiple choice questions that are graded by graduate assistants. "Reading this stuff is a real chore," one professor of student writing says, "so you line up T.A.s to do much of what little is done."[26] Most don't assign writing projects at all. "Students in our senior seminar for majors write a term paper," a University of Illinois associate professor says, "and their writing skills are inferior—punctuation, spelling, style, thought development. Even more discouraging is that many of them tell me that this is their first term paper."[27] A department chair says that in one course with many juniors and seniors, 80 percent have never had term papers assigned or any essay exams. But the situation is not easily fixed. "Many of our best faculty tell me they will leave if they are forced to teach undergraduate courses," a dean at the University of Illinois says.[28]

---

* The advantages of academia go beyond the light workload. A professor who is sick, for example, and misses a day of classes will not be charged for a full sick day, but only for his missed class hours. Where a regular state employee would be charged a full day, a professor would be charged only a single hour. As a result, the *average* UW professor who retires has accumulated more than $40,000 in "unused" sick leave credits. Three-quarters of University of Wisconsin faculty can expect *lifetime* tax-paid health insurance after they retire because of unused sick leave. (*Milwaukee Sentinel*, November 26, 1986)

The Academic Underclass

So who *is* teaching the undergraduates?

While they continue to publicly boast about the quality of their faculties, universities have filled the breach with a combination of graduate students (even, occasionally, undergraduates), part-timers and so-called gypsies, professors hired on a year-to-year basis who are, in effect, the coolies of the academic work force. For many students, these fill-ins are the only faculty they will ever see. "In four years I have had only one faculty member in my major," one senior at the University of Illinois says.[29]

The teaching assistants are the mortar of the system, cheap labor without whom the edifice of higher education would be reduced to rubble in a single fiscal year. Paid wages that most businesses would be embarrassed to pay their parking lot attendants, the teaching assistants are given almost complete responsibility for the education of freshmen and sophomores at many large universities.

The experience of the teaching assistantship is one of the most indelible lessons of graduate school. "As an initiation rite," a 1985 report by the American College Association charged, "the teaching assistantship is almost invariably a disaster: It says to the initiate that teaching is so unimportant, we are willing to let you do it. What is important, it says, is to demonstrate skills in the discipline, and the only way that matters is in research."[30] The report leveled a devastating indictment against the academy's use of T.A.s:

"The teaching assistantship is now a device for exploiting graduate students in order to relieve senior faculty from teaching undergraduates. The tradition in higher education is to award the degree and then turn the students loose to become teachers without training in teaching or, equally as ridiculous, to send the students off without degrees, with unfinished research and incomplete dissertations hanging over their heads while they wrestle with the responsibilities of learning how to teach. *Only in higher education is it generally assumed that teachers need no preparation, no supervision, no introduction to teaching."*[Emphasis added.]

Often living in Dostoevskian conditions, teaching assistants are expected to complete their own graduate work while fending off undergraduates who do not realize that T.A.s are not paid for any contact outside of class.

For many students, particularly freshmen bewildered by the size and complexity of their universities, the teaching assistant becomes their only contact with the institution. The T.A.s often have to assume the multiple roles of teacher, counselor, advisor, and friend—roles that fall to them by default. Success is understandably spotty. "Many graduate students have a siege mentality," Harvard's student-run *Confidential Guide** says. "First, many think students don't respect them, which is not really true. . . . Second, many grad students think they can only be popular if they grade easily. And finally, some are just unpleasant people."[31]

At Yale, T.A.s make up more than 25 percent of the people teaching and in a recent year filled 1,521 teaching appointments.[32] Student complaints about the quality of the T.A.s are commonplace. The student guide's evaluation of Yale's Anthropology 110b noted: "Students had nothing but criticism for the T.A.s who contradicted each other, showed little enthusiasm and appeared somewhat less than knowledgeable." Others students advised the school to "get rid of the supercilious and unpleasant T.A.s" who seemed "uninterested in the course."[33]

At Harvard, students complain that the teaching assistants are too preoccupied with their own work to be of much use to them.

---

* *The Confidential Guide* is published by *The Harvard Crimson* staff and is a notorious thorn in the side of both faculty and administrators at Harvard. The university publishes its own "official" course evaluation guide, known as the CUE Guide (after the Committee on Undergraduate Education), but there are periodic complaints that it is either censored or watered down, especially after an incident several years ago when a faculty member obtained an advance copy of the guide and attempted to change descriptions of some professors as "arrogant" and "condescending." *The Confidential Guide*, on the other hand, is unvarnished student opinion. (*The Harvard Crimson*, May 4, 1987)

In the Government Department, for example, the student guide warns that good section leaders are rare. "Chances are you'll get one who's more interested in his or her dissertation than in telling you what Hobbes thought."[34] Harvard's Econ 10 class has had more than 1,000 students. The teaching assistants are crucial because most of the actual teaching takes place in small sections. Jibes the student guide: "Most range from completely disorganized graduate students who are juggling two courses at both the law and business schools to Third World radicals . . . to tidy economics Ph.D. candidates who are working on a dissertation comparing the consumer indifference curves for strawberry French yogurt and Hawaiian grown alfalfa sprouts."[35]

The teaching assistants themselves are no happier about the situation. At Yale, the T.A.s complain that they receive no job training, no job descriptions, and no explanation for the level of their meager and often arbitrary pay.[36] Frustration was so great that T.A.s for a time picketed, carrying signs reading: "You Can't Eat Prestige," and "Ph.D. Need Not Stand for Poor, Hungry and Debt-ridden."[37]

The selection of T.A.s is symbolic of the status of teaching in the university. Many of the teaching assistants are drawn from the ranks of foreign graduate students whether or not they can speak understandable English. A student in Yale's Introductory Economics course complains of his teaching assistants that "95 percent of them do not speak English." Other students describe the T.A.s as either incompetent or "as confused as the students are."[38] A student at Brown who had an Asian T.A. in a chemistry section complains: "It was really difficult to understand what he was saying. And because it was so difficult, people tended to just not pay attention or ask the other T.A. questions during the lab. People tried, but you just could not understand what he was saying."[39] At Harvard, there are reports that the use of foreign T.A.s (T.A.s are called "teaching fellows" at Harvard) is so heavy that even students of French have developed Oriental accents.[40]

According to the National Science Foundation, about 23 percent of all graduate students are foreign, but that understates their concentration. At Brown, 67 percent of the graduate students in math, 50 percent of the graduate students in economics, and 45 percent of the engineering students are foreign.[41]

At Rutgers, a survey of students found that 61 percent of the foreign T.A.s were criticized for deficient English.[42] And when the University of Missouri at Rolla gave a spoken English exam in 1986, more than half of the foreign T.A.s failed.[43] None of the 20 foreign teaching assistants at the University of South Carolina was approved to teach in the fall of 1986.[44] Schools which require such tests are in the minority. The results, nevertheless, raise obvious questions about the quality of T.A.s in schools without screening programs.

But as the professoriate's flight from teaching gathered speed, the gap between the needs of the undergraduate program and the willingness of the faculty to teach grew so large that even the extensive use of graduate students was not enough to fill it. Increasingly loud complaints about the heavy use of graduate students also put pressure on the universities to find alternatives. The solution was relatively simple. With the tightened job market, the professoriate discovered it could also fill the holes with faculty members bearing full-fledged doctorates—part-time or even full-time—on a temporary basis. In 1970, the ratio of full-time to part-time faculty was 3.5 to 1; by 1982-83, it was 2.1 to 1.[45]

In other words, one-third of all faculty members in American higher education are now part-time. But this figure only partly reveals the scope of the situation: Many more are ostensibly full–time but have only a temporary status. These are the so-called gypsies. Many of them hold the euphemistic title of "visiting professor," or even "assistant professor," but their status is firmly defined by their one-year contracts. In California, one-third of the UC system's faculty members are now temporaries.[46]

They constitute an academic underclass—full-time instructors who are paid substantially less than the regular professors but teach substantially more. The part-timers and gypsies often work under appalling conditions.*

* At the University of Wisconsin-Milwaukee, a faculty committee found that many part-timers were actually making less money than the T.A.s they were

"For six years," says John Flynn of the Michigan Technological University, "I have shared one room with 15 other part-time instructors. Conferences and concentration are frequently impossible although, as a matter of fact, I frequently teach more students than full-time faculty."[47] A colleague puts the status of part-time teachers more graphically: They are "treated as pariahs."[48]

Cara Chell is typical of the gypsy/part-time teacher. "Three mornings a week I rise at 6 a.m., hit the road by 7 and drive an hour. I teach an 8 a.m. sophomore literature class, grade papers, and prepare class plans until noon, teach a noon freshman composition class, dash back to my office (the pronoun is deceptive since the office also belongs to two other instructors, but I've never seen them...) pack up my books and drive for another hour across town to another local university. I arrive there at 2 p.m., prepare, grade papers, and hold office hours; then teach a 4:15 advanced composition class. . . ." As a part-timer Ms. Chell is paid $1,000 a class, with no benefits. Part-timers are not paid for holidays, days off, or for student contact. Some gypsies teach four or five sections at various schools. They are, Chell says, "exhausted, degraded, and full of despair." Their status is so uncertain, Chell says, that "Old hands tell you to fail a paper for its comma faults, not for obvious plagiarism, because you don't want to risk a student's challenge."[49]

Christine Maitland taught at several community colleges in California and carried the equivalent of a full-time teaching load. But she was paid less than half as much as a regular faculty member. Eventually she quit, "because I had come to dislike teaching . . . I also quit because I was no longer giving my students a good education."[50]

Although many of the part-timers share her commitment to quality education, quality control is all but nonexistent when it comes to part-timers at some schools. "The department chairman called me three weeks before the semester began and asked if I

---

supervising. In one case, the report found, one temporary faculty member in the Chemistry Department "has been known to take over discussion sessions for the rest of the semester for T.A.s that could not speak understandable English, with no increase in salary." (*The Panther Herald*, April 6, 1988)

could teach a course for him," one part-time instructor recalls. "I took it, but I didn't know anything about the course. I didn't know what I was supposed to cover or where it fit into the curriculum. I ended up teaching it for three semesters, and no one from the faculty ever contacted me to discuss the class. No one ever came to observe me. And nobody ever asked me about it afterward. I could have taught them virgin sacrifice and I'm not sure anyone in the department would have known or cared."[51]

The teaching assistants, part-timers, and temporaries serve to demonstrate one of the iron laws of the university: The groups that are most integrally associated with teaching are invariably outcasts, with a status so low they fail even to show up on academia's normal scales of prestige. The part-timers and temporaries are divided from regular faculty by an immense gulf. They are normally not included in faculty meetings, cannot participate on committees, and are not expected to do any research.

The irony is striking. It is part of the academic orthodoxy that research is critical for the quality of teaching. "You cannot present the latest ideas in your field without being at the front of it yourself," says a Yale dean in a typical restatement of the creed.[52] But the universities have, in fact, turned over much of the teaching of undergraduates to teachers who have no such requirement. The status of the part-time/temporary faculty reveals the circularity of the argument about research. The academic establishment insists that only professors who do research can be good teachers, so they need to spend most of their time outside of the classroom; and because they are off researching (to become better teachers, remember), they are replaced by part-timers or temporaries who may do little or no research at all. Academia has an almost infinite capacity for ignoring such contradictions, especially when the payoff is so high.

The arrogance and highhandedness with which the professoriate uses part-timers and temporary faculty was particularly evident at the University of Texas.[53] As university enrollments skyrocketed, the school's English Department could no longer staff its many composition sections with regular faculty members, so it began hiring dozens of temporary instructors. They were paid 16 percent less than regular instructors, for teaching one-third more courses.[54]

Unlike most departments, however, UT's English faculty, in a spirit of democratic camaraderie, permitted the temporaries to vote in faculty meetings. But the professors' democratic spirit was sorely tested when the number of temporaries rose to the point where, if they voted as a bloc, they could outvote regular faculty. When plans to upgrade the university's writing program were announced, the department faced the prospect of hiring up to 150 temporary instructors, and the faculty's tolerance reached its limit. Rather than surrender its prerogatives, the regular English professors pressured the administration into suspending the new writing program—despite its crucial role in the school's core curriculum—and summarily dismissing all 65 of the instructors in the fall of 1985.

To make up for their departure, the English faculty hastily consolidated about a dozen sections of its sophomore-level literature course into large 250-student lecture classes. "Students wondered," one observer noted, "how they could take seriously educators who canceled whole courses for reasons that seemed to have nothing to do with their educational soundness."[55] The professors also made short work of the windfall—the money that would no longer be paid to the part-timers. They used it, according to one account, for "photocopying, for curriculum development, for travel, for visiting speakers, for conferences and so on."[56]

When it came down to it, the absentee professors had few qualms about wrecking the curriculum or sacrificing their students to preserve their perks. The temporaries were, of course, expendable, as the people who do the actual teaching in the universities always are.

Sidebar:
THE MASS CLASS

Professor Edward Kain is performing a striptease. Layer by layer he peels off his clothes and flings them toward his audience. Today he is demonstrating "social norms." In previous classes he has come dressed as the rock star Prince and once as a native Indonesian. He wears funny hats, occasionally dons a pig mask, and when he wants a student to answer a question, he'll throw a tennis ball into the audience — and it is an audience. Kain has taught huge classes with hundreds of students at Cornell University and at his current school, Southwestern University. To keep their interest for 50 minutes he has to be willing to try *anything*. "The single most important factor in student ratings," he is saying, "is not content but excitement and interest." This, in other words, is theater. And his audience is rapt as he explains his techniques.[1]

The room is packed not with students but with sociology professors from around the country attending the annual convention of the American Sociology Association. While some of their colleagues are down the hall discussing "The Morphographic Perspective and the Analysis of Educational Systems," several hundred sociologists have gathered to discuss more mundane matters: how to teach a mass class. For this group, a mass class is not 200 or 300 students; that is manageable. Even 500 students is merely large. The problem here is the cattle-call class of 800, 900, even 1,000 students packed into lecture halls of varying sizes and conditions, row upon row of blank faces waiting to be taught something, or at least entertained.

The sociology professors have all heard the horror stories. One speaker recounts tales of students who ordered pizzas to be delivered to class, students who brought dogs into the lecture hall (including one memorable visit during which the dog urinated on the podium), classrooms littered with beer cans after a lecture, and rumors of dark doings in the last few rows.

"There is an enormous difference between 400 and 700 students," says Ann Sundgren, who teaches at Tacoma Community College and at the University of Washington. "At 350 or 400, you can know if a stranger is in class, you can get a feel for the class. But when you go up to 600 or 700, you can't even see their faces. They can't even see your face. Once, after class, a student came up to me and said, 'I just came down to see what you look like.' "

"You are much more likely to run into psychos and schizos," Kain chimes in. "The odds are against you." In fact, data collected by another sociologist at the meeting suggest that the teacher of the average 1,000-person class can expect to have 25 psychotics, 120 illiterates, and 80 students who are "personally disorganized."

Professor Kain finesses such odds by treating his class as theater. He uses his T.A.s as ushers and his instructional staff as his stage crew, with some assigned to lights, others to props, while others work as costume designers. His pedagogical model is Phil Donahue, and he insists that teachers go through dress rehearsals before class.

"I love it!" he cries. "I'm a ham. What can I say?"

His enthusiasm is not shared, however, by Frederick Campbell, chairman of the Sociology Department at the University of Washington. "It snuck up on us," he says. "The economics of higher education demanded that more students be taught more cheaply. Sometimes great teachers rise to the occasion. But mostly, most people don't."[2]

There are other explanations, of course, for the mass class than simply "the economics of higher education." In an article in a campus newsletter called *Teaching at Berkeley*, Professor Richard Sutch of the Economics Department of the University of California at Berkeley vigorously defends the mass class, and in the process he reveals its importance in propping up the academic culture.

"Because it packs students into large lecture courses as freshmen and sophomores," Sutch explained, "the University saves a great deal of money which is then used to offer an amazing diversity of upper-division and graduate level courses.

"Since only a tiny fraction of the student body of a university are interested in the biosystematics of killer bees or the impact of inflation on worker-controlled industries in Yugoslavia, those students who are interested find their classes small and encounter a faculty eager to share their knowledge and time." His own department offers nearly 50 different courses of varying degrees of esoterica for upper-division students beyond the courses in basic economic theory. This embarrassment of riches, Sutch declares, is possible only because of the sacrifice of the lower-division undergraduates to the mass class.

"It allows the university to broaden the scope of undergraduate education," Sutch insists. But perhaps most important of all, it also allows the university to "maintain its graduate programs and the research pursuits of the faculty."[3] As long as that is the case, the mass class will be a staple of every university.

4 The Crucifixion of Teaching

THE banner that hung across the stage read simply: "Thank You, Alan Brinkley! We'll Miss You." As the young professor ended his last lecture, more than 500 students who filled the seats and aisles of Harvard's Sanders Theater rose in a standing ovation. By all accounts, Brinkley was one of Harvard's most gifted teachers, an electrifying lecturer whose vivid presentation of his material sparked both curiosity and enthusiasm among his students.[1] When he won the Levenson Award for Outstanding Teaching, he was described as a teacher whose students left the lecture hall "feeling not saturated but fascinated and hungry for more."[2]

Harvard's often acerbic student course guide said that Brinkley "brings alive one of the most turbulent periods in American history with an organization and fluid speaking style that few of his peers can match."[3] At 37, Brinkley taught the largest course in Harvard's History Department and had won an American Book Award for his study of the Depression era. He further stood out from many of his Harvard colleagues because of his open-door policy and willingness to meet with students one-on-one, even though, by some estimates, he taught one-third of all Harvard undergraduates in his various classes.

"Professor Brinkley was the first teacher who took an interest in me as a person," one student said afterward. "He advised me when I was choosing a concentration, helped me with my term paper for his class. . . ."[4] Charles Cohen, a senior in the History Department, later told *The New York Times*, "I did my best writing in Brinkley's courses because of his ability to infuse his subjects with energy and enthusiasm." One of his colleagues, Professor David H. Donald, himself a leading authority on 18th century American history, called Brinkley "a splendid young scholar and a superb teacher."[5]

In 1985, Harvard denied Alan Brinkley tenure and effectively fired him.

A slim majority of the tenured faculty members in the History Department (13 of 23) had voted to recommend tenure, but the favorable recommendation was overturned by the dean of Arts and Sciences.[6] Brinkley's case dramatically highlighted the fate of professors who emphasize teaching. It was particularly notable because of the contrast between Brinkley and his colleagues at the nation's most prestige-encrusted university. Harvard's history professors were notorious for the frequency of their absences from campus and the rarity with which many of them entered a classroom.

"There is little direction, little contact with professors, and so few courses offered each year," the student guide says, "that you'll swear they left half the course catalog on the floor of the registrar's office."[7] This is not much of an exaggeration. The course catalog denotes courses that are not being offered that year by putting them in brackets. So many history courses were bracketed one year that students printed up T-shirts reading simply: [History].[8] One recent year, almost all of the professors of American history were gone at the same time, gutting the curriculum and leaving undergraduates interested in American history at America's leading university to fend for themselves. "No one is looking out for the students," complained one major.*[9]

---

* For the 1986–87 academic year, the department listed 69 courses in modern European history, but 31 of them were bracketed. Of the remaining 38 courses, only 20 were offered in the fall semester; of these only 12 were taught by tenured professors and three of those 12 were courses intended for graduate students. So out of 69 possible courses, only nine courses with full professors were designed

Many of Harvard's professors are celebrated for their indifference to preparation, clarity, and civility in their dealings with undergraduates.* The student guide says that one prominent professor hadn't said a nice word to an undergraduate since 1964.[10]

But even if Alan Brinkley was the exception because of his teaching ability, the way his case was handled was hardly exceptional. Shortly before Brinkley's dismissal, another popular professor, Bradford A. Lee, an expert in modern history and, like Brinkley, a winner of the teaching prize, had also been dismissed. With Brinkley's departure, *three of the last four* recipients of Harvard's teaching award had been denied tenure.**[11]

Harvard is not the only school where the teaching award is a jinx.

At Stanford, says Stephen Ferruolo, a former associate professor, the attitude among senior faculty members (who make all the tenure decisions) is that "if you're a good teacher, you're not a serious scholar, that they're somehow incompatible. . . . Good teaching is a negative factor in tenure cases." Ferruolo, a widely known medieval history scholar, had won the 1982 Dinkelspiel

---

solely for undergraduates in the department. It was even worse in Brinkley's field—American history. Out of 44 total courses listed, only 10 were offered in the fall of 1986, and only one was taught by a tenured professor.

* This was, by no means, always the case at Harvard. At one time Harvard boasted such brilliant scholar-teachers as Henry James, Irving Babbitt (a teacher of T. S. Eliot), George Santayana, Joseph Schumpeter, and William Ernest Hocking. Two generations of Harvard students thrilled to Professor Samuel Beer's dramatic declamation of Voltaire's statement: "Men will not be free until the last King is strangled with the entrails of the last priest!" But he was a representative of a breed of teacher already obsolete in the academic culture. When he retired in the late 1970s, his course on "Western Thought and Institutions" was retired with him.

** The previous year, more than 1,100 Harvard students signed a petition urging the school to grant tenure to James R. Stellar, an associate professor of psychiatry who had also won the teaching award. But in 1986, after concluding that he would not receive tenure, Stellar resigned and took a position at Northeastern University. "The word is out that junior faculty at Harvard are viewed as transients whose job it is to do the bulk of the teaching and then leave," he said. (*The New York Times*, September 2, 1986)

Award for Outstanding Teaching at Stanford. But shortly after Brinkley was denied tenure at Harvard, Ferruolo was turned down for tenure at Stanford. [12]

At Yale, Bruce Tiffney also won a teaching award. He was informed of it in a letter from a dean. When he read the letter, he recalls, "I let out a whoop of laughter so loud my wife came in to see what was the matter." Two weeks earlier, Tiffney had been denied tenure after nine years as a junior professor. [13] Faye Crosby, who won the teaching award in 1982, was also denied tenure three years later. [14] "It's extremely unlikely," says Douglas Kankel, a tenured associate professor in Yale's Biology Department, "that if you are a professor with an exceptional teaching background, you will survive the tenure process." [15]

The promotion process at Yale, says David Blinder, a former assistant professor of philosophy, "manages to weed out some of the people who take teaching most seriously. To me, teaching was far and away the most rewarding. The most important moments in my education came in the teaching." Blinder, too, was denied tenure. Drawing the obvious lessons, an assistant professor at Yale told the *Yale Daily News*, "It would definitely be suicide to be a teacher as a junior faculty member." [16]

The pattern extends throughout higher education. Virtually every university in the country has a similar story. These cases are dramatic, irrefutable evidence that the academic culture is not merely indifferent to teaching, *it is actively hostile to it*. In the modern university, no act of good teaching goes unpunished.

Many academics try to justify themselves by blaming their students who are, they insist, often poorly prepared and uninterested in the subject matter. University professors are often loud in their criticism of the public elementary and secondary schools. Frequently they attempt to shift the debate on the failures of higher education to the failures at the lower levels. But when the Holmes Group issued its report on the reform of teacher education in 1986, it reversed field on the professors. Part of the reason for the widespread ineptness of America's schoolteachers, the Holmes Group concluded, lies in the universities themselves. "They strive to hire highly qualified academic specialists, who know their subjects well and do distinguished research," the Holmes Group said. "But few of these specialists know how to teach well, and many seem not to care. *The undergraduate education that intending teachers—and everyone else—receives is full of the same bad teaching that litters American high schools.*"[17]

At the heart of the system are the academic departments and their power over the system of tenure.* The process by which a young professor wins tenure—in effect, a lifetime job at a university—is widely misunderstood outside of the academy itself. Although university administrators often have the final say, the tenure system is controlled by the professors themselves. Because a professor once granted tenure is virtually immovable for life and ties up a spot in the department's budget for decades, the decision on granting tenure is the most important made in academia.

The procedures vary widely, but one basic model goes like this: At the end of a young professor's six-year apprenticeship as an assistant professor, he or she is evaluated by the tenured professors in the department. But because of increased competition for precious few tenure-track jobs, a growing number of schools have initiated an extensive review after only three years to determine whether a candidate is promising enough to be kept on for a second three-year term. Even if a junior professor passes this hurdle, he or she must undergo a much more searching review before being admitted to the land of academic immortality. In some departments a two-thirds vote of the tenured professors in

---

* In the mid-1960s, classicist William Arrowsmith wrote in his famous essay, "The Future of Teaching," the following analysis of the academic department: "At present the heart of university power is the department. It is this departmental power that now so vehemently promotes research and is hostile or indifferent to teaching. It is at the departmental level that the evaluation of teaching is subverted . . . it is here that the publish-or-perish policies are really promulgated; that the pressure for reduced teaching loads derives; from here . . . that the demand for early specialization arises, as well as the jealous specialism that fragments the curriculum, into warring factions. Put a mild and gentle man of broad learning into a department chairmanship, and within two years he will either be murdered by his colleagues or become an aggressive and vindictive *mafioso* of the crassest specialism." (From *Improving College Teaching*, edited by Calvin Lee, American Council on Education, 1967)

the department is needed to send a positive recommendation up to the administration. Other departments look for a consensus, but all votes are not equal. In some departments the opposition of a single heavyweight can derail a tenure bid.

Once a positive recommendation is made, some schools will appoint a panel of outside scholars—usually chosen for their eminence within their respective academic villages—to evaluate the candidate's scholarship. This theoretically protects against excessive inbreeding and also serves to keep any single department from straying too far from the orthodoxies of its discipline's mainstream. The evaluations are inevitably subjective. Some tenure candidates have gone down to defeat as a result not of criticism but of faint praise. One senior professor at the University of Washington who was asked to evaluate the work of a tenure candidate at the less prestigious Washington State University wrote back that the candidate "deserves tenure at WSU, even though he would not get it here." The candidate was denied tenure.[18]

The final decision on tenure is often made by the university's president, who usually ratifies the faculty recommendation. If he does not, the presidential veto is frequently based on reservations voiced by professors on the peer review committee, and so reflects the priorities of the academic villages.

Almost every school claims that tenure candidates' teaching abilities are weighed along with their published scholarship. The evidence to the contrary, however, is overwhelming. "Chancellors and vice chancellors say teaching is important," one professor at the University of Illinois says, "but no one believes it."*[19] Only a tiny percentage of schools ever sends faculty observers into a junior professor's classroom to evaluate his teaching. Even in

---

* Indeed, a 1987 survey of more than 1,300 academic vice presidents found that, for the most part, schools have put little time or money into improving the quality of teaching despite public claims to the contrary. The author of the report, Leslie H. Cochran, provost of Southeast Missouri University, said that the findings indicated that: "We're not strongly committed to improving and developing quality teaching. I hear a lot more rhetoric. But what we do not have on most campuses is a systematic plan." (*The Chronicle of Higher Education*, March 16, 1988)

those schools that do, however, professors have shown a marked reluctance to criticize their colleagues. In most cases, what little the senior colleagues hear about the junior professor's teaching is in the form of second-hand reports, often little more than gossip and hearsay.* It is almost an article of faith that teaching is simply something that cannot be judged.[20] What can be judged—because they can be measured, counted, weighed, and occasionally even read—are the candidate's published articles and books. Inevitably, they dominate the process.**

At the University of Illinois, where administrators have loudly declared their intention to upgrade the importance of teaching, Professor Richard Schacht, who heads the Philosophy Department, was named chairman of the school's new Council on Undergraduate Education. One of the council's main responsibilities is to encourage the faculty to take classroom responsibilities more seriously. I posed the following choices to him: Two junior professors are up for tenure at the University of Illinois. Professor A is an excellent researcher with an outstanding record of publication. But he is a terrible teacher. Professor B is an outstanding teacher,

* "Furthermore, it is evident that at least in the colleges of arts and sciences of leading universities little precise information about the teaching of individual faculty is secured. *To the contrary, there is evidence that what is known about someone's classroom performance is fabricated from gossip, rumor, ex parte evidence, and other random and unreliable means of intelligence.*" [Emphasis added.] (Lewis, Lionel, *Scaling the Ivory Tower*, Baltimore, Maryland, Johns Hopkins University Press, 1975 p. 23)

** Professor George LaNue, who has studied hundreds of tenure-related lawsuits says: "Schools all say we take teaching very seriously. But when pushed, it just disappears. They can't show they evaluate it very thoroughly or very consistently."

Harvard's Stephen Jay Gould acknowledges that teaching is seldom a serious factor in deciding whether to grant tenure. "I've never heard it seriously considered," he says. "There's lip-service given to it." A former member of the promotion and tenure committee of Northwestern's College of Arts and Sciences says: "Teaching is often discussed at some length in the deliberations. But in the final vote, it doesn't count for much."

"Over and over it always comes back to the person's reputation and promise as a scholar," concurs Joel Porte, the former chairman of Harvard's English Department.

skilled, dynamic, effective in the classroom. But he has a mediocre record in publishing articles. Would Professor A be given tenure? Professor B?

Schacht's answer cuts to the heart of the academic culture: Of Professor A (excellent researcher/awful teacher), he said: "We would try to find a place in our program for him that would cover for his deficiencies."

And of Professor B (outstanding teacher/mediocre academic publisher), he said: "Maybe he should go to a second-tier research university or to a liberal arts college. But not here."[21]

The treatment of teachers indicates academia's indifference to teaching, but it only hints at how deeply the contempt for it is ingrained within the academic culture. "It's the kiss of death," Associate Professor David Helfand, winner of one of Columbia University's General Studies Distinguished Teachers Awards, told *Newsweek on Campus,* "if you volunteer to teach two classes instead of one before tenure. They will say 'This guy is a *teacher.*'"[22]

Harry H. Avis, an instructor at a California community college, recalls his attitude as a young graduate student, immersed in the values of the academic culture. On reading an article that quoted an unnamed professor at the University of California at Berkeley saying "The sight of an undergraduate makes me sick," he recalled that his reaction was: "Someday I too, would be in a position to say those words." It took Avis years (and several lapsed grants) to realize that despite those early prejudices imbued from the atmosphere of the graduate school, he actually *enjoyed* teaching. Still, he confesses, many of his colleagues simply cannot understand his passion. "Some of them avoid me," he wrote, "some pity me as a failure, and most avoid talking about research in my presence."[23] In the academic culture, to be a teacher is to be a failure.

The indifference of the academic villages to teaching is readily understandable, given their commitment to research. But the virulence of the hostility is more troublesome. The contempt for teaching and the professoriate's ill-concealed embarrassment in its presence nevertheless provide an intriguing clue: The professoriate's teaching obligations are annoying reminders of their not wholly respectable professional roots—humiliating leftovers from the time before they were transformed into savants, gurus, and scientists. Professors were once mere pedagogues, and they have spent decades trying to live down the disgrace. The spectres of Ichabod Crane and Mister Chips are always hovering. Faculty members who actually enjoy teaching cast a shadow on the whole profession, like an eccentric family member who chooses to move out of an elegant, well-appointed mansion and back to a tacky one room walk-up above an all-night convenience store in the old neighborhood.

This attitude is captured in a recent article in the *Brown Daily Herald* by Brown University Professor Jacob Neusner. In the article, Neusner lectures his colleagues that to remain competitive with Harvard, Yale, and Princeton, "we professors [must] write books and articles, give principal addresses at scholarly meetings, organize research conferences, edit journals and monograph series, educate future scholars through doctoral programs, and also maintain post-doctoral programs as well, undertake collaborative research programs involving national funding, and on and on. . . ."

"In most fields, however, no one outside of Brown has heard of anyone in Brown," Neusner complains. "That is the difference between a teaching college *of amiable non-entities*, local icons, and a research university of productive, tough-minded, risk-taking sonofabitch scholars." [My emphasis.] Neusner goes on to characterize academics devoted to the teaching of undergraduates as "the non-publishers, the non-lecturers, the home-bodies, without ambition of an intellectual, let alone a scholarly character, the book-reading camp counselors. . . ."[24] If his language is inflammatory, it reflects the ideology of the academic village and, of course, the reward structure of virtually every American university.*

* In 1985, the Land Grant Association asked Professor Burton Clark, a professor of sociology and higher education at UCLA, to conduct a study on the future of state universities. He was struck by the radical disincentives to teaching that he found virtually everywhere. "Rare is the material or symbolic reward that does not push or pull the professor toward research and graduate students," he wrote in his report. "Something has to give and that something is the

"The heart of the problem," in American universities, concluded researchers Paul Baker and William Rau, who have been studying the academic culture for several years, "is that it is irrational for faculty to devote much time or energy to teaching. . . . From an economic point of view, undergraduate teaching does not count, and since it can't be counted there is little sense in devoting much time to it. . . ."[25]

The system seems to breed incompetence in the classroom. In their book, *The Academic Revolution,* authors David Riesman and Christopher Jencks note this as one of the peculiar marks of the modern Academic Man. "Many potentially competent teachers do a conspicuously bad job in the classroom because they know that bad teaching is not penalized in any formal way."*[26]

Professors have succeeded in using both tenure and their invocation of academic freedom—what sociologist Reece McGee calls the "freedom to teach badly"—to make their classrooms virtually inviolate.[27] Many schools use student evaluations, but they are seldom given much weight; students themselves are rarely if ever a formal part of the promotion or review process. Indeed, tenure itself means that questions about the quality of a professor's teaching are moot. Remarks a former department chair: "If a tenured professor decapitated the chancellor and raped his wife, he would have the right to 36 hearings over six years before university committees, retaining his tenure while his colleagues debated endlessly definitions and procedures. Fire a tenured professor for gross teaching incompetence? Forget it."[28]

---

undergraduate program. Someone has to come up on the short-end, and that someone is the freshman-sophomore student." Clark found that, since the end of World War II, teaching—once the center and sole purpose of higher education—"has drifted toward the margin of reward and interest. Why else would major universities, including private ones, year in and year out send away brilliant young teachers rather than give them tenure?"

* The opposite may, in fact, be true. "The more insufferably boring your courses and the fewer your students, the more leisure you have to publish and the better off you are. Small classes can perhaps wound the vanity of those few professors who think of themselves as great teachers, but never their pocketbooks." (Pierre van den Berghe in *Academic Gamesmanship,* New York, Abelard/Schuman, p. 73)

A tenured professor who misses three straight classes in mid-semester, or who cancels classes to do some consulting, or who reads lecture notes prepared 20 years before, or who refuses to show up for office hours can do so with little fear that it will ever be mentioned by superiors or colleagues.

Five Ways of Teaching Badly

The rape of classroom teaching in the universities takes several forms. First, of course, is the refusal to teach at all. But even within the classroom there are ways of minimizing the inconvenience of actually teaching. The neglect of teaching can be divided roughly into five major categories, with considerable overlap. Professors can:

(1) Merely regurgitate the textbook.

(2) Rely on notes prepared when they were younger, more ambitious, and without tenure.

(3) Dwell on their own specialties without bothering to translate the material from the arcane jargon of their specialty.

(4) Turn their classes into rap sessions, a tactic that has the advantage of being both entertaining and educationally progressive.

(5) Fail to prepare at all and treat their classes to an off-the-top-of-the-head ramble, leaping from topic to topic in what they think are dazzling intellectual trapeze acts but which usually are confusing, frustrating muddles for the students.

Tales of each are abundant.

Students in one Yale economics course described their professor's lectures variously as "uninteresting and somewhat confusing," "irrelevant and poorly prepared," "horrible," "poorly organized and boring" and "the most painfully boring experience I have ever had."[29]

At Harvard, both *The Confidential Guide* and the university's more staid official guide to courses, the so-called *CUE Guide*, are rife with student complaints of professors who are disorganized, vague, aloof, and unenlightening; and of professors known for their inability to make a point or finish a sentence, even, students report, a professor who "hasn't looked at his class for two years now."[30] And *The Confidential Guide* notes that one professor has been referred to as the "human Quaalude," for years.

A senior from the University of Michigan recounts his experience with a professor whose entire teaching strategy was taking the textbook and outlining it for his lectures. "Everyone figured that out after about four lectures. The class was abandoned after that. When I first started out here, I was really studious about going to classes. Even I didn't go after a while. I read the book. You could get his entire lecture in two days—you could read the whole book in a couple days. And the test was one of these fill-in-the-dot tests. Why go to class? You could just read the book, go in and take three tests, and you're done in two weeks. Why do you have to drag it out over a whole term? Why do you have to pay money for that? Just pay money for the damn book. It was just a damn travesty."[31]

Professors who rely on moldy notes generally fall into two categories: those for whom tenure meant the end of any serious effort and those whose esoteric research interests have little or no relation to the interests or needs of their students. One rule, however, seems to be that the moldier the material, the duller the presentation. One professor reportedly reads his lectures from notes yellowing with age in a droning monotone, guaranteed to cure any insomniac.[32] Students at another Ivy League school report that one instructor literally reads everything—including scripted jokes—verbatim from her notes.[33]

Perhaps the original sin of bad teaching is the professoriate's refusal to narrow or even acknowledge the gap between their own hyperspecialization and the need to translate their subject matter for undergraduates. Ideally, teachers should lead students to knowledge by showing them their own process of learning and thought. But this is hard work: It requires clarity, and that means both rethinking and reinterpreting the material. For many professors this is simply too much too ask. How much easier to simply take their work on the edge of whatever they happen to be cutting and present it to the students more or less undiluted.

The Confidential Guide described the problems with one literature course by noting, "Most of the lecturers have something in mind, but they are confounded either by (a) a terrific inability to say it or (b) the suspicious feeling they ought not to say it to undergraduates but rather should enlighten their colleagues and the grad students in the front rows with juicy little pieces of esoterica."[34] Take a professor from his own specialty and you risk disaster. One Harvard professor, for example, is an expert on modern literature who was required to deliver lectures on 19th-century authors. According to student reports, he made no effort to conceal his distaste; he reportedly began his lectures on the works of Tennyson with a harangue on his loathing for the Victorian poet. One report on Harvard's "Major British Writers" course captures the mood: "[The lectures] fail because the professors do not want to be there. The problem of highly specialized professors teaching introductory survey courses is twofold: Not only would they rather skip rudimentary explanations of what a spondee is, who Pope and Dryden are, and where England is, they would also rather not lecture on topics which lie outside their fields."[35]

The problems are even more serious in the sciences, where teaching has long been considered merely a distraction from the real business of research. One Harvard professor reportedly once told his Introductory Physics class: "You're not going to understand what I'm going to do for the next half-hour. . . . The math is about two years ahead of you, but because I suffered, you'll have to suffer through my presentation." The next year he was awarded tenure.[36]

That approach is by no means exceptional in the sciences. Harvard's Physics Department is renowned for the incredibly poor teaching of its faculty members. The philosophy of the department, *The Confidential Guide* says, "essentially thrusts the full responsibility for comprehension upon the student and equates high teaching ability with poor scholarship." The idea is that good students will understand that they need to learn physics by themselves "with only the occasional intervention of an instructor."[37]

The professor who simply refuses to prepare for class—because he is too busy, too lazy, merely indifferent—has two major options, both of them extremely popular within the academy: the ramble or the rap session.

The professor who begins each class with a wide-ranging discussion of the fortunes of the Bears (or Yankees or Broncos or Braves), or shows slides of vacations, or baits undergraduates with a topic like "Do we run from dogs because we are afraid, or are we afraid because we run from dogs?" can usually be assured of a reasonably docile class. The 50-minute rap session, pioneered by the seminar, has proven invaluable to several generations of harassed professors.

But rap sessions, of course, offer no escape for the teacher confronted with large lecture classes. After filling up the requisite number of classes with guest lectures, slides, and movies, the professor still faces the unavoidable fact that he or she has to go in front of the students and actually lecture. But if preparation is inconvenient, there is always the ramble. Evidence from student evaluations indicates that the practice of winging it is rampant, if not actually the norm. Some comments:

"He will do anything except make a point." [38]

"She can be very disorganized in lecture, confusing her audience by jumping from topic to topic."[39]

"Unable to translate his knowledge into well-focused, lucid presentations."[40]

"[Professor's] lectures are often unfocused, repetitive and monotonous. . . ."[41]

"[Students] also say that instead of going over basic theories, he jumps from topic to topic in a confusing manner and often rambles into tangential areas which are too complex for them."[42]

Sometimes it's hard to tell whether a professor suffers more from the studied incoherence of the specialist or is simply making it up as he goes along. Some combine the genres. Students report that one Ivy League faculty member who has been teaching the course on "Economic History of the North Atlantic: 1500 to the Present" is so poorly organized, prone to go off on unscheduled tangents, and to "make sociology soup out of simple economics" that the class never made it past 1688, just making it out of feudal Europe and never making it to industrial England.[43]

All of these permutations of lousy teaching reflect the academic culture's feeling that teaching well is simply not worth the effort or attention. In various ways they all reaffirm the subsidiary status of teaching: It is a job to get through with a minimum of time and intellectual investment.

More than 20 years ago, classicist William Arrowsmith wrote "The Future of Teaching," a moving tribute to and plea for the "ancient, crucial, high art" of teaching. It still carries a prophetic quality.

"Behind the disregard for the teacher," Arrowsmith wrote, "lies the transparent sickness of the humanities in the university and in American life in general. . . . At present the universities are as uncongenial to teaching as the Mojave desert to a clutch of Druid priests." And he poked fun at the practice of handing out token awards for teaching in place of genuine rewards. "If you want to restore a Druid priesthood you cannot do it by offering prizes for Druid-of-the-year. If you want Druids, you must grow forests."[44]

There are no indications that any such forests are about to appear in academia. If anything, the blight of the landscape is spreading. Traditionally, the younger professors, still fresh, energetic, and idealistic, have provided some of the best teaching on college campuses. But pressures on young professors to produce "scholarship" are growing increasingly intense; publications once required for promotion to full professor now are needed just to win tenure, while qualifications that would easily have won tenure a few years ago are now required simply to have a junior professor's three-year contract renewed.

Nancy Greenwood, a young visiting professor of sociology at the University of Missouri at Kansas City, reflects the dilemma faced by many junior academics. She enjoys teaching and does it well. "Sometimes when I am discussing methodology, I see a light go on in their eyes. It makes me wonder what goes on in other classrooms." But, she says, "they won't let me do that job. My mentors, my advisors all tell me I spend too much time on class preparation. I am very interested in teaching. But now I have to barricade myself from students and tell them they can only see me during office hours. What message do you think that sends to students?"[45]

Whatever message it is, it is a common one in the university. Discussing one of his professors in American Culture, a University of Michigan senior says: "He didn't even want to deal with students, it seemed like. He would just give a lecture and say, 'No, just deal with my T.A.' He didn't want to deal with us when we weren't in class."

The senior had a similar experience with another professor. "He was awful," the student says. "He got up there, and he would lecture, and he didn't really take questions or anything, and you always had to deal with your T.A. And he didn't have office hours. This professor—this tenured professor—is not available. I remember this because it was the last day of class. He was about to begin the lecture. Someone said, 'Before you continue, I'd like to know if we're going to be filling out course evaluations for this course.' And the guy said, 'No, we're not.' He didn't say why. He's tenured—it didn't matter to him what people thought, I guess. This is just amazing to me, because you can't get fired based on those, but you'd think at least he'd want to know. But apparently he didn't even want to know. He didn't really care."[46]

Professors indifferent to their responsibilities to their students manifest their contempt in a variety of ways. One of the most popular is in the form of reserve readings at the library. Some professors are notorious for putting only a handful of required readings on reserve at the library, thus sentencing hundreds of desperate students to a semester spent hovering around reserve desks waiting for one of the fugitive articles or books to appear.

Through all of this, the professors seem generally unaware of the impact of their behavior on their students or the impression that they make.

During the course of my research, I sat in on a meeting of the chairs of the various departments of sociology at the annual convention of the American Sociology Association.[47] Much of the meeting was spent discussing the various lures the chairmen used to attract top students for their graduate schools, including packaging grants with what they called "honorific distinctions" and even giving academic stars signing bonuses to get them to attend their schools. "The graduate applicants expect this, and you better give it to them," one chair warned.

The discussion of grants and perks and honorific distinctions had gone on for the better part of an hour before Eric Wagner spoke up.

Wagner, the chairman of Ohio University's Sociology Department, had a simpler recommendation. His department had sent students to some of the top schools, but they had come away unimpressed and in some cases disgusted by what they found. The professors in the elite departments, he said, "are so busy with their own research they don't have time to spend with our students." He told the group that students he sent to Stanford were so upset by the arrogance and apparent indifference of the professors there that "they wouldn't touch your fellowships."

His advice was simple: *"Just pay attention to them,"* he pleaded. "That may be more important than just throwing money at them."

The department chairs listened politely and went on to another subject.

Sidebar:
AN ENDANGERED SPECIES

Fred Gottheil is a teacher. A full professor of economics at the University of Illinois, Gottheil teaches an introductory class with more than 1,000 students and often lectures to SRO halls. Winner of numerous awards for his classroom performance, he is described variously as dynamic, enthusiastic, and inspirational.

"When I get up in front of the class it's like Dale Murphy of the Atlanta Braves," Gottheil says.[1] "*I know he can't wait to hit.* I feel the same way. I want them to think that this is the greatest course they'll have at the university.

"I always spend about 10 minutes at the beginning of every course telling them that this class is listed as a lecture/discussion, which is kind of ridiculous, but we are going to do that. I tell them that any question they have, any thought that occurs to them during that lecture, they are to raise their hand and pretend we are a class of 10 people.

"You want to get them to have an emotional as well as an intellectual feel for the material you are presenting. You've got to feel that the material is vital. If they think you walk up in front of them and it's just your job, hell, they'll walk away. If they see you are absolutely involved in it, they will pay attention. Especially when they see that what you are telling them is the most important thing in their life."

But how does he feel about teaching such a huge class? Gottheil's answer says a lot about the academic culture.

"You ask me if I like teaching large classes? Yes! Because if they don't get me, *they'll get them.* And my end in life is to prevent that. I'll teach thousands if I can keep my colleagues from getting them."

"The professor in the large class—most of them—what they are doing is looking for the one or two stars. 'You can speak my language? You understand Greek? Come here,

I'll train you; you can become a professor too.' The other 997, *screw 'em*. And they look on them with distaste."

Gottheil, however, is not able to completely insulate his students from the academic culture of his department. "I have 13 teaching assistants," he says. "All but one of them is a non-American. Some of them don't speak English. The whole structure of this department is not to put a qualified person in front of a class. It is to use the T.A. money to create Ph.D.s. Now you have to give them some bloody excuse. How can you give a guy $6,000? Well, you say, 'Let him T.A.' What he does in the T.A. sections, they have about as much interest in as in a soccer match in Bulgaria.

"So when I go complain and say, 'You can't put that guy in my class,' they say, 'What the hell do you want me to do?' I say, 'I want you to fire that son of a bitch because I want a person who can speak English.' And they say, 'Oh Freddy, give him a chance.'

"So we keep our factory going. We have a factory here. We're interested in making Ph.D.s. If I were the chair I'd just drop them, I'd cut the Ph.D.s down by one-third.

"But they want an empire. So if they can't fill the graduate student slots with Americans, they'll fill 'em up with Filipinos or horses or cows. But we still have in place the financial apparatus that puts them in front of a class. Some of these guys work out pretty well, but it's chance, because we don't show that much interest. It's a great accident. *They don't care.*

"[My colleagues] will concede everything I say, because they know they will do nothing. Because they are looking for *greatness*. We're channeling all our money into a supercomputer in the hope that somehow glory will descend on Urbana, Illinois, and people will remember we are a major university. We're going to have a supercomputer, and *we're going to be Harvard*. That's our shot at glory and these guys live on glory. All these guys in the faculty lounge talk about is what we are ranked; if we could get this guy in our department or get that guy in our department, maybe we can be ranked 15th. *Their aim in life is to be ranked 15th in the nation.* Well God save us! What good does it do you? *Zero.* But they think it is a reflection of great intellectual effort being made. They never entertain the idea of creating a real, diversified, intellectual experience down here in the heartland of Illinois. That never occurs to them. I don't think they see the university as a learning experience."

And if they cannot get greatness at Illinois, Gottheil says, they will simply go elsewhere. "Professors who have been here 20 years, you give them one dollar more, and they'd move to Iowa. They have no loyalty. We'd trade ourselves for a buck. They'd just as soon leave as stay, and the money goes to the people who have offers, and the offers go to the researchers."

Gottheil doubts that he would be given tenure if he were coming through the system now. "Not in a million years," he says. "I was lucky. I came in at the tail end of serious work in economics."

Over the last few decades, he has seen a dramatic shift in the values and priorities of his discipline.

"What bothers me is that we are turning out these students, and they are going to become the professors, and they will be incapable of teaching economics properly because they did not have training. We are creating economic illiterates. They can't even spell Adam Smith.

"Take a look at our graduate students. It's pathetic. The first thing we look at is his proficiency in mathematics. And if a guy can dance we bring him in. We put him through a graduate program of economic theory and econometrics, and we pound that crap into his head, and three years later we send him off into the market. *The guy can't even write a letter home to mother.* He's had no real, honest training, no intellectual thought. We tell the guy, 'You have about six years to turn out articles to get tenure.' He's about as interested in pursuing intellectual questions as the man in the moon, because intellectual thought is non-precise, it does not lead to well constructed arguments that can be published. If I have one original idea in my lifetime, I think, God bless me. And if I were to develop this, I would like at least 10 years to be able to think about it and develop it. But you can't afford that. The very first year a faculty member is up [for review], you look at the vita. And if it's blank you tell him, 'Why don't you try going somewhere else?' So the guy's interest is not to think about serious intellectual questions but to play the game. And we have journals constructed to handle that stuff and that's what we measure a man's work on."

Gottheil is pessimistic about the chances of reform, even though Illinois administrators insist that undergraduate education will be upgraded. The university's rewards still go to the researchers, not the teachers, and Gottheil sees nothing changing about that. Talk of reform, he says, has little to do either with improving the lot of the teachers or with real concern for students.

"It's like what Marx said about the British and India: 'They speak of God. They mean Cotton.' [Our administrators] speak of undergraduate education. They mean placating the legislature."

Sidebar:
THE STARS

The University of South Carolina finally won itself the national attention it so desperately wanted. But the publicity did not come in the form the university had hoped.

Under considerable pressure, university administrators acknowledged that they had paid $314,000 to Jihan Sadat, the widow of Egyptian President Anwar Sadat, for teaching a single course in Egyptian culture for three semesters. The figure included not only her fees for the course itself but also $94,283 for 44 round-trip flights on chartered airplanes for Mrs. Sadat and her security retinue, and more than $1,000 for gifts, including two porcelain figurines and a glass bud vase.[1]

Mrs. Sadat was not the only luminary the University of South Carolina had attracted to its campus in Columbia. Others included:

- Bill Cosby, who was paid $25,000 to deliver the university's commencement speech in the spring of 1986.

- Lyn Nofziger, a former aide to President Reagan who was paid $30,000 for lecturing *once a month* at the school.

- James Lehrer and Robert MacNeil, the hosts of PBS's "MacNeil-Lehrer News Hour," who were each paid $37,500 to lecture *twice a semester.*

- Gale Sayers, the former Chicago Bears running back, who was paid $25,000 a semester for being "a consultant" to the College of Education.

- Howard Simons, former managing editor of *The Washington Post,* who was paid $45,000 a semester for appearing on campus once a week.[2]

The revelations drew widespread indignation. "That hucksterism has replaced more genteel ways to raise prestige and cold cash is disquieting," *The New York Times* editorialized.[3] But the University of South Carolina was guilty only of being more flamboyant and extravagant than other schools. It was certainly not alone in trying to buy academic respectability and recognition by hiring high-priced stars.

In their mad dash for prestige, the one sure-fire route to prominence for universities is the Big Name, and price is often not an obstacle.

Relatively unknown George Mason University on the outskirts of Washington, D.C., has made its grab for eminence by hiring several stars, including James M. Buchanan, who recently won the Nobel Prize in economics. "Getting a Nobel validates a lot of things we are doing that weren't noticed before," exults George Mason's president, George Johnson.[4] Duke University has put itself in the vanguard of literary theory by aggressively hiring a pack of *au courant* critics at six-figure salaries. Even schools that are forced to cut classes for undergraduates to come up with the money for the stars have joined in the hunt. At the University of Wisconsin-Milwaukee, where a majority of the freshman class has to take some sort of remedial class, the Mass Communication Department recently hired a $75,000 research professor, even though it was forced to cut several sections for budget reasons.[5]

Throughout the higher strata of academe, salaries of $100,000 or more for prominent academics are no longer unheard of, nor are guarantees of research support, housing subsidies, travel allowances, light (or no) teaching loads, and even the authority to appoint other professors in their fields.

The new star system is a variation on what University of Chicago President Robert Maynard Hutchins called in the 1930s, the Great Man Theory of education.

"Under this theory," Hutchins wrote, "you pay no attention to what you teach, or indeed to what you investigate. You get great men for your faculty. Their mere presence on the campus inspires, stimulates, and exalts. It matters not how inarticulate their teaching or how recondite their researches; they are, as the saying goes, an education in themselves. . . . The fact is that the great-man theory is an excuse, an alibi, a vacuous reply to the charge that we have no intelligent program for the higher learning. It amounts to saying that we do not need one; we could give you one if we wanted to. But if you will only accept the great-man theory you will spare us the trouble of thinking."[6]

Neither the stars nor Hutchins' great men are hired for their teaching ability. Georgetown University, for example, has boasted of having former U.N. Ambassador Jeane Kirkpatrick on its faculty. But according to an account in *Newsweek on Campus,* Kirkpatrick, like many of the other stars, is an awful teacher. One student is quoted as saying, "She was rarely prepared. People would literally get up and leave in the middle of her lectures."[7]

The chief value of the stars is often their "halo effect," the glow they impart to the entire operation, regardless of their own contributions. "Most of the time," the Harvard student guide says, "all the stars offer are large lecture courses where you and 500 other people get to hear pearls of wisdom, and not all of the pearls are that shiny. Some of Harvard's most famous professors are also some of Harvard's most infamous lecturers. . . . Pack a telescope."[8]

The greatest impact of the star system, however, might not necessarily be on the students of the stars as much as on the atmosphere of the university as a whole.

"When you hire these stars," one Berkeley professor told *Newsweek on Campus,* "in effect, you're saying to the rest of the department: 'You're doing the dishes.' "[9]

And in the American university of the 1980s "doing the dishes" means teaching.

Sidebar:
THE SEMINAR

The modern university seminar is usually traced back to Woodrow Wilson, who sought to reform Princeton before trying his hand at remaking international politics. His success was about equal in both undertakings. The idea of the seminar was laudable enough: It would bring professors down from the podium and into more intimate contact with students. And it would replace the lecture's sterile one-way flow of information with a dialogue of scholars sharing their knowledge in an atmosphere of intellectual collegiality. What Wilson did not foresee was the convenience of the seminar for professors anxious to minimize their teaching responsibilities. [1]

By the 1960s, the seminar (Wilson, who was president of Princeton, had called it a "preceptorial") had become part of the teaching load of nearly every senior professor. To critics, the seminars were held up as living proof that universities were not neglecting close student-professor interaction, and their immense educational value was used to justify the mass classes to which freshmen and sophomores were being subjected. But what actually goes on in the seminar? John Silber, the president of Boston University, provided some insight when he was a dean at the University of Texas.

"The teaching load of many professors consists solely of one or two small seminars each week," Silber noted, "seminars for which they rarely prepare, at which they rarely do more than audit or at most comment briefly in an atmosphere of relaxed cordiality or hostility." The result was that Wilson's bastardized creation had become sessions in which "ill-prepared graduate students spend most of their time boring one another and wasting everybody's time, because the professor refuses to come to class fully prepared to guarantee an hour of intensive instruction for all participants. . . ."[2]

Another academic dissident, Professor Pierre van den Berghe, struck a similar note in his *Academic Gamesmanship*, when he wrote: "A graduate seminar in your field requires little if any preparation at all. You just distribute a reading list, assign topics to your students, let them do most of the talking, and confine your activities to two or three wise remarks a week."[3]

Little seems to have changed. Recounts one graduate student:[4] "I've taken six seminar courses, and in every one of them it's been almost impossible to learn a god damn thing. On the first day of class, the professor announces that everyone will write a paper. Sometimes he says that since the first paper writer will need about three weeks to get ready, there won't be a class for those three weeks. After that, all of the class periods will be spent having people read their papers aloud, with discussion to follow.

"When the professor asks who wants to go first, a woman volunteers. (It's almost always a woman.) The professor tells her that since she has less time to write than everyone else, her paper doesn't have to be as long as the others. She nods. Then she writes a 90-page paper, with 15 footnotes to the page. It is wordy, repetitious, and boring. It starts nowhere and draws no discernible conclusions. But she gets an A, and if you were planning a 25-page paper, you realize you have to bump it up to 35 or it will look like you blew it off.

In every seminar there is one guy who sits immediately to the left of the professor. He always gets there 20 minutes before class starts. He puts his attache case on the table and snaps it open, but he never pulls anything out of it. He monopolizes all the discussions and he likes to say 'in terms of.' Whenever he asks a question of someone who has just delivered a paper, it is never to learn something; the question is always phrased in such a way as to show how much he knows about the subject. This guy's paper turns out to be the weakest in the class, but he gets his A. In fact, very few students in seminars get B's, and in the entire history of seminars, no student anywhere who has shown up for some classes and written the paper has ever gotten lower than a B.

"You can learn more in two hours' random reading in the library than you can in a semester-long seminar. But if you take five or six seminar courses plus a colloquium or two, you can get to be a master of something, with a degree to prove it."

Sidebar:
AUDIO-VISUAL PEDAGOGY

A good deal of American higher education takes place in the dark. Literally. In an article in a campus newsletter, Professor Sam Davis of the University of California at Berkeley advises his colleagues: "Slides are invaluable if you are uncomfortable with your speaking or dramatic style, the ease with which you gesture, or the way you move around the podium. . . . With the lights out and visuals on the screen there is less emphasis on you. . . ."

Davis, however, admits there are drawbacks. "Given the opportunity to be in attendance but not seen, students often sleep."[1]

Indeed, slides and overhead projectors are popular.

Recounts a junior at the University of Michigan: "I had two chemistry professors my freshman year whose entire teaching method was based on the use of an overhead projector. They would merely put a transparency up on the screen and read it off to the class, sometimes adding a little professorial insight, but that was rare. The class would then rush to copy down the transparency before the professor finished going through it so they could get a few minutes of shut-eye, or fill in a few more blanks in their crossword puzzles. The faster you wrote, the more free time you got.

"To top it off, all the transparencies were on reserve in the libraries, so you could theoretically not go to any lectures and still get all the notes—you wouldn't miss a thing."[2]

5 Dare to Be Stupid: The Curriculum, a Short Course

"Everyone has won, and all must have prizes. . . ."
—Lewis Carroll

THE university curriculum is the flip side of the academic culture's attitude toward teaching.

"In an environment that is serious about the quality of teaching," the Association of American Colleges said in its 1985 report *Integrity in the College Curriculum*,[1] "the grand design of the curriculum will receive the attention it deserves." But, as we have seen, the actual environment of the university is anything but serious about the quality of teaching. And its attention to the design of the curriculum is reflected in the intellectual confusion, nonexistent standards, junk courses, so-called "guts," and blow-offs that are (or should be) the shame of American higher education.

But the curriculum is not completely without its rationale. Indeed, it bears the unmistakable mark of the professorial touch. As absurd as it is, the curriculum keeps the universities well-stocked and the students reasonably pacified, while demanding as little as possible from either students or professors. No other explanation can account for the melange of incoherence that confronts students at the modern university.

Roaming freely through the trackless wastes of registration, a

79

liberal arts sophomore at the University of Illinois bitterly laments his disappointment: "It seems like preregistration is a joke," he says. He had signed up for "Human Sexuality," but there were no available places. "I don't feel like taking bowling," he says. "I was looking forward to it. I guess there are a lot of undersexed people on this campus."[2]

Not so at Middlebury College in Vermont, where students have filed into a class that discussed the issues of "popular culture, eroticism, esthetics, voyeurism, and misogyny" as they are reflected in the films of Brigitte Bardot.[3] There are, in fact, few interests to which higher education does not cater. Auburn University offered a course in "Recreation Interpretive Services," which was described as "principles and techniques used to communicate natural, historical, and cultural features of outdoor recreation to park visitors." The school also listed in-depth courses in "Principles of Recreation," "Park and Recreation Maintenance," and "Recreation Leadership."[4] At Kent State, students have been offered a smorgasbord of intellectual offerings, including "Camp Leadership," a course that covers "the role of the camper and counselor," and "Records Management," in which students "set up, explain, and maintain alphabetic, geographic, numerical, and subject-filing systems." For the scholarly inclined, there is "Socio-Psychological Aspects of Clothing"; for the less rigorous-minded, "Basic Roller Skating," and for the adventurous, "Dance Roller Skating."[5]

At the University of Illinois, students have been able to work toward their B.A. by taking "Pocket Billiards," or the "Anthropology of Play," which is described as "the study of play with emphasis on origin, diffusion, spontaneity, emergence, and diversity."[6] The University of Massachusetts at Amherst has listed courses for credit in "Slimnastics" and "Ultimate Frisbee."[7]

Students at the University of Michigan who have taken "Sports Marketing and Management" have been given exams with such questions as: "Athletic administrators should be primarily concerned with two (2) groups: Name them." (Answer: players and coaches.) "True or false: At the Michigan Stadium a spectator can be readmitted to the game if he has a hand stamp visible." (Answer: False.)[8]

And students fortunate enough to gain admission to "Music Video 454" at California State University's Los Angeles campus can sit at the feet of Professor Alan Bloom,* who has declared, "I want students thinking" about television. Or at least about MTV. The class's only textbook was the *Rolling Stone Book of Rock Video,* and one class project has been a field trip to Hollywood where the students acted as extras in rock videos—for credit. On slower days, they have analyzed videotapes of Weird Al Yankovic singing "Dare to Be Stupid."[9]

"Central to the troubles . . ."

When the Association of American Colleges issued its report on the state of the curriculum in 1985, its conclusions were not surprising. "[W]hat passes as a college curriculum," the report said, had degenerated into "almost anything goes."

But what distinguished the AAC report from its counterparts—and indeed from most analyses issued over the last 50 years—was the directness of its indictment. "Central to the troubles and to the solution are the professors . . . ," the report charged.

> "Adept at looking out for themselves—departmental staffing, student enrollments, courses reflecting narrow scholarly interests, attendance at professional meetings—professors unquestionably offer in their courses exquisite examples of specialized learning. *But who looks after the shop? Who takes responsibility, not for the needs of the history or English or biology department, but for the curriculum as a whole? Who thinks about the course of study as it is experienced by students? Who reviews and justifies and rationalizes the academic program for which a college awards the coveted credential: a bachelor's degree?*"[10] [Emphasis added.]

The answer, of course, was nobody.

Even the major, the AAC concluded, had become "little more than a gathering of courses taken in one department, lacking structure and depth. . . ." The nature of the majors also "varies widely and irrationally" from one institution to another. The chair

* Not the best-selling author.

of the Committee for Economic Education of the American Economic Association confirmed that, confessing: "We know preciously little about what the economics major is or does for students."[11]

The problem of the university curriculum is no longer merely that there is no central body of shared knowledge at the heart of the university education—certain books that all educated men and women presumably would read. In the last several decades— a period that corresponds exactly to the professoriate's rise to unchallenged power—the bachelor's degree has been so completely stripped of meaning that employers cannot even be sure if its holder has minimum skills that were once taken for granted among college graduates. Somewhere in the professoriate's endless curricular shell game, the universities lost track of the need to teach critical thinking, writing skills, or even basic knowledge about the world.

Even as academia's claims of success—and pleas for money— grew ever more insistent, stories about the ignorance of college students became nearly clichés. Typical is the story of the Harvard *senior* who thanked his history professor for explaining World War I, saying, "I've always wondered why people kept talking about a *Second* World War."[12] When a literature professor asked a class of 200 students at a Midwestern school how many of them had heard of *Don Quixote,* only two students raised their hands. How many, she asked, were familiar with *The Man of La Mancha?* Not a single hand went up.[13] When historian Diane Ravitch visited one urban Minnesota university, she found that not one of 30 students in a course on "ethnic relations" had ever heard of the Supreme Court's landmark *Brown* v. *The Board of Education* case.[14]

The capacity of American higher education to turn out graduates utterly ignorant of international affairs and foreign languages continues to be the wonder of the world. Less than 15 percent of the seniors who were tested on their knowledge of world affairs in 1981 could answer even two-thirds of the questions correctly.*

* Not a single student scored higher than 84 correct answers out of a total of 101 questions. Most ominously, the group that scored lowest was education majors, who averaged a pathetic 39.8.

Another survey found that 75 percent of college students had studied a foreign language at one time or another, but only 7 percent thought they could understand a native speaker.[15] Occasional surveys of college students' knowledge of geography have yielded horrific results.*

This epidemic of ignorance can in large measure be attributed to academia's indifference. The professors are otherwise occupied and cannot be bothered. In his speech at the ceremonies marking Harvard's 350th birthday, Secretary of Education William Bennett said: "There's not that much effort to see to it, systematically and devotedly, that real education occurs."[16] That outraged the assembled academics. But the evidence is overwhelmingly on Bennett's side.**

The Numbers Game

The curriculum is a direct product of a fundamental paradox of life in academia. Even the most esoteric researcher scaling the highest peaks of scholastic sorcery ultimately relies on the undergraduates huddled in the foothills because they support his endeavors. This is particularly true in state universities where

* In 1984, a survey of University of North Carolina students found that 69 percent could not identify a single African country between the Sahara and South Africa (there are 28); less than half could name the two largest states in the U.S.; 88 percent could not identify the five Great Lakes; and only 27 percent knew that Manila is in the Philippines. In 1987, a survey at the University of Wisconsin-Oshkosh found that 25 percent of the students *in a geography class,* could not locate the Soviet Union on a world map. On a map of the 48 contiguous states, only 22 percent could identify 40 or more. (*The Philadelphia Inquirer,* June 10, 1987)

** A staff member of the National Commission on Excellence in Education found that few two or four year colleges required that a student demonstrate "true proficiency *in anything* as a condition for receiving a degree, fewer still that set clear learning objectives and unambiguous standards for academic performance. . . ." In fact, the American Council on Education found that only 15 percent of universities require tests for general knowledge; only 17 percent for critical thinking; and only 19 percent for minimum competency.

budget priorities are often closely tied to statistical measurements of enrollment. Because students are essentially hostages held by the universities to ensure society's continued good will (how long would universities survive if they dropped the pretense of educating undergraduates?), an elaborate numbers game colors the entire academic landscape.

In their study of academia, Professors William Rau and Paul Baker concluded that the SCH/FTE ratio—student contact hours to full-time equivalent faculty—"plays much the same role in academe that return on investment plays in corporate America, and in both instances the systematic misuse of these crude, reductionist measures has been the cause of . . . organizational decline. Taken to their extreme, SCH/FTE ratios turn undergraduate colleges into little more than body processing plants."[17]

The politics of this numbers game, particularly when money is tight, virtually dictates the destruction of traditional standards of performance and intellectual integrity. "Guts"—undemanding, unchallenging courses of notoriously low standards—are a symbol of the process. But the gut is not an aberration in the modern university: It is the inevitable byproduct of the professoriate's desire to expend as little time and energy on teaching combined with the imperative of keeping classrooms stocked with warm tuition-paying bodies. Nor is this limited merely to the lower end of the academic spectrum.

Not too many years ago students at Harvard could get credit for courses in "Scuba Diving," and "Sport and Political Ideology." Twenty-two students once studied Harvard's multiflex offense with the team's quarterback.[18] The University of Maryland is eager to break into the big leagues of major research universities with its high-tech research projects, but until recently, it also offered the so-called "Len Bias Major," named after the basketball star killed by an overdose of cocaine. Bias, along with many other athletes, majored in what the school euphemistically called "general studies" but which was generally known as "College for the Aimless," heavy on courses in such mind-bending subjects as "Rhythmic Activities," "Sex Roles," and "Recreation and Leisure."[19]

But this was an almost inevitable outgrowth of academia's manipulation of "democratization." The pressure to open admissions as wide as possible, argue Professors Rau and Baker, is academe's "original sin."

"Perhaps Socrates or Jesus Christ could educate this range of students, but most faculty cannot walk on water, nor do they care for the taste of hemlock," they wrote. But given the "grinding, impervious logic" of the numbers game, academia must make compromises. Among the first things to go, the authors argue, are any introductory textbooks "written at a 12th-grade reading level or above. . . . Since students can vote with their feet, introductory courses are typically geared to keep the bottom quarter of the skill range from fleeing in panic."[20]

The numbers game also virtually dictated the collapse of standards within the classroom itself. "If two-thirds of the students do not possess the skills necessary for professional success," wrote Professor David Berkman, a former chairman of a journalism department at an urban university, "there is no way you can flunk out a number anywhere near that percentage. *There is simply too much intimidation in the academic environment.* This is especially true for junior—meaning untenured—faculty members who teach many of the lower division courses where the bulk of the weeding out should take place. . . . No junior instructor who wishes to gain tenure will flunk out 67 percent in an introductory course." The result, charges Berkman, is rampant pandering.*[21]

---

* As department chairman, Berkman sent the following memo to faculty members: "[I]f we stress professional standards and if we demand quantities of work at which we, as students 20 years ago would never have blinked, and the result is that 40 percent of the intitial enrollment drops the course and we begin to hear how students are badmouthing us as sonofabitches, then it's only natural for us to begin to wonder if this is not a real reflection of something seriously deficient in us as teachers; and also to wonder, that as word of our reputation gets around, whether it won't raise as serious questions in the minds of our colleagues as well.

"The result is that we pander.

"We pander to the ignorance—or more likely the fears—of students who cannot and will not accept that as professional writers and speakers they will be expected to show professional competence in their writing and speaking. . . .

That often takes the form of an unspoken bargain between students and faculty throughout nearly the entire curriculum: Don't ask too much of me, and I won't ask too much of you.

The bargain works for both undergraduates and professors.

A three-year study of an urban community college in the early 1980s revealed the extent to which such "deals" can dominate the classroom. At the school, pseudonymously named "Oakwood" by researchers, administrators emphasized what they called "alternate instructional techniques."

"The good faculty members were those who did not require students to read, providing them with alternate means of getting the same information," wrote Richard Richardson, a professor of higher education at Arizona State University. "The belief that appropriate behavior in courses consisted of negotiating a set of minimum demands with faculty and then meeting these with the least possible expenditure of outside effort, was fostered by the absence for most students of any perceived relationship between being in class and educational objectives."[22]

The same phenomenon is captured by this account from a senior at the University of Michigan:

> "I had a communication class last year. Huge lecture, right. I'm not sure he wanted to do it. Here's the problem. It's 8 in the morning, a lot of people file in, stare at this guy for an hour while he talks, while he lectures. And then we have two midterms—both these fill-in-the-dot, standardized, computerized type of things where you know your grade the next day. No essay. This isn't a memorization class. 'Freedom of expression' is what it's called—it's definitely a theoretical class. There were no essays, there was no way to test

---

"We pander to student laziness—or to the past failures of colleagues to impose a challenging quantity of work—so that we pull back the first time seniors scream incredulously about the 20-page term paper, and in the future avoid ever opening ourselves to this reaction again. . . ."

"And, perhaps worst of all, we pander to that high school-guidance-counselor-mentality with which so many of our students are imbued, which manifests itself as a demand that our judgments and our grading be grounded more in a superficial, psychotherapeutic support, than on the professionalism in which the instruction and the kind of program we offer should be based."

your application of your knowledge at all. And I just thought, 'Gosh, what a waste this is.' It's a prerequisite for a lot of other classes, and it's not even a 'weeder' course—anyone that read the book and memorized it got a decent grade."[23]

Perhaps the clearest evidence of the extent to which the bargain came to dominate undergraduate education was the inflation of grades that accompanied the rise of the new professoriate. At Harvard in 1978, 78 percent of the student body made it onto the dean's list, compared with 20 percent in the 1920s and 26 percent in the 1930s.[24] The University of Michigan's 1974-75 freshman class had the weakest SAT scores in decades but was given the highest grade point average ever. In 1975, 70 percent of the grades at Princeton were A's or B's. At Stanford, the average grade was A— [25]

"A lenient grader," observed author Lansing Lamont, "could draw students to his course like sparrows to a feeder."[26]

The same pressures of the numbers game corrupted even the attempts to reform the badly rusting system. The most popular response to complaints about the incoherence of the curriculum was the introduction of new "core curriculums." But even the reforms were drawn into the professors' curricular numbers game.

In practice, Rau and Baker argue, the latent function of the core curriculum at most state universities "is to allocate student credit hours across colleges and departments."

> "In plain English, it is an academic pork barrel. Just as Keynesian economic policy attempts to stabilize fluctuations in economic demand, the core curriculum attempts to stabilize fluctuations in student demand. Little else will explain the hopeless muddle of core curricula."[27]

The fact is that curricular coherence is the archenemy of the academic culture. If the undergraduate were ever to be placed at the center of the university and the curriculum molded around the kind of education he or she should receive, the entire focus of the university would be disrupted, and the power of the academic villages badly shaken. The academy would be forced to revoke its *carte blanche* to the professors; and the villages would not only have to begin communicating within one another, they would have to make concessions to one another based on priorities other than their own. Some might even have to wither away. And the professors are not going to let that happen, at least not without an epic struggle in which they will use their entire arsenal of academic double-think.

The Ignorance Lobby

All of the academic maneuvering and posturing over the curriculum conceals one of the academic culture's most brazen coups: a startling transvaluation that has not only made mediocrity a way of life but something of an official ideology.

This was academia's problem: How could it defend itself from the inevitable backlash against its failure to educate its students? What could it say in its own defense when confronted with the monumental ignorance of its charges?

Could the professors somehow develop a philosophical justification that would make their abject neglect and the resulting ignorance of their students seem a virtue? This would, of course, involve turning the values of higher education almost literally on their head. But nothing is impossible in the academic culture for those who have faith.

The roots of the new ideology can be detected clearly in the 1947 statement of a commission appointed by President Truman which declared: "We shall be denying educational opportunity to many young people as long as we maintain the present orientation of higher education toward verbal skills and intellectual interests. Many young people have abilities of a different kind. . . ." The commission declared that such nonintellectual youngsters cannot receive a proper education if universities insist on recognizing "only one kind" of intelligence. The other kinds of "intelligence" specified by the commission included "social sensitivity and versatility, artistic ability, motor skill and dexterity, and mechanical aptitude and ingenuity. . . ."[28]

With his characteristic biting wit, the University of Chicago's

Robert Maynard Hutchins said at the time that much of the report "reads like a Fourth of July oration in Pedaguese. . . . It skirts the edge of illiteracy and sometimes falls over the brink. . . ."

But Hutchins was most concerned about the report's enthusiasm for greater "diversity."

"Since American institutions of higher education are already so diversified that neither the faculty nor the students can talk with one another except about the weather, politics, and last Saturday's game," Hutchins wrote, " the commission's advice is a little like telling a drowning man that he can improve his position by drinking a great deal of water."29

But the temptation was too much for academics to resist. The key was use of the words "diversity" and "pluralism," with their impeccable democratic credentials. Academics quickly found they exercised an almost mesmerizing effect on policymakers. But the rape of the language did not stop there. If curricular gibberish was now "diversity," then the traditional standards must be elitism, and anyone who advocated even a modicum of rationality in the curriculum must not only be anti-democratic, but potentially even fascistic.

The new labels proved to have almost an inexhaustible capacity for application in academic disputes. The University of Georgia, for example, was convulsed when an English teacher was fired for protesting favoritism to failing athletes. The case drew national attention, but an interesting footnote involved the vice president for academic affairs of the university, Virginia Trotter, who had implemented most of the policies at issue. Trotter had her Ph.D. in home economics. Her publications included pamphlets with such titles as "The No–Stoop, No–Stretch Kitchen," and "Cleaning Supplies—Keep Them Handy." Dr. Trotter attributed criticism of her academic credentials to "elitism."30 And such was the culture in American higher education that no one had any doubt whatsoever that she meant it as a pejorative term. Administrators understand that unreasonable academic standards or "elitist" curricula are not only ideologically wrong but, more importantly, incompatible with the financial health of their institutions.

The new ideology of diversity and anti-elitism was a potent new weapon for the professoriate in protecting its gains against inconvenient reforms. In the mid-1970s, for example, the Carter administration summoned academic leaders to Washington to discuss the possibility of holding a White House conference called "Liberal Learning in the 1980s and Beyond." Harvard had just introduced its Core Curriculum, and the administration had noted with interest the apparent enthusiasm for reform among the nation's academic leaders. But when confronted with specifics, they found that the academics were less forthcoming. Many professors bitterly opposed any effort to develop even a minimum curriculum, because they saw it as a reactionary infringement on their own prerogatives. Some were concerned over simple turf issues: Would their own academic arabesques on Sumerian sodomy be included in any such core? But in public they took a different, and by now predictable, tack: They expressed lugubrious concern over the problems of defining any curriculum in light of the diversity of the student body, particularly the so-called new learners, who would not be in schools if they were forced to conform to traditional standards.

After two days of wrangling, the organizers dropped the goal of defining liberal learning and in a burst of inspired profspeak changed it to "legitimizing diversity in the solving of common problems." Plans for a full-dress White House parley were quietly scrapped.[31]

As if to prove that this was not a fluke, a 1983 conference sponsored by the National Endowment for the Humanities came to a similar "conclusion." At the NEH conference, representatives from 11 institutions of higher learning could agree only that "the curriculum should reflect the particular goals and character of the institution. There is no single effective education, and what works well at one institution may be a disaster at another. . . ."[32] In other words, they punted. But deciding not to decide was itself a powerful ratification of curricular disintegration because it left the academic culture untouched.

A slightly different variant of the new ideology can be seen in Brown University's hot new curriculum.

More aptly, it is a non-curriculum. When it was introduced in the late 1960s, it abolished all course requirements and most of the other traditional standards of academia as well. The grade "D" was summarily dropped. But that hardly mattered because Brown students could take any number of courses pass/fail.[33] And if by chance they did fail, that also did not really matter. Under the new dispensation, failures were not recorded on transcripts. ("I regard recording [failures] for the external world both superfluous and intimidating, or punishing," a Brown dean explained.)[34] A Brown student could also fail as many as four courses and still graduate—with the equivalent of seven semesters of work at most schools.[35]

An article in *The New Republic* by former Brown student Philip Weiss provided a revealing glimpse of the culture at work, complete with courses like, "Introduction to Cinematic Coding and Narrativity"—dubbed "Clap for Credit" by students. Weiss also described a course officially titled "Rock 'n' Roll Is Here to Stay," and quoted one student enthusing, "You could go to class and listen to the *White Album*," to which another student responded, "You don't have to go to class. I'd turn on the stereo and raise my hand in bed."[36]

Not coincidentally, after the New Curriculum was installed, Brown quickly became the hottest school in the Ivy League, if not the country. It has become, in fact, one of the nation's first designer colleges. At one time or another in the 1980s, it boasted such luminaries in its student body as Amy Carter and the daughters of Jane Fonda, Geraldine Ferraro, Barbara Bach, Claus von Bulow, and Prince Michael of Greece.[37] For a few years it was the trendiest school in the country, even topping Harvard in the number of applications.[38]

It is also a museum piece of the academic mind in its purest state.

Dean Walter Massey explained that the genius of the New Curriculum is that it focuses "on the student as the subject of concern, *not on areas of knowledge* [my emphasis]," and that it puts a premium on intellectual independence over intellectual breadth.

"If the flexible curriculum runs the danger of allowing academic narrowness in students," he explained, "the overly prescribed curriculum runs the dangers of encouraging students to believe they are educated when they finish college."³⁹

In the past, of course, people went to college specifically because they *did* believe that when they were finished they would be educated. *That was the point.* That was why they paid so much money for it. That was why they devoted four years of their life to study. But at Brown, the gurus of the academic culture succeeded beyond their wildest dreams—not merely in abolishing traditional standards but in inverting the very purposes of higher education.

Of course, the reality is that at the heart of the New Curriculum is neither a body of knowledge nor concern for the students or their "intellectual independence." A Brown dean hints at the actual agenda that underlies the ideology of the New Curriculum when he said: "What a lot of people don't realize is that the faculty has much more freedom than students do under this curriculum. . . ."*⁴⁰

Unfortunately, the worst effects of the new ideology of mediocrity are felt not in the uplands of the Ivy League but at the lower levels of academia, where even basic literacy may be at stake.

When the College Board, for example, made the modest suggestion in 1983 that college entrants ought to be competent in such things as standard English (vocabulary, sentence structures, and what not), Professor James Sledd, an emeritus professor of English at the University of Texas, weighed in with an indignant rebuttal in the *English Journal.*

The College Board had noted that "Without such competencies, knowledge of history, science, language, and all other subjects is unattainable." To Sledd this was "transparently false."

"A person (need one say it?) can learn a huge amount without

---

* Under cover of their trendy curriculum, Brown's professors have pulled off their own coup. One dissident administrator, Ed Beiser, notes that Brown now has mass lecture classes with several hundred students. "When a freshman can pass through two semesters without any member of the faculty even coming to grips with his work, it's difficult to train that student to be an active participant in his education." (*Brown Alumni Magazine,* April 1987)

being able to read or write at all . . .," Sledd declared. "Quite simply, it is a gross injustice to demand a mastery of standard English from students who through no fault of their own, have had no chance to master it." That is because standard English is "the language of privilege" that is now "essentially a tool and instrument of the dominant for purposes of domination." Sledd also writes that applying such elitist standards as literacy would "close the doors of our colleges to millions of students—and" (perhaps more importantly) "thousands of professors."[41]

Sledd echoes the position staked out by Professor William Lasher, one-time chair of the University of Cincinnati's committee on linguistics and director of undergraduate studies of English, who excoriated his colleagues some years back for objecting to students who wrote such sentences as, "We was at the ball game last night" or "Mary had five card," because they were "clear and logical" attempts to simplify the language, by abandoning the reactionary strictures of what he termed the "experts' rule."[42]

None of this is merely theoretical; it has concrete implications for what happens in the classroom. And most ominous of all, the various trends of the academic culture toward mediocrity and officially sanctioned ignorance tend to filter down and collect in the Schools of Education.

Richard Mitchell, the author of *The Underground Grammarian* and a trenchant critic of the depredations of the educationists, notes that it is "a bizarre article of faith" of the educationists that "superior intelligence and academic accomplishment [are] traits not suitable to schoolteachers."[43]

Indeed, that attitude seems deeply ingrained in the teacher factories. A special state study committee, for example, found that Massachusetts' teacher education programs were distinguished, particularly at the graduate level, by "low or no admission standards . . . redundant course work, low exit standards and poorly constructed programs." At some Massachusetts schools, education students had SAT scores as much as 135 points below the national mean.[44]

The lack of meaningful standards in schools of education seems to act like a magnet for some of the lowest achieving students in higher education. The schools then make the very least of this material by creating an environment where the emphasis is on "language arts" rather than literature; "values clarification" rather than the study of philosophy or ethics; "student outcomes" instead of learning; and the study of self-actualization, the relationship of nonredundant personological variables, and transpersonal education rather than anything remotely relevant or comprehensible. It also attracts students who know that A's in education classes are as easy to come by as sun in Jamaica. At the University of Illinois, in a recent semester, 50 percent of the grades in 300-level education courses were A's.[45]

The product of this sort of educationist ideology is no longer a mystery. Even though teacher-certification exams are themselves notorious guts, 17 percent of the education graduates nevertheless manage to fail them.[46] The philosophy of mediocrity remains entrenched among the educationists. In that sense it is education's version of the trickle-down theory. What begins in the upper reaches of the academy inevitably works its way down into the classrooms of elementary schools where the basic issues of literacy are at stake.

Ultimately, the legacy of the gut culture is a generation of kids with self-esteems well intact, but unable to read, write, or do even basic math—in other words, self-satisfied illiterates. It is hard to avoid the conclusion that despite its thinly veiled contempt for the lower level schools, the university is, in fact, the home office of educational mediocrity in America.

Sidebar:
GREAT GUTS

The Yale senior proudly anointed himself the school's premier "gutmaster."[1] He was, he claimed, a certified expert in hunting out the most inane, easiest A courses in the syllabus. "Introduction to Interpersonal and Group Dynamics," for example, was a sure bet: "Lots of in-class fun and games. No tests. Very little reading. And a paper or two (one of which, purposely, is a group exercise)."

But this was nothing, he later recounted in a column in the *Yale Daily News*, compared with his discovery of "The Greatest Gut of Them All."

The course, "Contemporary Sociological Theory," theoretically met on Tuesdays and Thursdays. On the first day of class, the professor announced they would never meet Thursdays.

Also, there was no syllabus, no midterm, no final, and no term papers.

"What about readings?" a student asked. "Oh, we'll read a book and discuss it in class each week." Grades would be based on "participation," he said.

It got better.

During the fourth session of the class, the professor announced: "I like how the discussions are going so much, I'm going to give everyone an A for the course."

Reported the astonished but delighted gutmaster: "More people started coming to class late, being less prepared, and taking catnaps during discussion. But he kept his word about the grades."

There is no definitive explanation of the source of the word "gut." *The New York Times* once took a stab at it by quoting etymologists who speculated that it could refer to courses so easy they could be passed with no more preparation than "gut instinct."[2] (At some schools different terms are used; at Northwestern University, guts are referred to as "micks," in tribute to their patron saint, Mickey Mouse.)

Whatever its source, the gut is a much sought-after fixture in the university, especially in the ostensibly more demanding schools where competition for grades might be stiffer. The gut has even developed refinements of its own. There are two kinds of guts: work guts and grade guts. Sometimes they are found in the same course: These are the "flaming guts."

There is no shortage of any of the variations.

Guts at Harvard are particularly well-documented and even nicknamed ("Heroes for Zeroes," "Nuts and Sluts," "Snowmobiles," "Spots and Dots") in part because of the zeal of the student-run *Confidential Guide*, which diligently searches out and advertises the most outrageous examples. Many of the most incendiary turn up, to the immense embarrassment of Harvard's administration, in Harvard's much-touted Core Curriculum.

In "Popular Culture in the Modern Context," for example, there were no papers and no required sections. Sometimes the section leaders didn't bother to show up for the few that were scheduled. No one seemed to mind. The course is nicknamed "TV." ("If you've ever watched TV or seen a J. L. Goddard or an Alfred Hitchcock movie, you can't fail.")[3]

After nearly half the students in the Core course on "The Atmosphere," got A− or better, the course was quickly redubbed "The Gutmosphere."[4] And the student guide reported that "Coins of the Roman Empire," (no midterm, no final, no readings) was said to attract "the shrewdest scholar-athletes and other hardened gutseekers," because it was offered "at an intellectual level that would not have challenged a third grader."[5]

Although "Theories of Choice" has been the linchpin of the Core's emphasis on moral reasoning, its modest requirements (the midterm has been take-home, and the final has always been multiple choice), the course is affectionately known among students as "Theories of Multiple Choice."[6]

But the king of Harvard guts has been "The Concept of the Hero in Hellenic Civilization," known as "Heroes for Zeroes," a course that has traditionally required little reading and the slightest effort for the maximum grade.[7]

Some of the most reliable guts have been found in the Psychology Department. Even so, students have been warned to avoid the intro courses in the fall "when the professors are reputed to be the ultimate in Harvard boredom." But a spring semester gut can leave even confirmed gut-chasers feeling queasy. "After the course is over," *The Confidential Guide* reports, "you leave wondering if you've learned anything you didn't know before thanks to magazine articles or common sense."[8]

"Of course you have no idea what your data or analysis of the data mean, but then again, even if you did, would you care?"[9]

Research

6 *Through the Looking Glass: An Introduction to Academic Research*

"The leaders of thought have reached the horizons of human reason; but all the wires are down, and they can only communicate with us by unintelligible signals."
—Anonymous, quoted by Winston Churchill.

TIIE debate over higher education often pits teaching versus research. But that begs the question, because it presupposes that the professors really do as much research as they claim and that the research they do actually has some value. What is not in question is the importance research has in the academic culture. "Published research," Harvard President Derek Bok says, "emerges as the common currency of academic achievement, a currency that can be weighed and evaluated across institutional and even national boundaries."[1]

But how much research is really being done? And is it worth anything? Assistant Secretary of Education Chester Finn posed those same questions a few years back, before he went to work for the government. Of the 850,000 working academics in the country, Finn asked, how many really make any contribution to the "enlargement of human knowledge"? After eliminating the "horde of papers, articles, and books whose publication or presentation accomplished nothing save, perhaps, for the author's curricula vitae," Finn estimated that the answer would be that only 1 in 10 professors makes any contribution at all.[2]

He was being charitable. But Finn was highlighting one of the most embarrassing facts in the academic culture. Although the assumption that professors are busily at work on the frontiers of knowledge is the justification for their featherweight teaching loads, 60 percent of all college faculty members have never written or edited a book and one-third have never published even a single journal article.[3] The vast majority of the non-publishers are tenured, senior professors who came into the profession before the great research push began, and they are, inevitably, clustered in schools near the bottom of the academic heap. But even in the better schools, a grant of tenure is often an invitation to scale down or even retire from the arduous business of creating knowledge. Academia, to use Finn's phrase, is often "a very congenial facade behind which very little work of any kind is done. . . ."[4]

But to hear academia's boosters tell it, the scholarship that *is* produced by the professoriate is the glory of the academic enterprise and, indeed, something of a national treasure.

"In these days when foreign economic rivals seem to be surpassing us in one field after another," Henry Rosovsky, the former dean of Harvard's faculty of arts and sciences, exulted in a 1987 article in *The New Republic*, ". . . there is one vital industry where America unquestionably dominates the world: higher education."[5]

Indeed, all parents forced to take out a second mortgage on their homes to pay college tuition can take heart, knowing that their efforts have made it possible for America to maintain its edge by supporting one professor's research into the "Evolution of the Potholder: From Technology to Popular Art," complete with a chart tracing the "Distribution of Potholder, and Hot Mat Design Motifs by Decade," (including the frequency of "fruits and nuts," "animals, birds, insects, fish," and mottoes).[6]

Students sweating through second-shift jobs at Midwestern foundries can take comfort from the knowledge that they make it possible for "Women's Shopping: A Sociological Approach" to see the light of day.[7] Undergraduates living off popcorn and piling up a lifetime of debt can do so with the realization that they are supporting breakthroughs in "A Linguistic and Pedagogic Exegeses of Some (Jieng) Dinka Tongue Twisters, Riddles and Song and Dance Games."[8]

Probably only American higher education could have produced something like one professor's study of the phenomenon of high school cheerleading. The researcher concluded that cheerleaders are not only an "erotic icon" but are engaging in an "institutionalized-biological ritual," which can be compared to religious symbols described in a passage cited by the researcher as "polysemous, affective, and prescriptive signs, deriving their power from their multireferential or multivocal nature and their ability to encode a special model of reality."[9]

It is not necessary to insist that *no* worthwhile or valuable research is being done at the universities to recognize that much of what passes for knowledge creation makes only the most piddling contribution to the pool of human wisdom. Much of it is merely humbug. But research is also the intersection point where all of the major threads of the academic culture cross. For it is here that four faces of the professoriate are most clearly seen: high priest, witch doctor, bureaucrat, and hustler.

The research culture is founded on an almost religious faith in the search for new knowledge, and professors have a marked tendency to drift toward pietistic unctiousness in describing the importance of their work. In practice, however, a more apt parallel for the professors is with the alchemist, sorcerer, and witch doctor who relies on the power of obscure incantations, obfuscation, and the infinite capacity of mind-darkening jargon to intimidate and mystify the uninitiated. The professoriate's success with this sleight of hand is evident in its continuing dominance over higher education and its $120 billion wallet.

But despite the image he projects to the awed world at large, there is an unusual duality in the soul of the professor. Within the fraternity itself, the professoriate enforces its regulations with a rigidity, inflexibility, and utter unimaginativeness that would shame all but the most officious bureaucracy. The dominant theme is careerism, and it colors every aspect of the enterprise. Unread and unreadable, the product of the professoriate is seldom intended to expand the horizons of human knowledge as much as to keep the academic machine running smoothly, the journals filled, the libraries well-stocked, the resumes bulging, and the grants awarded. Volume rather than insight is what counts, and conformity rather than originality is what is rewarded.

Research is, above all, the ticket to academic riches—publications, tenure, promotion, research grants, sabbaticals, consultantships, and lately even a piece of the action in related businesses. Whatever claims the professoriate may make about their work at the cutting edge of their fields, their product is very much for sale, even if that means the topic, methodology, and even the results have to be skewed to obtain a marketable product.

Above all, however, modern-day academic research is a window into the academic mind. University administrators will invariably point to their faculty's work on curing cancer or developing superconductors. But the reality is that much published research is more on the order of "Submerged Sensuality: Technology and Perceptions of Bathing,"[10] or "A Functional Approach to Interruptions in Conversation, a Mathematical Analysis," complete with diagrams and formulas that might have been devised by a nuclear physicist on the number and significance of the "ers" and "uhs" in conversation.[11] Or "The Influence of Contextual Variables on Interpersonal Spacing," in which the author writes that "room size and shape influenced interpersonal distance," but that "interaction indicated that room size affected distance only in rectangular rooms."[12]

For every breakthrough on the mysteries of the atom, there are thousands of articles dealing with issues like "Intimacy in Conversational Styles as a Function of the Degree of Closeness Between Members of a Dyad," in the *Journal of Personality and Social Psychology*, which found, in part, after 10 pages of mathematics and complex formulas that "acquaintances were generally more similar to strangers than they were to friends."[13]

Foundations have not been immune. "Does Foraging Success Determine the Mating Success of Male Tungara Frogs?" for example, is a question of considerable interest apparently not only among Tungara frogs but also among the people who hand out grants for the Smithsonian Institution.[14]

Television has become a rich source for the exercise of the professorial mind, including the study: "Using Television to Alleviate Boredom and Stress: Selective Exposure as a Function of Induced Excitational States." That one concludes: "All in all, the findings lend strong support to the utility of the selective exposure propositions." In particular, they support the notion that "subjects make intelligent program choices—mostly intuitive but sometimes following comprehension of the circumstances—when using television to alleviate boredom and stress."[15]

And a good deal is on the order of the study on Mickey Mouse in which one academic concluded about his features that "Roundness is the essence of the neotenous configuration. . . ."[16] Another scholar posed the question "Are pigeons and children different?" (To which she answered, in part: "The answer to this question must wait until the science develops innovative methodological procedures. . . .")[17]

And one of the nation's more prestigious universities granted a doctorate to a woman for her dissertation on the subject: "An Investigation of Instructor Use of Space," in which the researcher watched 24 instructors in their classroom. She explains: "The observation system provides for six separate and distinct areas of classroom space. These are: (1) use of the blackboard (2) area behind the teacher's desk or table (3) the territory in front of the teacher's desk or table (4) the location outside the last side row of desks . . . (5) the area behind the last row of student desks . . . (6) the teacher's sitting or standing next to a group of students." And she concludes, in part, "Instructors whose students sit in a traditional arrangement use space significantly different than instructors whose students sit in a non-traditional arrangement."[18]

As much as academics might try to disown some of these examples of scholarship, the fact remains that they are the misbegotten children of the academic culture and they bear the unmistakable mark of the academic mind.

J. Scott Armstrong, a professor at the University of Pennsylvania's Wharton School and editor of the *Journal of Forecasting,* conducted his own analysis of academic writing and concluded that professors who wish to be published in the academic press must: "(1) *not* pick an important problem, (2) *not* challenge existing beliefs, (3) *not* obtain surprising results, (4) *not* use simple methods, (5) *not* provide full disclosure of methodology, sources and findings, and (6) *not* write clearly."*[19]

The reasons for the professoriate's apparently limitless attachment to the ridiculous, the insignificant, and the absurd is embedded deep in the academic culture itself; it might even be the essence of the culture.

No matter what an individual's capacities or talents, the academic culture demands that every professor and would-be professor produce research that is "original," breaking previously uncharted ground. Unfortunately, originality is no more commonplace among academics than among any other sector of the population. But the requirement in the universities today is universal and enforced without exception or appeal.

Jacques Barzun calls this an example of academia's "preposterism."

"Consider the assumption behind the [Ph.D.]," Barzun wrote in *The American University.* "It is noticed that trained minds who investigate a subject and write a book about it sometimes make a contribution to knowledge. Valuing knowledge, we *preposterize* the idea and say to every intending college teacher: 'you shall write a book, and it shall be a contribution to knowledge' . . . everybody shall produce written research in order to live, and it shall be decreed a knowledge explosion."[20]

But if the Ph.D. is an example of preposterism, the requirement that young professors produce a dozen or so articles for the learned journals to win tenure is the *reductio ad absurdum* of the research mentality, because it assumes that academics can make original discoveries every few months or so. By 1970, the number

---

* One of the favorite labors of the modern literary academic is the production of updated critical editions of classic works, complete with elaborate notations noting every trivial difference between various manuscripts and texts. The process was epitomized by the epic labor in which twenty-five academics once read through Mark Twain's texts—backwards—to count how many times "Aunt Polly" was printed as "aunty Polly." (Edmund Wilson, "The Fruits of the MLA," in *The Devils and Canon Bacham*, New York: Farrar, Straus and Giroux, 1973)

of Ph. D. s had reached 398,000, almost four times the number in 1950. But under the pressures of academic expansion the number reached 750,000 by 1984, and a huge proportion of those aspiring academics were faced with the absolute requirement that they remain on the cutting edge of their field.[21]

"At the University of Illinois, in our department," a professor says, "seven articles would be weak [for a tenure candidate]. We don't put much emphasis on books. A person who is spending all his time on a book is wasting his time, because a book will take a couple of years to bake, and in the meantime there is nothing to eat. It's all in the oven, and you'll just get chopped to pieces when it comes to merit increases. It doesn't pay to write books."[22]

It also doesn't pay to write for the wrong journals. "If you have an article in a journal that is sort of interdisciplinary, they just about discount it. If it's a technical journal they adore you."[23]

At one time, a thinker like Immanuel Kant could afford to wait until he was 57 to publish his *Critique of Pure Reason.* Many senior professors still on the payroll slipped into tenure with only a handful of publications or even none at all. But the pressure to publish now is so great that few junior professors can afford to risk taking on a large or meaty problem or wait until their judgments are considered or mature.

How much safer to put research in bits and pieces, to capture some small corner of reality and present it in a manner designed to emphasize the profundity of the discovery.

The key is originality, whether that originality is applied to an incredibly narrow sliver of knowledge and whether it has the slightest importance or interest for anyone other than the author.

It is here that profspeak is indispensable.

7 Profspeak

'Twas brillig, and the slithy toves
Did gyre and gimble in the wabe. . . .

PROFESSOR David Berkman calls it his Cocktail Party Theory.

"There's a faculty reception," he says, "and a bunch of profs are standing around introducing themselves to one another. Professor A states his specialty is the application of thermodynamics to metal stress; Professor B announces that hers is economic trend prediction, while Professor C is completing the definitive re-definition of Aristotelian logic. When inquiry is made of Professor D, he responds, 'Television—as in *Leave It to Beaver*, *Dynasty*, and the *Love Boat*.'

"Clearly," Berkman notes, "we who are the professor D's of academia have some real ego and status problems."

The solution for professors of the new and quickly growing field of media studies, Berkman says, was to follow the paths already laid out by their predecessors in the softer sciences who "decided that by adopting with a vengeance those traditional academic trappings such as required doctorates, rhetorically escalated theoretics, lots of footnotes, and tables with funny looking Greek symbols," they too could be real professors. Now when Berkman's Professor D is asked at faculty receptions about his specialization, he can respond weightily, "Mass Communication—with a research specialty in agenda setting."

"Which," Berkman says, "you gotta admit, sounds pretty damn impressive—as long as that prof doesn't reveal that what our field claims as its leading-edge research [is] the mind-boggling discovery that people will talk tomorrow about what led the evening newscasts and was headlined in the paper last night."[1]

Professor D has discovered profspeak.

In Berkman's scenario, the inflated verbiage, obscure jargon, and trivia-enhancing qualities of profspeak are used primarily to prop up the academic ego and provide a subtle status boost. Profspeak is the *lingua franca* of the modern university: Wherever two or three professors gather, it is in their midst.

But why? How is it that normally intelligent, occasionally articulate, sometimes even eloquent men and women become pompous, opaque, and incomprehensible the moment they enter academe? What could possibly seduce them into such rhetorical buffoonery? The answer again goes to the heart of the academic culture. Profspeak is a direct product of the culture's Triple Imperative of Obscurantism. The slavish use of obscure jargon, convoluted syntax, and the symbols and trappings of mathematics are essential for any academic because:

(1) They can make even the most trivial subject sound impressive and the most commonplace observation immeasurably profound, even if the subject is utterly insignificant.

(2) They make it much easier to avoid having to say anything directly or even anything at all. And, most important,

(3) It is easier than real thought or originality.

Whatever lofty claims they might make about their ideals (and there are few claims they do not make), academics share the same motives that animate the soul of every bureaucracy and closed guild. From the Internal Revenue Service to the local sewage district, every petty bureaucrat recognizes that power rests in large part on the ability to cloak his or her knowledge behind a veil of inflated and intimidating jargon. Theirs may actually be the second oldest profession. Persian treasury officials, sociologist Max Weber pointed out, actually invented a secret script so as to maintain control over financial affairs.[2] The lesson was not lost on academics.*

The use of jargon, obfuscating convolutions and "nebulous verbosity, " Stanislav Andreski noted in his classic *The Social Sciences as Sorcery,* "opens a road to the most prestigious academic posts to people of small intelligence whose limitations would stand naked if they had to state what they have to say clearly and succinctly." Andreski proposed a formula of his own: Verbiage increases to the extent that ambition exceeds knowledge.[3]

Andreski noted that social scientists can spread a patina of profundity over their work merely by substituting such terms as "need autonomy" for self-reliance and "need affiliation" for sociability. Thus, the sentence "They manifested high need autonomy, need achievement, and need order," would mean that the subjects were self-reliant, ambitious, and orderly.[4] But the first version sounds so much more . . . impressive.

Even this can be improved on, Andreski noted, by using the letter "n" in place of the word need, "because of its status-bestowing properties stemming from its frequent appearances in mathematical formulae. So by scribbling the letter 'n' all over their pages, some people have succeeded in surrounding their platitudes with the aura of the exact sciences in their own eyes as well as those of their readers, who might have seen some books on mathematics without being able to understand them."[5]

Andreski provides an example of how the process works with this paragraph:

"The preliminary results of our research project into the encoding process in communication flow indicate that (owing to their multi-

---

* In his 1987 book, *The Last Intellectuals,* author Russell Jacoby noted the crabbed, jargoned sound of academic writing, but attributed it to inattention. "In their haste, they did not linger over the text. Academic intellectuals did not cherish direct or elegant writing; *they did not disdain it, but it hardly mattered.*" (p. 16) This misses the fundamental importance of profspeak in the academic culture; professors fall back on impenetrability not because it doesn't matter, but precisely because it *does* matter so much—for the vast majority of academics, it is an essential element on the building of careers in the modern academy.

plex permutations) it is difficult to ascertain direct correlates of 'n Aff.' On the other hand, when on the encephalogram 'dy' divided by 'dx' is less than 'O,' 'n Ach' attains a significantly high positive correlation with 'n Bam,' notwithstanding the partially stochastic nature of the connection between these two variables."

Translation: "Owing to the waywardness of human nature, it is difficult to find out why people join a given group, but observation of how people speak and write clearly suggests that, when the brain is slowing down, a desire to achieve often gives rise to a need to bamboozle."[6]

The lush vistas that opened up for the professoriate after World War II, with their seemingly endless possibilities for advancement, cash, and freedom from teaching, meant that profspeak could be the ticket to the promised land. By creating new words for things that don't really need names or fancier terms for commonplace phenomena, and by substituting formulas for simple declarative sentences, each scholar added to the appearance of doing work that is crucial to society—or at least valuable enough to warrant continued lavish support from foundations and the federal government. Each piece of pseudo-science could raise the stock of the entire shared enterprise; the fate of each is the fate of all.

So university libraries are flooded with such articles as: "Analyzing Utterances as the Observational Unit." The authors are students of human speech. But they would be unlikely to dazzle their colleagues, foundations, or family members by announcing their discovery that people say things for a variety of reasons and choose the sort of words appropriate for the occasion. What they wrote was: "Speakers generate utterances to satisfy cognitive, affective, or aesthetic urges, selecting specific lexical combinations from a personal lexicon determined by the content of the interaction."[7]

The same problem faces the professor who writes about the scholarly implications of a television show like *The A-Team*. She is hardly going to win many points for saying the show is about a bunch of macho guys who hang around together doing macho things. But subjected to the transforming power of profspeak, *The A-Team* serves to demonstrate the application of "articulation theory to popular texts," including the insight that in *The A-Team,* "the male group is ubiquitous in colonizing the conventional spheres of interpersonal activity as a self-sufficient autonomous unit."[8]

Quantification serves many of the same purposes as jargon. Even eroticism is reduced to mathematical formulas by scholarly researchers. From the *Southern Speech Communication Journal,* "Sexual Acts and References in Prime-Time TV: A Two-Year Look," comes: "The frequency of sexual acts and other than implied intercourse increased substantially from 1978 (130) to 1979 (243: X^2 (df = 1) = 34.23, p. 001)."[9]

In the academy, no subject is too minor to be made intimidating, remote, and mysterious. A recent issue of *Social Science Research* includes "Multiple Modeling of Propensity to Adopt Residential Energy Conservation Retrofits." That work of scholarship rolls out the whole spectrum of weaponry from a multivariate log-linear/logistic model to a multivariate structural probit model with latent variables all to determine what sort of people add storm doors or windows, insulation, or weatherstripping.[10]

When former vice presidential candidate Geraldine Ferraro made a commercial for Pepsi Cola, she probably had no idea that she would be the subject of "The dialectic of the feminine: Melodrama and commodity in the Ferraro Pepsi commercial" in the scholarly *Communication Journal.* A sample sentence: "In using the five codes devised by Barthes in S/Z—the referential/cultural code, the hermeneutic code, the proairetic code or code of action, the semic code, and the symbolic code, we need to conceptualize narrative not as a system of meaning, but as a system of exchange or an economy."*[11]

As the obsession with jargon and mystification seeped downward, it seemed to settle most solidly in the ranks of the educationists. Alongside their darkly incantational mutterings, even

---

* Sample: "Ferraro, in the Pepsi commercial, attempts to speak a reordering of the symbolic code of binary opposition. . . ." In the same issue of the journal, another article examines *Miami Vice,* describing television as "a realm of mediation in which the fictional is explicitly collapsed into the real in the interests of commodification."

the social sciences seemed models of clarity. Richard Mitchell recounts in *The Graves of Academe* the story of one scholar who in the process of becoming a doctor of education developed the concept of "transpersonal teaching," buttressed by commensurate model analyses and stepwise regression strategies, including the discovery that "the R2 of Self-Regard is .0123 and of Inner-Directed, a hefty .4544." Educationists, Mitchell says, come up with concepts like "transpersonal teaching" and develop terms like "micro-teaching" to describe small group exercises for obvious reasons. "You cannot write dissertations and articles, you cannot teach courses in teacher academies, you cannot get grants of public money, you cannot hire out as a consultant, you cannot set up a project and assemble a staff, if all you're going to do is talk about very small classes and the fact that a teacher will often help one student."[12]

"Who among us," asked sociologist Robert Nisbet, "has not learned to his advantage or disadvantage of the hypnotic fascination that is exerted upon foundations, research committees, and certain editors by phraseology?"[13] Indeed, such committees seem unusually vulnerable to the lure of profspeak. Jacques Barzun recalls that as a member of a committee evaluating proposals for Fulbright scholarships, he had to consider a proposal to study "The Influence of Psychic Images on Obesity in Singers." Testifying to the impressive powers of academic obscurantism, Barzun says that "it took two of us an appreciable time to persuade the others that the psychological fantasy was not worth a Fulbright."[14]

There is evidence that prolonged exposure to profspeak can be deadly not merely to the higher critical faculties but to common sense itself. That proposition was tested by a puckish researcher in the early 1970s. He gathered a group of distinguished educators, psychiatrists, psychologists, and social workers and told them that they would be hearing a lecture by Dr. Myron Fox, an expert on the application of mathematics to human behavior, on the topic "Mathematical Game Theory as Applied to Physician Education." But Fox was neither a "doctor" nor an expert. He was an actor.

The researcher coached him "to present his topic and conduct his question and answer period with an excessive use of double-talk, neologisms, *non sequiturs,* and contradictory statements. All of this was to be interspersed with parenthetical and meaningless references to unrelated topics." After his hour-long presentation, the academics were asked to evaluate his talk. Not a single one saw through the charade. In fact a majority rated him favorably, with some of the professionals calling him, "extremely articulate," "knowledgeable," and crediting him with "good analysis of subject that has been personally studied before."

Perhaps most damning of all, one academic said he found the talk "too intellectual."[15]

*The Weird World of
the Academic Journals*

RESEARCH, of course, is not enough. It must—somehow, some-place—be published. But not in something as plebeian as *The Atlantic Monthly* or *Harper's*, for that would entail no prepublication approval by peers and would be considered catering to popular (i.e., nonacademic) taste. The research, festooned with footnotes, sources, and elaborate explanations of methodology, must be published in such scholarly publications as the *Journal of Humanistic Psychology* or the *Quarterly Journal of Speech*, unread by the masses, for obscurity is vital.

If academia revolves around research, then research revolves around the process of academic publishing, particularly in the learned journals. By one estimate, academics in the sciences turn out articles for their 40,000 separate journals at the rate of two every minute, 2,880 every 24 hours.[1] That's more than a million a year—a million new nuggets of created knowledge, the product of academia's labors at the frontiers of wisdom. And this does not include the acres of prose turned out by the economists, sociologists, political scientists, historians, or literary critics for their own learned journals. There are 142 journals in sociology and 71 in philosophy alone.[2]

Collectively, these publications represent the heart of the academic enterprise. They are the expression of the academic mind in its purest form. If universities are knowledge factories, as Clark Kerr insisted, the published research of the professors is their primary product, the justification for society's support and indulgence, and the reason that teaching loads are so small, classes so huge, and undergraduate teaching the orphan of higher education.

Because the articles are what Harvard President Derek Bok has called the "currency" of academia, the vast majority of what passes for scholarship is intended neither to expand the bounds of knowledge or make a genuine contribution to a discipline. Says one critic: "The overwhelming function [of the research] is to get onto the vita of the person publishing it and to help out with promotion and tenure."[3] But even this explanation falls short. The academic journals play a central role in shoring up academia's prestige hierarchy, bolstering the authority of the academic villages and helping academia's ever-vigilant Thought Police stamp out heresies and other unwelcome challenges to the status and orthodoxies of the village elders.

Academic journals, of course, were never intended to serve merely as the hard currency of the academy. They began in the 17th century as a sincere effort to keep scholars from being inundated by what then seemed to be a sea of books.[4] They were a convenient method of disseminating new information rapidly throughout the scientific community. Theoretically, even now, the academic journals represent scholarship at its most meticulous. The journals are governed by a system of peer review under which every article that is submitted to a journal is (theoretically) evaluated by a group of academic specialists in the same field to determine whether it makes a valid contribution. Only those articles that pass such rigid scrutiny ever see publication. But under the pressures of the academic culture and what one critic calls "knowledge politics,"[5] the process has been distorted almost beyond recognition.

One expert on the scholarly journals is Gerald W. Bracey, who notes that he probably knows "less about more" than any other living American. As the writer of the "Research" column for the educational monthly, *Phi Delta Kappan*, Bracey has to read or skim through 100 to 200 scholarly journals in the behavioral and social sciences and education for discoveries and breakthroughs that he could summarize for his readers. For Bracey, the director of research for Cherry Creek Schools in Englewood, Colorado, and holder of a doctorate in psychology from Stanford, the experience of wading hip-deep through the muddy profspeak on "minutely incremental research projects" is grueling and disillusioning. "Some months," he wrote in *The Chronicle of Higher Education,* "I am tempted to turn in my 14 odd pages blank but for the comment, 'Nothing happened.' "[6]

Most of the "experiments" reported were trivial and involved pathetically limited data. The average length of experiments in one area was one week. Data were, moreover, difficult and often impossible to verify. When researchers were asked for material to support their conclusions, much of it turned out to have been destroyed by the researcher. Attempts by one researcher to reproduce or check the results claimed by another researcher—the heart of the scientific method in the hard sciences—were almost unheard of in the social sciences, Bracey found, because "such activity counts for nothing with those who are counting publications. . . ."[7]

One of the reasons such sloppiness is tolerated may be that few academics bother to read much of what passes for scholarship these days, even as the number of journals continues to mount. "More and more people are writing more and more articles that fewer and fewer people are reading," Bracey says.

Studies of the phenomenon of the journals have led to the promulgation of what could be called The One Percent Rule. Among scientists, half of all technical reading is done in less than 1 percent of the scientific journals. Less than 1 percent of all journal articles have anything more than the tiniest readership, while any given article is probably read by less than 1 percent of the journal's readers. "Needless to say," remarked one researcher, *"the motivation to read appears to fall far short of the motivation to publish."*[8]

"We seem to be headed toward a situation where 'knowledge production' (as they like to call it in universities) is an exercise in solipsism," Bracey says. "The chief beneficiary is the author, who gets promotions, tenure, prestige, and more grants to write more stuff that won't be read." One particularly outrageous career-making gambit is the practice by some professors who publish the same findings over and over again under separate headings. The result is what Bracey calls the "Thanksgiving Turkey Vita."

"I've seen 80-page resumes with separate listings for data reported at local, state, regional, and national meetings, as an interim report, an article, and a chapter in a book," Bracey says. A related maneuver is the practice of multiple authorship, so that several professors can reap professional rewards from a single paper. "Can it be," Bracey wonders, "that six people at four institutions really 'authored' a five-page article?"[9]

Although they play such a large role in their professional lives, even the professors themselves admit that the journals are largely useless. A survey by the American Council of Learned Societies found that a solid majority of professors in seven disciplines (classics, history, language or linguistics, literature, philosophy, political science, and sociology) admitted that it is virtually impossible "to keep up even minimally" in their field. "There are far too many journals, and most of what they publish is ignorant drivel," one respondent said. The survey found a majority agreeing that the journals' peer review system, in which panels of supposedly neutral professors review articles submitted for publication, is biased in favor of well-known professors, those from prestigious schools, and those who use "currently fashionable approaches." One respondent charged that the leading journal in his field is controlled by a "small circle of prima donnas who shut out challenges to the theories on which they have made their reputations."[10]

The driving force behind the academic journals is the atomization of knowledge: the dividing and subdividing of tinier and tinier bits of information about smaller and smaller subjects. In English, for example, the journals include: *Shakespeare Quarterly, Blake Quarterly, The Dickensian, Texas Studies in Literature and Language, ESQ, A Journal of the American Renaissance, American Literary Realism: 1870 to 1910, Early American Literature, Western American Literature, Studies in American Fiction, The Great*

Lakes Review, The Southern Literary Journal, The Southern Humanities Review, Modern Fiction Studies, The Review of English Studies, The Mark Twain Journal, The Thoreau Quarterly, Poe Studies, The Wallace Stevens Journal, The D.H. Lawrence Review, James Joyce Quarterly, Browning Society Notes, Doris Lessing Newsletter, Evelyn Waugh Newsletter, Jack London Newsletter, The Baker Street Journal: An Irregular Quarterly of Sherlockiana, and even the *Menckeniana Quarterly Review.*

Within this environment to be published is to specialize; to prosper is to hyperspecialize. *The Walt Whitman Quarterly,* for example, which exists for the sole purpose of analyzing and reanalyzing the work of that singular American poet, publishes such articles as "The Art of Walt Whitman's French in *Song of Myself.*" In that article, the professorial author writes that "Whitman may not always be getting full credit for his use of French," and then spends several hundred words righting this injustice, even though *Song of Myself,* the author says, has a total of only two purely French words. [11]

Other disciplines are affected differently.

In economics, the combined pressure to publish frequently and the need to use fashionable methodologies have resulted in a kind of academic economics that has little, if any, relation to the real world. Wassily Leontief, 1973 Nobel laureate in economics and former president of the American Economics Association, accuses his colleagues of having a "preoccupation with imaginary, hypothetical, rather than with observable reality." When Leontief studied articles published in *The American Economic Review* from March 1977 to December 1981, he found that 54 percent of the articles were mathematical models *without any actual data from the real world.* "We found exactly one piece of empirical research," Leontief later wrote, "and it was about the utility maximization of pigeons." [12]

History has been similarly affected. "Quite obviously," Historian David Oshinsky of Rutgers says, "a point has been reached where few historians bother to read the articles in major historical journals unless they touch directly upon their particular area of expertise. The material is simply too dull—a mass of footnotes, quotations, and bibliographical data that have no meaning to the vast majority of potential readers."[13]

Among those who, theoretically, *must* read this scholarly effluvia are the administrators and colleagues who have to pass judgment on a professor's qualifications for tenure or promotion. But there is evidence that not even they read much of it. Researcher Lionel Lewis, for example, who studied the tenure system intensively, concluded that the public insistence on the importance of scholarship is "largely a fraud" to cover more subjective judgments.

"So many factors other than the quantity or quality of articles or books enter into decisions departments make about those who are accepted or rejected as members that it is humbug when the question of someone's productivity is raised," Lewis wrote in his classic study of the academic tenure system, *Scaling the Ivory Tower.*[14] Instead, after examining numerous cases, he found that one constant was the professoriate's preference for colleagues with "an inoffensive personality." Graduate schools with their often brutal socialization processes weed out most rebels and individualists; the rest is done by professors in the promotion process. Lewis argued that the professoriate's claim that it based judgments on the quality of research was really "a protective device to conceal the true reasons why someone is forced to leave a department. Second, it keeps those who are fearful of losing their position in check; research and writing (even if a good deal of it is useless) diverts their attention from departmental affairs and helps maintain the status quo. Third, it promotes the idea that an objective standard is utilized in arriving at decisions which are made subjectively."*[15]

The stories of deans and department chairmen who keep scales in their office so they can simply weigh a candidate's publications are probably apocryphal. But if they don't weigh, they can count. A book known as the *Social Sciences Citation Index*, for example, keeps track of which scholars are being cited in the all-important

---

* "If nothing else," wrote Lewis wryly, "the data . . . leaves one with the incontrovertible impression that university faculty are not overburdened with staggering teaching and research commitments."

footnotes by other scholars. The *Index* painstakingly monitors more than 3,000 social science journals. At a glance, you can look up a scholar's name and find every time he or she has been cited. Inevitably this huge tally sheet has come to play a growing if somewhat *sub rosa* role in the process of hiring and promotion, since it provides a relatively painless alternative to suffering through the professor's scholarly output and is a reliable indicator of his or her status within the discipline.* The *Index* actually lists the top 50 "scientists" each year in order of citation frequency. A couple of banner citation years can get you out of the Three I League into the big time. "The *Citation Index* can be used to identify fast-rising rookies, players at the peak of their careers, and over-the-hill performers, along with those who peaked too soon," notes critic Jon Wiener. "One imagines the eventual establishment of a social science ticker tape which would spread citation rates to the offices of deans and department chairmen instantaneously. (A burst of noise from the ticker; the dean rushes over and reads off the sputtering tape, 'Dan Bell up 6.')"[16]

Through the footnotes, the journals create a vast network of cross-validation—the academic equivalent of *I'm OK, You're OK*. Reassurance and reinforcement are passed out in the form of footnotes. The system naturally has its own side-effects: It encourages generous self-citation (not at all unheard of in a profession where modesty is the mother of oblivion) and networks of back-scratching mutual-citers. Thus, the most trivial or obscure point can find itself rushing through the academic village within months of its birth.

Failure to play the journal game, on the other hand, can result in a career whose high point may be an instructor's job at South-

---

* "The conclusion is inescapable," writes Political Scientist David Ricci, "when a scholar knows that his associates are unlikely to judge the quality of his work by reading it directly, he will seek to publish frequently, in hopes of making at least the length of his publications list impressive." Ricci says that the "persistent failure to communicate," among academics is reflected "in the contemporary scholarly habit of reading only the introduction and conclusions to published works, leaving unexamined the central parts. . . ." (*The Tragedy of Political Science*, New Haven, Yale University Press, 1984)

west North Dakota A&M.* The journals are thus a powerful instrument of regulation by the academic villages, particularly when it comes to suppressing unpopular ideas.

The Academic Thought Police

In 1976, Professor Michael J. Mahoney of the University of California at Santa Barbara attended a conference of psychology professors on the subject of behaviorism. Mahoney expected some controversy. Some of his work had been at odds with the work of some senior members of the field, and some of it had even called into question major tenets of behavioristic orthodoxy. But he was not prepared for what actually happened.

"I was called into an empty hotel suite and told in no uncertain terms that my research and writing . . . were antithetical to the tenets of behaviorism and 'dangerous'. . . . Although most of the attack was emotional and intensely *ad hominem*, the final message was to stop publishing what was essentially considered heresy. . . ." The experience was "very damaging to my scientific innocence," Mahoney says.[17]

The incident inspired Mahoney to an unconventional experiment. "Needless to say," he explained, "I was (and am) puzzled and intrigued by such displays of intolerance. . . ." He wanted to determine the depth and pervasiveness of bias in the peer review process of his field's journals. This process of peer review is crucial because the peer panels hold veto power over the journal articles that not only determined academic livelihoods but the direction of the science itself. One sociologist calls the peer reviewer "the linchpin about which the whole business of science is pivoted."[18]

To test for bias, Mahoney prepared two sets of an experimental

* "The scholar who forgets to cultivate his or her image will end by busing dishes," writes critic Bernie Fels. "Endless sociological studies of the academy confirm the tautological nature of reputation. Where everything is skin-deep, mirrors are profound. Reputation is constituted out of reputation; to be reputable means to be cited and mentioned; to be cited and mentioned supposes reputation." ("The Academy and Its Discontents," *Telos 31*, 1977)

report for 75 reviewers. The two versions of the article were identical except that the results in one instance appeared to support the theoretical orientation of the peer reviewers, while the other version had the same data but contained a conclusion that seemed to challenge the peer reviewers' perspective. The methodology was the same, but only the conclusions differed. Although the peer reviewers supposedly were paragons of scientific objectivity, in practice they tended to approve the articles supporting their own positions, praising the reasoning and methodologies employed. The articles with the unwanted conclusions were ripped for their allegedly shoddy research and technical deficiencies. "The very same experimental procedures, for example, were applauded or strongly criticized depending on the direction of the data," Mahoney said.[19]

When Mahoney published his findings in the journal *Cognitive Therapy and Research*,[20] demonstrating how the journals blindly perpetuated their own orthodoxies and suppressed results that challenged them, he provoked an outraged uproar. The outrage was not from academics concerned about the unscientific bias and "knowledge politics" at the heart of their enterprise but from professors furious at being embarrassed. Several leading behaviorists tried to have Mahoney reprimanded or fired.[21]

A similar reaction followed a study by Douglas P. Peters of the University of North Dakota and Steve Ceci of Cornell University. They also sought to test just how well the journals' vaunted system of peer reviewing worked. In the process, they raised questions not only about bias but about whether scholarly articles were even read by journal editors and reviewers who passed on their publication.

Specifically, their experiment was designed to determine whether a published article by someone from a top-flight school like Harvard would have been published if it had been written by a professor from an unknown or backwater school. What would happen if the very same article were evaluated by the same journals—but with the titles and names of the authors changed? Would the reviewers and editors notice that the article had already appeared in their publications (did they really read the articles they published?) and if they did not notice the duplication, would they make the same decision the second time around?

Peters and Ceci chose 12 articles published in prominent psychology journals, many of them published by major professional organizations. All 12 articles had been written by professors from "prestigious and highly productive" departments and each of them had been cited more than the average in the 18 to 32 months since they had appeared. To test the review system, the two investigators then *resubmitted* the articles to the same journals that had originally published them. The only changes made were cosmetic; fictitious names were substituted for the authors, and they were given new, less revered institutional affiliations, such as the "Tri-Valley Center for Human Potential."

What Peters and Ceci found was startling. Of the 38 editors and peer reviewers, 35 (or 92 percent) failed to recognize the resubmissions. Of the original 12 articles, nine continued through the same review process that had previously approved them. This time, however, *eight of the nine were rejected*. The reviewers gave a variety of reasons but generally turned down the resubmitted articles because of "serious methodological flaws." Since these flaws had either been nonexistent or completely overlooked previously by the editors and reviewers, Peters and Ceci concluded that the explanation for the rejections lay elsewhere. "The most obvious candidates as sources of bias in this case," they wrote, "would be the author's status and institutional affiliation." Thus, they had found evidence that the elaborate peer review process was a thinly veiled old-boy network and that the claim that the articles were judged by merit alone was largely fraudulent.[22]

Not surprisingly, the academic establishment was not amused by Peters and Ceci's findings. After a lengthy delay, their paper was first refused by *Science*, and then by the *American Psychologist* before it finally appeared in a journal called *The Behavioral and Brain Sciences*. Peters and Ceci were reportedly ostracized after their study was published and all 'indirect' support (secretarial assistance, photocopying, postage) was withdrawn.[23]

The virulent reaction of their colleagues and the harassment with which Mahoney, Peters, and Ceci were rewarded for exposing the weaknesses of the journals' review system was revealing because it showed that the professors' *coup d'etat* had not, after all, been very different from other revolutions.

The old-fashioned benign monarchy of the universities had fallen. In its place, new oligarchies had risen up, and their power over individual faculty members was far more insidious than anything attempted by the most autocratic university president. Under the *ancien regime,* the individual professor faced with threats from above could always invoke academic freedom and could often count on the support of his peers. But academic freedom had never been more than an abstraction for anyone other than tenured professors; and now that all the traditional barriers had been overthrown, the junior faculty and graduate students found themselves at the mercy of the elders of the academic villages.*

Through their control of the journals, the elders could now dictate not merely what subjects their juniors should research, but how they should go about it. The methodologies of the elders became *de rigueur* for young academics who hoped to make their way in the university as well as for more senior professors eager to move up the prestige pyramid by moving to a better school. Fads and fashions quickly became orthodoxies. The recalcitrant quickly fell into the many black holes that academia reserves for the out-of-step.

The tightened job market of the 1970s and early 1980s merely tightened the stranglehold of the elders, because with fewer opportunities for their juniors, they could more easily enforce their standards. Social scientists slow to adopt the intricate techniques of quantification and the use of mathematical formulas in

---

* "Overall, research and reflection on the policies of modern science editors have rendered some very disconcerting conclusions," writes Mahoney. "It is clear, for example, that refereed publication has become a tyrant that must be dealt with by those who aspire to a career in academic science. It is also clear that the quality of research has been seriously influenced by the growing pressure to publish voluminously. In a very real sense, current publication policies dictate what can and cannot be viably studied, what methodologies are acceptable . . . and so on." ("Scientific Publication and Knowledge Politics," *Journal of Social Behavior and Personality,* 1987, Vol. 2, No. 2)

their articles gradually found the doors of their disciplines closing to them. Literary critics who failed to keep up with the latest theoretical permutations of structuralism, post-structuralism, and deconstructionism found outlets for their scholarship drying up. In each discipline, new orthodoxies were enthroned and methodologies codified into holy writ. Professors who failed to fall into line often found themselves unpublished, unrecognized, and unemployed.

The power of the academic villages was illustrated by the case of Paul Starr. An assistant professor of sociology at Harvard, Starr tried to make an end run around the profspeak, obscurantism, and trivia of the academic journals. In the process he committed the two cardinal sins of the village:

(1) He wrote about subjects of great importance for a general audience.

(2) He wrote in lucid and compelling prose rather than the ponderous quantitative profspeak so popular with his fellow sociologists.

His greatest success, ironically, was his greatest apostasy. Starr won the Pulitzer Prize and the coveted Bancroft award for his book, *The Social Transformation of American Medicine*.[24] He was the first sociologist ever to receive either distinction. The book was considered an original analysis of the history of medicine in this country. But to many of his colleagues, it was merely another in a long list of Starr's heresies. Starr not only wrote books for the general literate public, he also wrote book reviews, essays, and even op-ed page pieces for newspapers.

"Paul Starr was objected to by some because he won't publish in the itty bitty academic journals," said his mentor, sociologist Daniel Bell, who calls Starr "the most brilliant sociologist of his generation."[25] In the academic villages of the social sciences, the rules about this sort of thing are very strict. A social scientist who writes essays in clear and lucid prose is considered a mere "journalist" or even worse, a "popularizer."

This animosity burns particularly hot among the quantifiers of the social sciences. "Touchy about being unable to substantiate their claims," Stanislav Andreski says, "the worshippers of methodology turn like a vicious hunting pack upon anybody branded as impressionistic, particularly if he writes well and can make his books interesting. Often enough, their motive is sheer envy, as the ability to unearth something really interesting and present it in a lively style demands a special gift and cannot be acquired by mechanical cramming, whereas anybody who is not a mental defective can learn to churn out the tedious door-to-door surveys which pass for sociology."[26]

When Starr came up for tenure at Harvard, his department voted 7 to 3 in his favor, making him the first junior faculty member in 16 years to be recommended for tenure by the department.[27] But the opposition to Starr and all that he represented was adamant. For some years the department had been divided between the number-crunchers and the so-called "armchair theorists."

A few years previously, a special advisory committee had claimed that the department was too heavily weighted with "theorists," "thinkers," and "savants" who approached social issues from an impressionistic, historical, and interpretive mode. "Harvard is what hard-boiled sociologists in the mainstream would call a department full of brilliant journalists," History Professor Stephan Thernstrom told *The New York Times*. "They do soft, perceptive, intelligent work, but it isn't science."[28] The advisory committee recommended that Harvard get on the stick and move into the sociological mainstream. And there was no question what that was. William H. Sewell, Vilas professor of sociology emeritus at the University of Wisconsin, told *The New York Times:* "The mainstream of sociology is empirical and quantitative. And I would guess about 85 percent of sociologists are of that persuasion."[29]

The forces of orthodoxy had a powerful ally in Harvard President Derek Bok. To review Starr's bid for tenure, Bok named a special review panel weighted with elders from the academic village, and when it came back with a negative recommendation on Starr, Bok sacked the young professor.[30] Starr immediately accepted a tenured professorship from Princeton. The case is an interesting look at an academic execution.

Members of the *ad hoc* committee sniped that Starr was "overrated" because he "merely synthesized old research and presented no new information."[31] Despite his Pulitzer and Bancroft awards, the professors on the committee complained that "he did not raise purely sociological questions." Bell and the other traditionalists were outraged. "Anyone who would dare say that his work is inadequate is a fool," Bell said. Said another colleague: "I think this decision has sent a disastrous signal to the younger generation of American sociologists."[32]

But it was, nevertheless, a clear signal. The news of Starr's dismissal was accompanied by the sound of young sociologists breaking out their calculators and looking up the mailing addresses of the most technical journals in their field. The message was unmistakable: Power in sociology was firmly in the hands of the elders of the academic villages, and the days in which a younger sociologist could hope to survive outside the itty bitty journals were gone.

But Starr's fate had also exposed the underbelly of the academic culture, graphically revealing the ever-widening gap between academia's pretentions and its realities. Starr, of course, was not denied tenure because his scholarship was inadequate or because he was not a hard enough worker. He was dumped by Harvard because he challenged the reigning orthodoxies of the academic village.

In fact, Starr's fate, combined with the research of Mahoney, Bracey, Lewis, and Peters and Ceci leads to an almost unavoidable conclusion: that the system that undergirds the entire academic enterprise and on which the professors have built their elaborate and costly network of status and prestige—which they use to justify their abandonment of the classroom and their endless hunt for new grants; the system that is the excuse for their perks, privileges, leaves, sabbaticals, travel, and their cushy and enviable lifestyles is, at bottom, *little more than an elaborate myth*.

But it is a myth with teeth.

Sidebar:
THE ACADEMIC BOOKSCAM

Like the academic journals, the university presses are controlled by faculty committees, and their products bear the unmistakable stamp of the professorial mind.

"The accusation that university presses have served the educational community primarily in validating accepted hiring and promotion policies seems to me right on target," says Kenneth Arnold, director of the Rutgers University Press. "For years I have heard (and said) that authors do not need royalties from us because they are rewarded with promotion and tenure. We are truly part of the university personnel system and too often publish books whose primary reason for being is the author's academic advancement, not the advancement of knowledge. . . . Our complicity in the tenure game is one of the main reasons that university press books do not sell. Many of them are not meant to."[1]

As long as university libraries feel honor bound (or are pressured) to maintain their subscriptions and to buy the latest works in any given specialty, the professoriate is certain of a market. Harvard University, which has more than 11 million volumes in its libraries, adds more than 200,000 a year; it subscribes to 102,000 current periodicals and spends nearly $31 million a year on its collection. Even the University of Nebraska subscribed to more than 23,000 journals and periodicals and buys 63,000 volumes a year. There are 35 universities that spend more than $10 million a year on libraries alone.[2]

A brochure titled "How to Publish," distributed by the Edwin Mellen Press at a convention of sociologists, explains how the system works: The publisher puts out only 250 to 300 copies, charges $40 to $50 a copy, and still makes a profit. How? The brochure explains the economics of scholarship: "Every book which makes a contribution to the development of scholarship must be read by scholars in its problem area. . . . If there are only fifty scholars who must read your book because they are working on the frontier problems of a discipline, then your book has a viable market." The $40 to $50 tab would be too high for book stores, the brochure notes, "but [university] libraries regard this as a very low price."[3]

Professors have also managed to use the economics of textbook publishing for their own benefit. The practice of professors assigning their own high-priced texts to their classes is well known. But a more recent development is the apparently widespread professorial black market in textbooks.

According to the Association of American Publishers, professors who receive complimentary not-for-sale textbooks frequently sell the books for their own personal profit, even though such practices not only cut the author's royalties but drive up the already steep cost of the books for their students in the long run. Thus far the publishers' appeals to the professoriate to stop its profiteering have been futile.

The publishing group's estimate of the professors' black market profit: $80 million in 1986 alone.[4]

The
Academic
Culture
in Action

9 *Academic License*

HARRIS HALL was seething.

Contra leader Adolfo Calero had not even arrived for his speech, but the hall was packed. For weeks, a local radical group known as the International Committee Against Racism (InCAR) had promised to disrupt the speech sponsored by a conservative student organization on the Northwestern University campus. On the night of April 13, 1985, InCAR members were out in force. Several members mounted the podium to chant slogans and deliver short speeches. Then, minutes before Calero was scheduled to enter the room, Barbara Foley came onto the stage. Witnesses later said she spoke in loud but measured tones.[1]

"This monster that they're bringing here tonight is not a human being, he's a monster," Foley declared. "Adolfo Calero is going to get up here, he's going to try, and in a few minutes he's going to talk about freedom and democracy, and liberty. . . . He's coming up here with the blood of thousands, just about literally, on his hands. He has no respect for the free speech, much less the right to live. . . .

"He has no right to speak tonight, and we are not going to let him speak." After a pause, she said: *"He should feel lucky to get out of here alive."*

When, minutes later, Calero took the stage wearing a dark suit and a bulletproof vest, a protestor rushed the stage and splashed him with red liquid (it has been variously described as paint and animal blood) while InCAR members chanted "Death to the Fascist/ Fascists Have No Right to Speak!"[2] Unable to give his speech, Calero quickly left the hall.

Afterward Foley exulted, "I think it's terrific that people saw the fascists. . . . They should have no freedom of speech."[3]

By an odd coincidence, the incident marked an intersection of sorts between Foley's curricular and extracurricular activities. Two days after the Calero shoutdown, Foley was again in the Harris Hall auditorium, to teach her Monday afternoon class in American literature.

Foley was an assistant professor in Northwestern's English Department.

As she began her class, the red paint/blood still stained the carpet and floors of the classroom. "I think it's highly significant that the university did not clean this room," Foley said. "I think it was left that way to make people angry with the protestors."[4]

But that was not necessary; reaction to the shoutdown was already harsh. The student newspaper, *The Daily Northwestern*, called the incident a "brutish attack" and "intolerable," and said of Foley that "she embarrassed not only herself but the entire university."[5] The administration let it be known it was considering asking Foley to resign but decided against such a precipitous action. Instead, a special *ad hoc* committee of professors was appointed to look into the incident.

It was the beginning of a process that would stretch out for more than two years and become one of academia's most celebrated academic freedom cases—revealing along the way the priorities of the academic culture as well as the new definitions of academic freedom on the modern campus.

Birth of an Ideal

Academic freedom is one of the noblest products of the American university—the guarantor of the freedom of inquiry and the free interchange of ideas, scratched out case by case from the hard soil of the 19th-century university. It was an ideal long before it was a reality. In founding the University of Virginia, Thomas Jefferson had declared: "This institution will be based on the illimitable freedom of the human mind. For here, we are not afraid to follow truth where it may lead, nor to tolerate any error so long as reason is free to combat it."[6]

But for most of the 19th century, universities were held in thrall by men of commerce, distinguished by the peculiar arrogance of the businessman who regards his own success in his chosen line of commerce as irrefutable proof of his superior intellectual powers in every other sphere as well. Since these men felt they had, in effect, paid for the universities, they did not think it unreasonable that they could also purchase the ideas and opinions of their employees. And for most of the century, university professors did not have any greater leeway in the expression of their opinions than the average employee of the railroads, steel companies, or other conglomerates whose magnates controlled the universities' boards of trustees. Academic freedom was what the magnates said it was, and often their definition was not particularly broad.

Professors lost their jobs for teaching the concept of evolution; Edward Bemis was fired from the University of Chicago for even daring to meet with Pullman strikers in 1894; James Allen Smith was sacked at Marietta College for criticizing monopolies.[7] In 1915, Scott Nearing, a self-proclaimed socialist, was fired from the University of Pennsylvania for reproaching coal-mining companies for using children as laborers. A powerful mine owner sat on the university's board of trustees, which was argument enough for Nearing's head.[8] Professors were driven out of their universities for raising questions about the abuse of immigrant labor, for endorsing free trade and bimetalism, and for running afoul of public opinion on matters military, particularly during World War I.[9]

Jeffersonian idealism aside, the real impetus for the recognition of academic freedom in this hostile environment was the growing identification of the universities with the sciences. The scientific ethic required "a special conception of truth and a formula for tolerating error," that required new status and protection for the professorial profession. "Academic freedom, then, came to rest on the spirit of suspended judgment and changing truth that animated the laboratory or the scholar at work among his manuscripts," writes historian Frederick Rudolph.[10]

As with so many other aspects of the new American academy of the late 19th and early 20th centuries, the concept of academic freedom drew inspiration and impetus from the German universities. In Germany, academic freedom had two separate, but related aspects: *Lernfreiheit* and *Lehrfreiheit,* which roughly translate into the freedom to learn and the freedom to teach.[11] The former was the freedom of students to study what they liked, live where they would, and to travel about in search of the education they chose. *Lehrfreiheit* was the freedom of the academic to pursue truth in his studies wherever it led him. Inevitably, however, something got lost in the translation into the American university. Almost from the beginning, academic freedom was seen as almost exclusively the right of the professors, while the concept of student freedom took a decidedly secondary status.

By the middle of the century, despite setbacks here and there—administrators reacted with typical timidity and inconsistency in the face of the McCarthyite onslaught of the 1950s—academic freedom was firmly entrenched in the academy; its principles were carved in granite all over campuses, and its invocation by university presidents was invariably accompanied by dilated nostrils and misty eyes.

But academic freedom had also become caught up in the other changes sweeping through the universities, including the vastly expanded powers and privileges of the professoriate. Bundled together with such notions as peer review, tenure, and "faculty self-governance," academic freedom became a bulwark of the increasingly elaborate and intricate system of faculty power and privileges. Faculty members found it a convenient weapon to use in their struggle not merely with nagging legislators and political critics, but also with their own administrations and even their students.

The gradual hardening of academic freedom into bureaucratic dogma is reflected in the proliferation of protections that sprang up for professors even in cases that had little or nothing to do with the question of free expression at all. Ostensibly, most of those barriers were created to protect the professors from violations of their academic freedom. But over time, they fossilized, taking on an existence of their own, unrelated to their original intent, except as they continue to insulate the professoriate from accountability. Probably the best example of all is tenure itself.

Tenure is justified on the basis that a lifetime appointment is essential to provide professors with the security and assurance that their freedom to pursue truth will be unhindered. In other words, academic freedom is the rock on which tenure is founded, and tenure is the heart of the academic enterprise.

But tenure is also the ultimate protection from accountability. "Mental deterioration, sloth, abandonment of professional standards, gross immorality in or outside the university, flagrant breach of academic position, none of these on the evidence is likely to affect the permanence of appointment once tenure has been granted," noted sociologist Robert Nisbet, an outspoken critic of the system. [12]

In practice, tenure is also— ironically—the source of academia's most brutal thought control. Untenured junior profs— and below them instructors, lecturers, and graduate students— are, of course, absolutely at the mercy of the senior faculty, so academic freedom is very much a relative concept in their cases. *
The tenuring process is academia's ultimate control mechanism, and it is often used ruthlessly to snuff out dissent among uppity junior profs who deviate from the standard line, either in their scholarship, their methodology, or their politics. But once through the portals of tenure, the young professor finds himself girded about with procedural armor that provides him with a security unheard of in any other profession.

An example of the disciplinary machinery that must be mobilized to dislodge a tenured professor is the recent case of a

* David Helfand, an associate professor of physics at Columbia University, turned down tenure saying: "At the same time tenure does little to safeguard academic freedom for those who have it, it powerfully suppresses the academic freedom of those who don't." (*Washington Monthly*, June 1986)

professor at a large state university. After serious charges of professional misconduct were made against him, he exercised his right to have the allegations investigated by a committee appointed by the faculty senate. The committee of professors held hearings that lasted *46 days*—longer than most murder trials—and heard more the 250 hours of testimony before recommending that the professor be dismissed. Even that was not a final decision, since the ultimate authority to dismiss faculty rests with the university's board of governors. The professor himself made it clear he would take the case to the courts if the university finally ruled against him. [13]

Such cases of professorial misconduct have little if anything to do with freedom of expression, but they demonstrate the way that the mechanisms designed to protect "academic freedom" can be manipulated.

The result is that, by and large, professors are untouchable. Of course, there is a lesson in all of this.

In the passion to protect faculty rights, there is little consideration of the rights of students victimized by faculty. A professor's right to hold his job is considered an inalienable moral and constitutional entitlement, and it doesn't always seem to matter what is happening in the classroom—or if anything at all is happening there.

Some professors, for example, have argued that any monitoring of their teaching—even if done by their colleagues—is an infringement on academic freedom because it violates the sanctity of their classrooms. The inviolability of the classroom was reflected in some of the reactions to reports that a conservative group calling itself Accuracy in Academia was planning to monitor professors in their classrooms.

In Wisconsin, nervous academics and friendly legislators sought to put teeth into the protections. State Representative Marlin Schneider introduced a bill that would make it a *felony* to sit in a classroom against the wishes of the instructor. [14] Violators would be subject to a fine of up to $10,000, a two-year prison term, or both, *for sitting in a classroom.*

While the application was extreme, Schneider's bill was merely an extension of the tendency among professors to invoke academic freedom to place their classrooms absolutely off-limits and their classroom conduct beyond the possibility of challenge or censure, no matter how awful their teaching or outrageous their conduct.

The hermetically sealed classroom has been accompanied by another modification of the application of academic freedom. Originally, it was invoked to ensure the free exchange of viewpoints, particularly in the classroom. Writes historian Rudolph: "What finally happened was the assumption within the academic walls of a posture of neutrality on controversial matters; in the classroom the American professor used his professional competence and his scientific knowledge of the facts to present controversial questions in such a way that his own neutrality protected the students from indoctrination."[15]

But over time that consensus also decayed. Now the principle that once guaranteed diversity of ideas in academia is used not only to silence opposition but to turn classrooms into pulpits for propagandizing.

Students who happened on an Ivy League course on "Caribbean Societies: Socio-economic Change and Cultural Adaptations," have encountered one professor's distinctive approach to his pedagogical duties. "He utters dogma, not reasoned ideas," says the student course guide. He has made such declarations as: "The Europeans freed the slaves in the Caribbean and in doing so set up their own definition of freedom. . . . In fact, though, there were slaves remaining right in Europe—those slaves were the workers who were enslaved to the capitalists."*[16]

The refusal to hold professors accountable for their conduct in the classroom is not limited to academics. Colman McCarthy, a

---

* "A difference that never fails to astonish me," wrote Joseph Epstein in another context, "between undergraduate education now and then—then being roughly 30 years ago, when I was an undergraduate at the University of Chicago—is that now university teachers who have strong political views feel no need to suppress them in the name of fairness or disinterestedness or a higher allegiance to the subject being taught." (*Commentary*, September 1986)

guest professor who taught American University's course in "The Politics of Non-violence," acknowledged to *The New York Times* that he assigned little homework and that he allowed students to grade themselves, a policy, *The Times* noted, "that brought an 'A' to most of them." When American University dropped McCarthy, its move was met by the outraged reactions of 18 members of Congress who wrote letters to the school's president supporting McCarthy.[17]

Sometimes whole programs seem designed around political rather than scholarly goals. At the University of California at Berkeley, the Peace and Conflict Studies program included no political science courses, "apparently due to a feud with the Political Science Department," one critic notes. It did include economics courses, but many of them are not taught by economists. "More disturbing is that many of their included courses are clearly inappropriate," charged Professor Jeffrey Perloff after investigating the program. "Indeed, one [course] appears to have been included only because of the Marxist bent of the instructor." Perloff found that there was "little or no supervision or planning" in the internships program, except that "many of the possible required internship programs listed as appropriate by [the Peace Studies program] appear to be chosen for their political connections rather than because of their relevance to peace and conflict studies."[18]

"[M]ost of us know of some departments that have an unhealthy degree of ideological uniformity," says Robert Ehrlich, chairman of the Physics Department at George Mason University.[19] As a result, students who want to complain about a biased professor may find that the department chair is an ideological clone. "In such cases," Ehrlich writes, "students understandably tend to consider any complaint futile."

In the old days, writes Joseph Epstein, the editor of *The American Scholar*, a department chairman might take a professor aside and tell him that it was all right to publish attacks on the bourgeoisie to his heart's content but that as a teacher he should stick to the text. "Today, however, our chairman would be accused, at a minimum, of McCarthyism, fascism and troglodyticism."[20]

Treading Lightly: The Case of Barbara Foley

Barbara Foley made no secret of her politics. Marxist professors are no longer a rarity on campuses, but Foley distinguished herself by proudly adding to her Marxist label a hyphen and the term "Leninist." She had sought notoriety for her political beliefs both inside and outside the classroom. As a graduate student at the University of Chicago, Foley was suspended for two quarters for some of her activities in connection with protests.[21] Soon after joining the Northwestern faculty she had assumed an active, high-profile role in the International Committee Against Racism (InCAR).

Joseph Epstein, who teaches at Northwestern, wrote a memorable description of the group:

> "The students who belong to InCAR manage to achieve a grayness, a grimness, a joylessness that almost seems studied. There is a dimness about their dress, a bleakness about their response to the pleasant surroundings in which they live—Northwestern's is a lush campus set along the shore of Lake Michigan in Evanston, Illinois—that does not seem altogether natural. Whatever the season, winter seems to be in their faces as they stand near the rock, blaring the word through bullhorns or passing out leaflets for one or another of their causes—leaflets . . . that resemble not so much political argument as a ransom note."[22]

Foley's academic interests can be guessed at from the names of the courses she taught: "Race and Racial Attitudes in American Literature," "Proletarian Writers of the 1930s," and "The American Dream: Myth or Reality?" Her approach to literature was also distinctive. When one student mentioned in class that her favorite poet was Emily Dickinson, Foley told her categorically that Dickinson was only a minor poet because she had ignored politics in her work.[23] But Foley's activism was not limited to poetry criticism.

Even though she was a faculty member, Foley put in her time with the bullhorn at InCAR rallies. She handed out announce-

ments of InCAR meetings after class and even tried to sell a
student a copy of the Progressive Labor Party newspaper.[24]

"She was acting as if we were all interested, as if we were all
going to become her disciples," junior Andrew Shain told *The
Chicago Tribune*.[25] Explained Foley: "It's completely impossible
for any professor to teach without being political. My students
won't all end up as Marxists, but I would hope that some of them
become more politically active as a result of our discussions."

Even so, it is unlikely that Foley's politics would have ever been
an issue had it not been for what happened on April 13, 1985, in
Harris Hall. The day before Calero's scheduled appearance, Foley
urged her students to attend.[26] Afterward, she remained unre-
pentant. Foley declared that she was the target of a "witch hunt,"
and she hinted darkly that if she were punished even tenured
professors might eventually be purged because of their politics.[27]

The first indication that the faculty could not be counted on to
take a stand against Foley's actions came in January 1986. In the
spirit of faculty self-governance, the matter had been turned over
to an ad hoc committee of professors, which bore the unwieldy
handle UFRPTDAP (University Faculty Reappointment, Promotion, Tenure and Dismissal Appeals Panel). The group spent
months reviewing Foley's conduct at the Calero shoutdown before
issuing its report. It found that Foley's actions were "violative of
the speaker's right to speak and be heard and of the audience's
right to hear," which constituted "grave professional misconduct"
and was "violative of academic freedom."[28]

But even so, the panel recommended little more than a slap on
the wrist: a "formal letter of reprimand," accompanied by a warning letter for her file. ("Dear Ms. Foley, Please do not suggest that
visitors to our campus will be lucky to get out of here alive"?)

And as far as many of the faculty were concerned, that was that.
Shortly afterward, Foley came up for tenure. Even before they
addressed the merits of the case, her colleagues in the English
Department specifically decided *not* to discuss her politics.

"Whether she was pushing a clear and hard political line in her
classes," Epstein later observed, "whether it was appropriate for a
member of the faculty to be a major figure in a radical student

organization, whether the teaching of literature was a proper occasion for attacking what Professor Foley deemed the rampant racism and brutalities of capitalism in American life—all this, apparently, was proscribed from discussion. . . . As for Professor Foley's behavior during the Calero event, this, too, was apparently ruled out of bounds for discussion."[29]

In the end, the vote of the tenured faculty in her department was 10 to 5 in Foley's favor, with one professor reportedly abstaining. The apparent insignificance of her "grave professional misconduct" was reflected by the ease with which her promotion subsequently was endorsed by the university's *ad hoc* tenure committee, the College of Arts and Sciences Promotion and Tenure Committee and the dean of the College of Arts and Sciences.[30] The question was also presented to outside (non-Northwestern) English scholars for their own "peer review." In Foley's case, some 35 outside readers were asked to evaluate Foley's scholarship.

Foley's scholarship includes a book titled *Telling the Truth: The Theory and Practice of Documentary Fiction*. At least within her academic village, Foley's work can be considered mainstream. *Telling the Truth* is littered with terms like "contextualization," "hypostatization," "reconcretization of the referent," "intertextuality," and "extratextuality," and is crammed with adoring references to the politburo of modern literary theory. No one would accuse her of being a bourgeois popularizer.

"We may be grateful to Derridean deconstruction for calling our attention to the ideological agenda that is inevitably attached to the binary opposition fiction/nonfiction," she writes in a typical passage.[31]

Throughout the book she alternates between ideological purity and theoretical impenetrability. There are 16 references to Karl Marx, seven to Engels, and an equal number to that well-known literary critic Lenin. ("The most useful definition of ideology remains that of Lenin. . . .") The two streams merge in passages like this on page 235:

> "Recalling the Leninist conception of ideology as partisan discourse outlined in Chapter 4, I contend that the procedures of analog-

ous configuration and ideological abstraction are as embedded in
counter-hegemonic mimetic works as they are in texts that project
propositions assimilable to dominant systems of belief."[32]

Asked to sit in judgment on the merits of Foley's critical writ-
ings, the three dozen outside readers reportedly delivered an
overwhelmingly favorable verdict. That may, in itself, be a commentary on the state of literature studies today.

This celebration of faculty collegiality and good fellowship, however, came to an abrupt halt when Northwestern's Provost Ray-
mond Mack announced that despite the recommendations of the
English Department, the two tenure committees, and the Arts
and Science dean, he was denying tenure to Foley. "Tenure is not
an entitlement," Mack explained. "It means the position we've
offered is for someone who is worthy of permanent status in the
university."[33]

The outrage that had been so noticeably absent among the
faculty over the Calero incident now found its voice. Typical was
that of Professor Barbara Newman, one of Foley's colleagues on
the English Department faculty. "I, myself do not approve Professor Foley's participation in the shoutdown . . .," she said. "But I
don't think that one incident should outweigh all these positive
factors in her record."[34] Newman collected 44 other faculty signa-
tures in a letter to *The Chicago Tribune* that declared that the
administration's actions in the case were "a blatant abuse of the
tenure process and *therefore a powerful threat to academic freedom at Northwestern.*"

"It is the right to peer review, faculty self-governance, and due
process which is fundamentally at stake," the signers declared.

Note here how the bureaucratic bulwarks of professorial
power—"peer review" and "faculty self-governance"—had
become in the minds of the Northwestern faculty *synonymous*
with academic freedom. But they were not alone in this remarkable leap of logic.

The local representative of the American Association of University Professors also denied that the union was defending Foley's
disruption of the speech, insisting that his concern was "due

process and the constitutional guarantees that should govern her punishment and the procedures for tenure."[35] The national AAUP also endorsed Foley's tenure appeal. Jordan Kurland, the group's associate general secretary, said that Mack's decision was "contrary to the principles of peer review."[36] The Modern Language Association also declared its solidarity with Foley's cause, and letters of support poured in from universities around the country.[37]

Much of the indignation on Foley's behalf was directed at her victim, Calero. Richard Kieckhefer, a professor of history and literature of religions, publicly questioned Calero's right to speak on campus in the first place, saying: "From a moral viewpoint, I have serious problems with a university campus being a forum for privileged discourse."[38]

The subtext beneath all of this appeared to be the assumption, seldom explicitly stated, that academic freedom meant not the freedom to exchange views and ideas *except by professors.* In their letter to *The Chicago Tribune,* the 45 faculty members made the remarkable claim that Foley could not be accused of violating Calero's academic freedom because "Calero was neither an academic speaker nor a guest of any academic department at NU." Outside of academia, they were saying, there can be no salvation.*

There were, of course, voices raised in support of Mack's decision. "If you're an intellectual bigot, which she is, you don't have a place in the university," Kenneth Janda, a political science professor, said.[39] But at one point 85 Northwestern faculty members had signed a letter to Mack, expressing concern that denying tenure to Foley would "stifle free political debate on campus."[40]

Foley herself claimed that she was the victim of sex discrimination and filed a complaint with the EEOC, threatening prolonged litigation against the university.

The pressure was such that in October 1986, Northwestern appointed *yet another* committee to look into Foley's case. The

* Joseph Epstein noted that the controversy took a decidedly Orwellian turn when posters began appearing around campus saying: "Support Diversity of Opinion, Back Foley!" and "Retain Civil Liberties, Keep Foley!" (*Commentary,* September 1986)

panel was chosen from 22 candidates. Foley was granted a veto and used it to strike the names of 12; Mack disqualified four.[41]

In January 1987—a year after the first *ad hoc* committee's report was issued and 21 months after Foley declared that Calero should feel "lucky to get out of here alive"—the committee rejected Foley's charges of sex discrimination and violation of academic freedom. But it said that the provost's action in ignoring all of the favorable recommendations by the committees "cast doubt" on the peer review process. And although it had been expected to make a recommendation for or against tenure, it chose to avoid the issue, punting the question to Northwestern President Arnold Weber.[42]

Shortly afterward, the vast majority of Northwestern's faculty of Arts and Sciences voted to endorse Foley's position. "If the decision goes against us," Professor Paul Breslin of the English Department declared, "I don't want it to be because we were shy or irresolute about making ourselves clear."[43]

Despite faculty solidarity in support of Foley, Northwestern President Arnold Weber refused to play along. In February 1987, saying that it "would be anomalous to ignore a severe transgression against a central value of the university when considering whether or not to confer on a candidate the institution's most prized status," President Weber denied tenure to Foley.[44]

"Tenure is intended to protect the most aggressive pursuits of truth—for which freedom of speech is essential—and not to shield those who seek to abridge the freedom of others to speak and to hear," Weber wrote in a 13-page decision.[45]

Reaction was predictable. "I'm disgusted," barked the local AAUP representative.[46] Foley herself struck an ask-not-for-whom-the-bell-tolls posture, declaring that "there is a witch hunt going on against leftist faculty at Northwestern. I don't find it inconceivable that even a tenured professor could be fired for political reasons at Northwestern."[47]

The English Department at Northwestern loudly mourned her departure. "She certainly leaves a great hole," Martin Mueller, the department chair, told the student paper.[48] But not to worry.

Foley was quickly hired by the English Department at Rutgers, but was liberated from the need to actually teach by a timely grant from the taxpayer-supported National Endowment for the Humanities. With that grant, she was able to spend the next full year working on a book on "the proletarian literature of the 1930s," before joining the department at Rutgers. To sweeten the deal, Rutgers agreed to pay the difference between her grant and salary.[49] Academia had more than taken care of its own.

Foley could also look forward to an active political life as well. Rutgers has an active InCAR chapter, and Foley said: "I do very much intend to continue as an activist in InCAR. InCAR is an important aspect of my political being. I wouldn't have gotten up there (at the Calero incident) and did what I did if I had not been a member of InCAR."

Regrets? She's had a few, but apparently not about the Calero incident. "I said I wouldn't do the kind of things that happened with the Calero incident again," she said. "But that doesn't mean I regret it."[50]

Sidebar:
HANDS OFF THE
"HANDS ON" PROFESSOR

Sexual harassment is far more prevalent on college campuses than many academics care to admit. Part of the reason is that universities do little or nothing about it.

One survey found that one in six female graduate students in psychology had had sexual contact with a professor; nearly one-third of psychology Ph.D.s said that they had been "subjected to unwarranted sexual advances," many from their own advisors. And half of those women reported that their professors had retaliated against them when they rebuffed their advances.[1] A survey of women in the 1980 senior class at the University of California at Berkeley found that 30 percent reported "unwanted and objectionable sexual behavior" by at least one instructor in their college careers.[2]

Although sexual misconduct is remote from questions of freedom of expression, the way it is handled by universities reflects the way the professoriate has manipulated concerns over academic freedom into an array of protections that insulate professors from accountability even for their most outrageous misconduct.

An undergraduate at a big university tells a story that is unfortunately common on university campuses. On one occasion, she recounts, she went to see her teaching assistant about her grade on her midterm. When she brought up the subject, he told her, "I know how you can get a better grade." In the past, the instructor had been more explicit, asking her to sleep with him, explaining, "We're not student/professor," anymore. The young woman rebuffed him and subsequently received a D for the course. Upset over the harassment and what she saw as her teacher's retaliation for her refusing to have sexual intercourse with him, she complained to the authorities at the university but quickly came face to face with a system designed for the sole purpose of protecting the faculty. The only official action was to advise the T.A. to attend a "workshop" on sexual harassment.[3]

Another undergraduate had a similar experience. She got a paper back from one of her teaching assistants with this note attached: "On the first day of class this fall you wore a skirt and a purple top held up by thin straps; I think there were beads somewhere—it showed your breasts a little—it was lovely and it fit the atmosphere (mood and weather) of the day. I can't get that image out of my mind and want to photograph it and get it out of my system despite my interest in you as a writer, thinker and student and all that. . . ." The student later reported that the same T.A. also made sexual advances toward her at a party and toward two other women at different times. No action was taken against him.[4]

At another big university, the matter was even more serious, and the university's reaction even more timorous. An assistant professor was hired in the fall of 1984 to teach a basic news reporting class, despite the fact that he had no journalistic experience and his heavy foreign accent made him unintelligible to many of his students. Soon after he arrived, several women students accused him of offering to trade high grades for sex. After a warning by the department chair failed to deter the professor, a hearing was held by a department committee, after which complaints were heard by a designee of the chancellor. Then the case went to a special committee that, like the other committees, found the charges to be supported by reliable testimony and ordered him suspended, with pay, from teaching.

Because the professor had a three-year contract, as do most new appointees, he was entitled under university rules to an 18-month notice of nonrenewal. The result was that he was permitted to remain on the payroll until an absolutely final decision was made. For that to happen, the case had to go to yet another university committee, after which it was sent up to the chancellor for eventual transmission to the board of regents. The women complainants, whose numbers continued to grow while the university dithered, had to repeat their testimony a half-dozen times to separate hearings. All the while, the professor was being paid his full $23,000–a–year salary for not working. And because his salary was not available to pay a replacement, his summer and fall classes—for which students had registered—were canceled by the university.[5]

10 *The Deformation*

REFORM may be the most popular leisure activity of the American university. The history of higher education is littered with grandiose blueprints for change—the debris of dozens of well-intentioned but ultimately failed efforts. But the rhetoric of reform is one of the proudest traditions of the academy.

This is because the pressure for reform is a constant: Every few years the failures of academia—teachers who don't teach, students who don't learn, overcrowded classrooms, lousy instruction, the hyperspecialization of the faculty, and the incoherence and narrowness of the curriculum—become too flagrant for the public to ignore. And because the universities still subsist on the public's good will, academics are forced to go through the motions of self-purification, at least publicly.

But nowhere is the power of the academic culture more evident than in its success in sabotaging reform.

The pattern is, by now, a familiar one. Because the modern university administrator refuses to challenge the power of the professoriate, all attempts at reform are:

- Designed by professors.
- Approved by professors.

- Implemented by professors.
- Reflections of the values of the academic culture itself.

As a result, the very reforms designed to correct the ills of the academic culture end up ratifying the same values that created the problems in the first place.

The situation at the University of Wisconsin is typical. There, the flight from teaching by the professors over the last 20 years has resulted in huge classes, impossible scheduling problems for undergraduates, and a hopelessly jumbled curriculum that now forces the average student to spend more than five years getting a bachelor's degree from the school. But when administrators addressed themselves to calls for reform, their solutions focused on *giving the professors raises.** The response was a hopeless *non sequitur,* but not unusual within academia.

When Harvard's curriculum was descending from farce to utter absurdity in the 1960s, for example, the faculty's proposals for reform urged greater flexibility and "innovation," which was exactly the problem in the first place. Schools with notoriously lax intellectual standards adopt reforms that aim at increasing "diversity;" institutions distinguished by their obsession with research decide to involve undergraduates directly in esoteric research projects; universities with superspecialized curriculums adopt core curriculums that celebrate the virtues of specialization; and universities where the faculty's teaching loads are microscopic and the neglect of students is rampant implement reforms that call for more generous sabbaticals and leaves for the professors.

In the end, after all the dust has settled, the academic villages are stronger than ever and the autonomy of the professors untouched. In public, the university president simply declares victory, goes back to his residence, and waits for the next uprising. Of academia's many frauds, its reforms are the most predictable and the most pathetic.

What follows are three stories of reform, academic style.

* A three-year catch-up pay plan approved in 1985 boosted the average full professor's salary to $52,000 by 1987. (Chronicle of Higher Education, June 7, 1985)

Berkeley
The Revolution that Failed

On a warm early spring day, Sproul Plaza still blossoms with booths representing political causes. Itinerant Maoists and pro-Palestinian groups are scattered among other miscellaneous out-croppings of campus radical chic. But the changes at Berkeley are obvious. They are outnumbered by displays for Bible studies, groups like the Asian Business Club, a vision screening program, and an outfit advertising "California Adventures." A man with a microphone singing "Ain't She Sweet"—off-key—entertains a group of students near the student union.

At the height of the Berkeley Free Speech uprising in 1964, angry demonstrators had seized Sproul Hall and were removed by police; throughout the attempted revolution Sproul retained a symbolic importance.

Twenty years later, it remains one of the main administration buildings on campus. Typical of university buildings frequented mainly by students, it seems modeled on the principles of Eastern European architecture: giganticism married with squalor.

Now, more than 20 years later, it is easy to see who was the real winner in the struggle for Berkeley.

The student revolution that began at Berkeley with the Free Speech Movement spread across the country, afflicting the great and the meek alike (although many of the great turned out to be rather meek when their turn came). Beneath the turmoil at Berkeley, the great higher education debate of the 1960s began to take shape. Under Clark Kerr's leadership, Berkeley had quickly emerged as one of the nation's first great research universities. Its professors were held in international esteem for their work in the laboratories and libraries but not in the classroom. When they did venture into the classroom, classes of 1,000 or more were not uncommon. Contact with faculty was rare and superficial. The vast majority of classes were taught not by professors, but by graduate students. Two-thirds of the school's small classes were

taught by teaching assistants and 4 out of 10 freshman and sophomore classes were taught by graduate students. [1]

Students thought they were mere interlopers at a vast institution devoted to causes that were not theirs and to which they were
largely irrelevant. They felt like orphans, and to a large extent
they were right.

In 1963, Kerr had virtually predicted the student uprisings of
the decade, noting that "the undergraduate students are restless."
Although he had been largely responsible for the new entrepreneurial university, he acknowledged that recent developments
had done the students little good—"lower teaching loads for the
faculty, larger classes, the use of substitute teachers . . . the fragmentation of knowledge into endless subdivisions. . . ."[2]

When the campus began to seethe with the unrequited passions
of its students, the university was quick to begin its own ordeal of
introspection. The result was a document that would influence the
reforms at countless campuses across the nation. The Muscatine
Report was named for a little-known English professor named
Charles Muscatine, the chair of the special committee of the
faculty senate that proposed Berkeley's own cultural revolution.
The report was a sensation.[3] On the surface it gave students all
that they could possibly desire, including the abolition of most of
the school's traditional requirements. "Our student body is too
large, too various, and too changing to be susceptible to many
universal formulations," it declared in what remains the guiding
creed of the multiversity.[4] It also struck the decisive blow for
"relevance," by calling for the elimination of those courses "that
have through obsolescence lost their contact with vital human
concerns."[5]

It seemed certain to ignite a firestorm of reform.

But 20 years later, the vast majority of classes for freshmen and
sophomores are still taught by teaching assistants; many of the
lectures are vast crowd scenes.[6] The curriculum is an even greater
monument to wretched academic excess than it was in the 1960s.
Berkeley today offers more than 8,100 courses that would take a
student nearly 1,000 years to get through if he or she took them

all. Even so, a majority of all freshmen are crammed into a mere 60 lower division courses (or well under 1 percent of the campus' offerings).[7] The result is chaos and nightmarish confusion.

One commission that looked at undergraduate education in the 1980s concluded that education for freshmen and sophomores at Berkeley and other UC campuses was little more than a "hit-and-miss" affair and that the system made it "virtually impossible for many lower division students to work even a semblance of intellectual coherence into their academic programs."[8] The casualty rate is high. Almost one-third of Berkeley's students have no degree even five years after entering as a freshman.[9]

In fact, a state commission found, the entire freshman and sophomore years at the University of California tended "to fall between the departmental cracks, as it were."[10] In some departments at Berkeley, the majority of introductory courses are taught by graduate students "under some supervision," and in other subjects more than two-thirds of the courses are taught by T.A.s.[11] Throughout the UC system, more than one-third of the faculty are part-timers.[12] Given their importance, it might be expected that the school has devoted considerable resources to the selection and training of these faculty members, but a state commission found that, in fact, both T.A.s and part-timers were in a "status of relative neglect."[13]

In 1984, on the 20th anniversary of his original report, Professor Muscatine looked over the wreckage and declared the undergraduate curriculum "miserable . . . one that hasn't been redesigned in 30 or 40 years. . . ." The problem, Muscatine said, was that the university was run "like a religion."[14]

It is also still—after all these years—impersonal. "It's like an overnight teller machine, " student Nick Pacheoc told *The Los Angeles Times*. "The service is there, but the contact isn't. It isn't warm. . . ."[15]

The Berkeley "reforms," are, in a sense, a model of all of the academic reform movements of the last several decades. On the surface, the Muscatine Report appeared to be a radical document that called for sweeping changes in the academic environment.

But in reality, it was a blueprint for the extension of the academic culture's most cherished values. "Nowhere," the report said with unusual firmness, "do we suggest a diminution of the research activity of the faculty." Research (rather than teaching), it declared, "is of the very character of this campus; without it Berkeley would be indistinguishable from other kinds of schools."[16]

In another crucial respect, the Muscatine Report was the model for almost every other report on reform that would follow. As Professor Martin Trow later pointed out, it had "the virtue of not affecting anybody who does not want to be affected by it . . . virtually all of its many recommendations can be ignored by those who are simply not interested."[17]

The record of the last 20 years makes it clear that the faculty at Berkeley was "simply not interested."

In the years since, however, Berkeley's administrators have kept its essential ideology intact. The buzzwords that helped build the multiversity are still useful in fighting off more recent reform attempts.

"There will never be a standardized or a core curriculum at Berkeley," declares Nancy Scheper-Hughes, one of Berkeley's many deans, "because of the vast changes of the student population. Because of the *diversity* of the students' interests . . . it would be almost impossible to come up with a single core curriculum into which you could force every student."[18]

None of this is likely to change. A faculty report on academic planning for the rest of the decade was sharply critical of education at Berkeley, bemoaning the heavy use of teaching assistants, the large classes, the indifference of the faculty. But the report left no doubt about the relative importance of Berkeley's students and its professors. "At the heart of the university and the paramount concern of this report," the authors wrote in an echo of the Muscatine Report, "is the quality and integrity of the faculty and its scholarship and research. . . ." And they even warned that "continued preoccupation" with teaching undergraduates "will undermine the ability of the departments in Letters and Sciences to . . . enhance the quality of their faculty."

"Notwithstanding the heavy and complex responsibilities in undergraduate education . . . *continuing excellence in research and scholarship remains [Berkeley's] primary objective.*" [19]

Inevitably, such pieties shape what passes for reform and innovation on the Berkeley campus today. Under some desultory pressure from parents and legislators to do *something* about the squalor of the undergraduate program, the professoriate has developed several programs for improving contact with undergraduates. Although the root of the problem is the focus on research, hyperspecialization, and the values of graduate education, their solution has been to involve Berkeley undergraduates directly in the professors' own research and to simply declare this a reform.

One undergraduate, for example, was given a fellowship to do work on "Self-Management in Yugoslavian Firms," while Scott Hodges in biology wrote a paper on "Interpopulation Nectar Variation in Nemophila menziesii and Nomephila atomaria." A university publication afterward quoted Hodges: "It was great! I had thought about graduate school before, but when I was having too much fun with the research, I decided to apply." [20]

Harvard
"A Bogus Core: Or the ABCs of Curricular Reform"

"Theoretically, I should be immune to the impact of any label or symbol, but the Harvard label has always bothered me," S. I. Hayakawa, the famed linguistics expert, university president, and one-time United States senator once confessed. "Something happens to me when I'm in the presence of a Harvard man—I sort of lose my confidence, even though I know some of them are really stupid asses." [21]

Harvard often has that effect. The mystique of America's premier university has given it an authority that often, over the last 350 years, has exceeded its merit. "For generation after generation," Henry Adams wrote, "Adamses and Brookses and Boylstons and Gorhams had gone to Harvard College. . . . Any other education would have required a serious effort, but no one took Harvard College seriously."[22] No less an authority than Benjamin Franklin lampooned the school's earliest pretensions, writing that Harvard students

> "learn little more than how to carry themselves handsomely, and enter a room genteelly (which might as well be acquired at a Dancing School), and . . . they return, after an abundance of trouble and Changes, as great Blockheads as ever, only more proud and self-conceited."[23]

Even so, it is the alma mater of six presidents of the United States and legions of presidential confidants and, as such, has long had a disproportionate influence over business, government, the churches, and even the conduct of war. But its sway over the academic community has been even more dramatic and immediate. From its position at the pinnacle of the academic pyramid, Harvard has set academic fashions for more than a century; every innovative curricular twist out of Cambridge has been the object of slavish imitation in every two-cow-and-a-professor school in the country. The Core Curriculum was typical.

When Harvard introduced its Core Curriculum in the late 1970s, it was hailed throughout the country as "a quiet revolution" in academia; the boldest stroke in half a century in the effort to restore intellectual coherence and rationality to the undergraduate curriculum.[24] But by the mid-1980s, the Core had become a model of reform gone awry. The student course guide pointed out that the distinguishing characteristic of core courses was that they were "easy and overcrowded," as well as often poorly taught.[25] Bloated into a 200-course potpourri of whatever-the-professors-wanted-to-teach, the Core had also raised intellectual incoherence to new heights. But by then it had already shaped "reforms" in universities throughout the country.

The Core was merely the latest in a long string of Harvardian reforms to become the academic rage nationally.

The first major upheaval occurred in the late 19th century when Harvard President Charles Eliot, in the words of Oliver Wendell

Holmes, "turned the whole university over like a flapjack," with his sweeping reform of the curriculum.[26] In the spirit of the German universities, Eliot decreed lighter teaching loads and higher salaries for the professors, and abolished many of the course requirements for the students. He ushered in one of the first great boom periods for the new professoriate. In 1870, Harvard had only 32 professors who taught 73 courses. By 1910, the number of professors had quintupled to 169, while the number of courses had ballooned to more than 400.[27]

This first outbreak of the professorial revolution foreshadowed much of what was to come. Most of the new courses were highly specialized, matching the professors' own increasingly narrow interests. Nearly half of Harvard's courses had fewer than 10 students, while a full quarter of the students were clustered into 13 massive courses. As their counterparts in this century would do, the students, free from requirements, gravitated toward the 19th-century precursors of "guts"—courses with ridiculously easy standards—and Harvard soon got a reputation for turning out graduates with academically eccentric backgrounds.[28]

The turmoil was finally settled by Eliot's successor, A. Lawrence Lowell, who restored some of the standards and requirements scrapped by the zealous Eliot. For a time, the curricular center held. But the forces of specialization and the rise of the new professor—unleashed by Eliot's reforms—continued to gather power and momentum.

Harvard's next major burst of reformist zeal occurred in 1945, with the issuance of a report that would be known as the "Redbook."[29] It was essentially a call for the renewal of liberal education through the establishment of a program of "general education." The idea was not an original one. Columbia University had inaugurated a General Education program in 1919, and the University of Chicago's brilliant young president, Robert Maynard Hutchins, had been pushing for a return to "the Great Conversation" of Western literature and thought for more than a decade. As one critic put it, the Redbook was a "variation of Hutchins' *Higher Learning* without the wit."[30]

But still, this was *Harvard,* and it had a dramatic impact on curriculums throughout the country. Unfortunately, at Harvard itself, General Education was dead on arrival.

The Redbook had recommended at least a partially prescribed curriculum: certain courses that would provide the basis of the shared intellectual experience. Specifically, the Redbook proposed that every Harvard student take a course in "Western Thought and Institutions," another in "Great Texts in Literature," and have a choice of two courses in the physical and biological sciences. Looking back, it was perhaps the last gasp of a tradition of education based on the common discourse of educated men and women. But Harvard's professors were not eager to surrender any of their gains.

When the General Education reforms came before them for approval, the Harvard faculty asserted its prerogatives and voted decisively to scrap the Redbook's curriculum, substituting a watered-down version replete with electives and loopholes. At the very outset of the reform, wrote critic Kenneth Lynn, the professors had "utterly destroyed the rationale of a shared intellectual experience for students." But killing General Education, Lynn said, "made sense to a faculty that saw no compelling reason not to let professors stage their own shows as usual."[31]

"Harvard," one administrator later wrote, "made its peace with specialization."[32]

Under the guiding hand of the faculty, Gen Ed, as it became known, quickly descended into irrationality and self-parody. The number of courses proliferated, and students took full advantage of the almost limitless freedom of the program to compile course loads designed for their painlessness rather than their educational value. In 1963, a committee headed by Biochemistry Professor Paul Doty tried to arrest the decline of Gen Ed, but its efforts were soundly rebuffed by the faculty. Instead, the professors urged the university to take "a somewhat more venturesome and experimental view" of the program and to become "quite sensitive to innovation and change."[33]

This marked the end of any intellectual integrity or coherence on Harvard's Gen Ed program.

In time, Gen Ed would be larded with courses like "Classical Music of India, Pakistan, and Bangladesh," "The Making of Australia," and "The Role of Women in Irish Society."

"With few exceptions," wrote Lynn, who taught for a time at Harvard, "such courses were academic boutiques into which trendy shoppers were enticed to browse."[34] They were also symbols of the extent to which the Gen Ed program had lost sight of its original goals. Between 1963 and 1969, the number of courses in Gen Ed jumped from 55 to 101.[35] Harvard's course guides began to look like oversized telephone books. And although Gen Ed was packed with relatively interesting nondepartmental courses, the idea of a shared intellectual experience was utterly destroyed.

But the impact on the curriculum was never more than a sideshow for Harvard's faculty. This was the Golden Age. Between 1952 and 1974, the number of professors at Harvard had grown *more than seven times faster* than the number of undergraduates. But even with this explosion in professorial talent, the proportion of courses available to undergraduates had, in the same period, *actually declined by 28 percent.*[36] The numbers lent strong credence to the notion that Harvard's professors had far more important things to do with their time than to worry either about their students or what they were learning, if anything.

The faculty's indifference was endorsed, if indirectly, by the new philosophy of education preached by University of California President Clark Kerr, who had introduced the idea of the multiversity. In Kerr's multiversity, there was no single community, goal, set of priorities, or values. In practice it was a formula for virtual anarchy, and the professors made the most of it.

"The chaos unleashed in the campus reign of political activism and cultural radicalism in the late 1960s," writes Harvard administrator Phyllis Keller, "merely confirmed and heightened trends that were well under way."*[37]

* Wrote Keller: "This new conventional wisdom of curricular flexibility, variety and choice—which became a hallmark of the American multiversity—led to near chaos by the late 1960s. *It was not, after all, the product of a coherent educational philosophy but rather the sum of piecemeal, special interest reforms. These were designed, in the first instance, by faculty members who*

The Core

Years after assuming the presidency of Harvard in 1971, Derek Bok recounted a yarn about advice he received just before he took office. According to Bok, "an old acquaintance," (he provides no name) urged him to consider a bold step to reform Harvard: Bok, the anonymous counselor urged, should abolish its undergraduate program altogether. Such a step, Bok quotes his tempter as saying, would "clearly acknowledge that teaching undergraduates has become an anachronism in the modern university. Professors are equipped to do research and to train their graduate students to do research. Teaching introductory economics to freshmen or European history to sophomores is a waste of talented scholars. . . ."[38]

Bok's tale is similiar to the story of the University of Chicago's Robert Maynard Hutchins, the century's leading higher education reformer. He too had been urged to dump his school's undergraduate program on roughly the same grounds. But the similarities between the two men stop there.

Even in his own account, Bok did not react to the suggestion with horror or reject it out of hand. In fact, his first reaction was to consider some "practical problems."

> "Who would occupy the classrooms, live in the huge undergraduate Houses, make up the lost tuitions? What on earth would we do with the football stadiums?"[39]

If Bok was not quite the visionary Hutchins was, he was also not the same sort of university president as Hutchins.* In the 1930s,

---

wanted to ease the burden of general requirements on the ablest students so that they might concentrate on advanced work. . . . There seemed to be no common understanding among a highly professionalized faculty as to what could or should be expected of an undergraduate population that was diverse in abilities, preparation and interests. Nor, as time wore on, did the faculty seem inclined to even consider this question." (in *Getting at the Core*, pp. 133–4)

* The contrast between the two men is captured in this description of Hutchins by Frank K. Kelly, a longtime associate: "He was challenging, aston-

Hutchins had set out to remake the University of Chicago more or less in his image: He dropped the university's football program and remade the curriculum, attempting to turn back to an emphasis on the traditional masterpieces of Western civilization. Hutchins considered these books to be the intellectual inheritance of the civilization and the core of the "permanent studies which every person who wishes to call himself educated should master."[40]

Hutchins' Chicago Plan broke apart the narrow departments into four general areas: physical sciences, biological sciences, the social sciences, and the humanities. Most radical of all, he created a four-year liberal arts program to begin in the junior year in high school. Throughout the 1930s, he lead an attack on all the newly minted deities of the academy, including vocationalism, empiricism, and what he saw as anti–intellectualism masquerading as an emphasis on "experience." Said Hutchins: "If we want to give our students experiences, we should go out of business. The place to get experiences is in life."[41]

Bok, on the other hand, was very much a modern university president, keenly aware of the limits on his power. A university president, he noted in his first annual report, "must recognize that the progress of the University will always depend fundamentally upon the imagination and ability of the faculty, students and staff."[42] Unlike Hutchins or Harvard's President Eliot, Bok was not an articulator of any broad vision of educational reform, and certainly none that would challenge the fundamental values of the academic culture. He was a compromiser. And he never got too far out in front of his faculty. That posture would shape the Core from the very start.

In 1973, he appointed Henry Rosovsky as dean of the Faculty of

---

ishing, witty, ironic, sometimes very warm, sometimes cold, sometimes humble and exhausted, sometimes imperious, yet always searching, always learning. Sometimes he appeared to be Zeus on a mountain called Olympus. Sometimes he viewed his life as an avenue of ruined monuments." (in *Court of Reason: Robert Hutchins and the Fund for the Republic*, The Free Press). In contrast, most of his successors as university presidents appear pint-sized.

Arts and Sciences. That same year, Rosovsky and Bok began laying the groundwork for the Core Curriculum. In his first report as dean, Rosovsky reviewed the collapse of Gen Ed. He noted that the number of departments and degree-granting committees had risen by 30 percent in the last 30 years and that some of these academic outposts had come to look on themselves as "elite and restricted enclaves remote from the general College population."[43]

But Rosovsky was not mounting an assault on the entrenched academic villages. And despite the faculty's consistent sabotage of Gen Ed, he would entrust the fate of the new Core to their mercies. In fact, he prided himself on the number of faculty he included in the process. "No one," Phyllis Keller later wrote, "least of all Rosovsky, contests the faculty's position as head of the household."[44]

But it was a contentious household. Every department was adamant in protecting its turf and every specialist insistent on maintaining his specialized courses intact. The process launched by Bok and Rosovsky quickly degenerated into a large-scale brawl of warring bureaucratic fiefdoms, each insisting on getting its own in the process. According to one critic, the process of developing the Core was similar to the way the House Public Works Committee goes about putting together a budget, by handing out a bit of pork here and a bit there to the various constituencies.[45] Rosovsky had originally had in mind a program with a relatively small number of courses to replace the bloated Gen Ed program. But the faculty was determined to accommodate everyone and quickly enlarged the Core to no fewer than 80 to 100 courses.

But the central problem was the old one: How do you get highly specialized professors to teach generalist undergraduates? A genuine program of liberal education would require some significant retooling. It would require specialists to develop new courses designed not for their own acolytes but for students who might not even major in their field.

The professors' strategy was simple, if not completely straightforward. Instead of developing a Core that was based on creating what Rosovsky called the "shared experience," they simply redefined liberal education to fit their agenda. In place of a core curriculum aiming at a common ground of shared discourse, they pushed forward what they vaguely called "approaches to knowledge." Eventually that would evolve into something called variously "modes of thought" or "modes of inquiry."

A recent Harvard publication explains the difference between emphasizing "modes of thought" and other curriculums based on more traditional values.

"[The Core] does not define intellectual breadth as the mastery of a set of Great Books, or the digestion of a specific quantum of information, or the surveying of current knowledge in certain fields. Rather, the Core seeks to introduce students to the major *approaches* to knowledge in areas that the faculty considers indispensable. . . ."[46]

In literature, for example, the faculty committed itself only to exposing students to "a variety of *critical approaches*," which meant they could continue to teach their own particular esoteric theory, rather than Milton or Dante.[47]

"Modes of thought" meant that the emphasis was on *how a specialist goes about studying* a given subject. In practice, it meant that the professors would not have to change much of anything to adapt to the new curriculum. Thus, one of the major reforms of higher education that set out to deal with the academic disasters created by the academic culture *ended up, instead, ratifying and strengthening that culture's most basic features.*

One of the most memorable critiques of the Core Curriculum comes from Harvard graduate Peter Engel writing in *The Washington Monthly*:

"Getting a handle on this 'core philosophy' isn't easy, so heavily larded is it with academic hokum. . . . In the end, it's hard to avoid the conclusion that such talk is, at bottom, an elaborate ruse to avoid facing the fact that there are few professors at Harvard who are willing to teach an introductory blockbuster like 'Western

Thought and Institutions' . . . only a lot of professors willing to
expatiate on their specialty, be it 'The Thirty Years' War,' 'Chinese
Painting,' or 'Monuments of Asia.' All the Core asks is that they
wrap their small sausages of knowledge in thick casings of 'method'
and 'context.' "48

Ironically, Harvard was able to sell this new jerry-built apparatus to the world as a major, perhaps even epochal, reform, a
return to the basics of liberal education. *The New York Times*
called it "a radical departure from established methods of undergraduate education;" *The Washington Post* declared the coming of
the academic millennium, saying: "Not since 1945 had the academic world dared to devise a new formula for developing 'the
educated man.' "49 Rosovsky himself added to the sense of drama
surrounding the Core by letting it be known that he had turned
down a chance to be president of Yale because he regarded his
work on the Core as being so critical.50

The public relations explosion and prestige machinery of Harvard effectively drowned out many of the early critics. Harry
Levin, a professor of English at Harvard, commented that
" 'Modes of thought' are all important to be sure, *but they should
have something important to think about.*"51 But this was not the
focus of the Core. As Engel wrote:

> "There is nothing in the Core that requires any two Harvard gradu-
> ates to have been exposed to the same book or author in their four
> year terms. Plato may still be easily avoided, as may Shakespeare,
> to say nothing of Voltaire. . . . If you visualize the academic en-
> terprise as a vast archeological dig, with scholars chipping away at
> the frontiers of knowledge, one approach takes the student to an
> observation tower at the center, where he can see the vast sweep
> of the enterprise, the most important questions being asked, the
> places where progress has been made and where, on the con-
> trary, the landscape is shrouded in mystery. *The 'Core' approach
> whisks the student directly up to the rock face, hands him a
> shovel and pickaxe, and tells him to start digging. 'These are
> my tools,' says his specialist guide, 'and this is what it's like doing
> my job.*' "52

It is almost a given among faculty and administrators at Harvard that student opinion can be dismissed out of hand. But it was an editorial in the March 8, 1978, *Harvard Crimson* that identified another of the Core's central weaknesses. "Whether faculty members will be willing to teach the types of courses outlined in the report is not clear," it said. "The core proposal might well set up the type of lecture courses that no one likes to teach and no one likes to take." (In fact this was exactly what eventually did happen.)*

Specifically, the editorial warned that the Core could actually lead to the widening of the gap between students and professors because it could create even more courses taught by "busy graduate students who are much more interested in pleasing their doctoral advisers than accommodating the students in their classes." (Again, the student editorialist's prophecy would prove to be right on the mark.)

The story of the Core reads depressingly like the story of Gen Ed. But tragedy returns as farce. Derek Bok had derided Gen Ed for having such specialized courses as "The Biology of Cancer" and "The Scandinavian Cinema," and for blimping up to 120 courses at its most bloated and irrational. But the Core quickly passed that number, surpassing even 150 courses within a few years, including such Gen Ed throwbacks as "Tuberculosis in the 19th Century" and "Nationalism, Religion and Politics in Central Eurasia."[53]

As the *Crimson* had predicted, the Core also became home to some of the largest, most unwieldy classes on the Harvard campus, along with some of the most notorious blow-offs.

For a few brief months in late 1985, the Core was subjected to public scrutiny when Secretary of Education William Bennett delivered a scathing attack during a speech at Harvard's 350th

---

* The Core was plagued with problems almost from the start. In his 1979–80 annual report, Dean Rosovsky complained that it was extremely difficult to provide any continuity in the courses, because of the traditionally erratic schedules of the faculty. "Our professors have heavy departmental and research commitments," he wrote. "There is also significant turnover among members of our untenured faculty. The problem of leaves and sabbaticals is especially acute for those who are in charge of planning the core."

birthday party. "There is an extraordinary gap between the rhetoric and reality of American higher education," he declared. He had the Core very much in mind when he complained that "not only do students now tend to lack a knowledge of their own tradition, they often have no standpoint from which to appreciate any other tradition, or even to *have* a sense of tradition."[54]

Bennett got unexpected support for his position from the Crimson's course guide, *The Confidential Guide*, which said simply, "He's right."

"That's because the core is designed not to teach any select body of knowledge, but to introduce presumably eager undergraduates to different 'modes of inquiry'. . . . Thus after four years you will hopefully be able to flip a mental switch and think like a historian, or an economist or a scientist. And you better be able to, because the Core won't give you a coherent picture about Western history, scientific advances or philosophical thought."[55]

Nor has the Core changed the normal routine of the professoriate at Harvard. As usual, the Core courses rely heavily on graduate students to teach the sections. Even that process reflects the inattention of the faculty. An article in the *Crimson* describes the problem:

"At the beginning of each semester, there is a desperate scramble for graduate students to lead sections in oversubscribed core courses with course advertisements for TFs [Teaching Fellows] on departmental bulletin boards. Yet these last ditch section leaders provide the only personal instruction students get in large lecture classes."[56]

For their part, Harvard professors continue to regard the Core as a great success.

Illinois
"Operation Wheelspin"

By the mid-1980s, the University of Illinois was like a drunk who had taken a vow of abstinence—40 or 50 times. Unlike Harvard or Berkeley, it had never undertaken any single major reform effort.

But it had been naming committees, study commissions, and task forces for half a century to try to arrest the centrifugal forces in the curriculum and faculty. Between 1935 and 1958 alone, the university had addressed itself to developing a coherent core curriculum *at least 10 times* but without any success.[57] As early as 1962, a major university committee had warned:

"The faculty shows some evidence of having fallen into the academic trap, consciously or otherwise, of dividing the traditionally inseparable duo of the academic structure—teaching and research—into its two components and severing the invaluable bonds which keep them pulling together as a team. . . . Course content has tended to be increasingly specialized without the breadth and inter-connection which are integral parts of general education."[58]

Despite the warning, however, the situation grew steadily and progressively worse over the next two decades. In many ways the University of Illinois' fate was typical of many of the large state land-grant universities in the 20th century. It had grown into an immense mega-institution—36,000 students on the Urbana-Champaign campus and an annual budget of well over half a billion dollars. But despite its size and wealth, it had developed what one observer would later call "an institutional inferiority complex resulting from the desire to be equivalent—in fact—and in perception—to the Berkeleys, Cornells, Harvards, Michigans, and Stanfords."[59] The result was an almost single-minded obsession with research. And the price for this was large classes, inaccessible professors, a heavy use of teaching assistants, and, ultimately, the sacrifice of undergraduate education.

It was not that Illinois administrators did not recognize that something was terribly wrong with the school and it was not their lack of good intentions and earnest reform efforts. But they were unable to break the old habits.

In April 1985, a young administrator at the University of Illinois began an unusual mission of exploration into his own institution. Lawrence Mann had been at Illinois since 1969. He had received his master's and doctorate in education there and since 1976 had worked in either the office of a dean or the chancellor. But Chancellor Thomas Everhart gave Mann a decidedly atypical assignment: He wanted him to venture out into the campus and interview students, faculty, and even other administrators to find out what had gone wrong with undergraduate education at the school.

From the beginning Mann was confronted by an irony. A recent survey of more than 600 university chancellors and presidents had rated the University of Illinois as ranking eighth nationwide in the quality of its undergraduate program.[60] But the reality, as Mann discovered, was very different:

- Student writing was poor and almost uniformly neglected by the faculty.
- The advising program was spotty at best: nonexistent in some programs and the object of faculty indifference in almost all.
- Because of their emphasis on research, U of I professors had left their classrooms in the care of teaching assistants, many of whom were ill-trained or spoke inadequate English.
- The curriculum was badly fragmented and a liberal education more a matter of chance than design for Illinois students.
- The faculty was convinced that good teaching was seldom rewarded and had no confidence whatsoever in any attempts at reform.*

Not a single one of these problems was new. As he pored over university files, he discovered that all these problems had been addressed repeatedly by a variety of committees, administrators, and critics over the last 30 years and that in most cases *little or nothing had been done about them.*

* Unless otherwise noted, all citations and quotes are taken from Mann's report.

One faculty member with 23 years of experience on the campus put it bluntly to Mann: "Our institutional attention simply isn't focused on undergraduate education." In fact, as he conducted his interviews Mann found "substantial consensus" that undergraduate teaching had never been a top priority at the University of Illinois.

"It has been clear for many years," one senior faculty member told Mann, "that this campus does not put a premium on excellent classroom teaching. When push comes to shove—promotion and salary increases—it doesn't count."

The state of student advising was typical. At the heart of the problem, Mann found, was the inaccessibility of the professors. In fact, he concluded that students "tend to know their teaching assistants better than the faculty." One dean complained to Mann: "Faculty advising should be seen as serious business, but I talk to my faculty until I am blue in the face and most still don't take it seriously." His comments were echoed by an associate professor who serves as a departmental advisor. "That advising is done badly by a lot of people is a reflection of the research emphasis," he said. "Advising is part and parcel of teaching, and even though it is required of faculty in this college, many faculty do a terrible job because it doesn't count in the reward structure."

Their complaints were little different than those raised 20 years earlier, in 1966, when the student body president wrote to the provost complaining that students were "generally ill–advised," and thus found themselves in the wrong courses or even in the wrong curriculum. He urged the provost to create a committee to look into the problem, but the provost took no action. Complaints surfaced again in 1972 when one of the university's periodic study committees declared that urgent reforms in student advising were "mandatory." No action was taken. In 1979, a conference on Undergraduate Education at Illinois again took up the issue, noting: "It is the view of many faculty members that few incentives exist for them to make a greater commitment to academic advisement [sic]." Four years later, in 1983, the issue was *again* raised at yet another conference on undergraduate education with, Mann noted dryly, "no apparent result."

Mann also heard numerous complaints about the quality of student writing on campus. One stunned department chair told Mann that in an introductory course that included many juniors and seniors, he found that "for 80 percent of the students this is their first term paper and first course with essay exams."

University committees had been complaining about this problem for more than a decade. In 1975, a Committee on the Use of English had documented volumes of deficiencies on campus and made a series of recommendations for tightening requirements; those proposals were again made by yet another panel in 1981 which went over the same ground, with the same conclusions. Even so, in 1985, Mann found that "little has been done to give greater emphasis to communication skills throughout the undergraduate curriculum. . . ."

The story of the use of teaching assistants was depressingly similar. In 1977, one study found that almost 70 percent of the large introductory courses were taught by T.A.s. "Many students indicated they were surprised by the extent to which instruction is provided by graduate students," Mann wrote, "and concern continues about the English speaking ability of some foreign teaching assistants. Some students noted that they selected the Urbana-Champaign campus largely because of the excellent reputation of the faculty, but have found little opportunity to interact with faculty due to large classes and a preoccupation, by many faculty, with research and graduate education." One senior told Mann that he had only had a single professor in his major field in four years.

"If nothing else it's a question of credibility, of what we promise and what we deliver," says Mann. "If you read some of the brochures we send out, it says the reason you want to come to the University of Illinois is that you are going to rub shoulders with and you are going to interact with the great faculty. We may not say so explicitly, that we guarantee that you are going to be in classes with those people, but that's clearly the conclusion that people draw when they read this stuff.

"But the average undergraduate who comes here is not going to be hanging around with those people. They aren't going to be sitting in their rooms or in their office or in their labs. The interaction is much more limited than the people would believe."[61]

The problems with teaching assistants were also not new. In 1972, a "Committee on the Nature of Undergraduate Education" had noted: "The use of poorly qualified teaching assistants is one source of considerable dissatisfaction with the instructional program." In 1979, another conference called for "the development and improvement of adequate training and supervision programs for teaching assistants." Despite all of those good intentions and calls for reform, Mann found that "oversight appears to remain uneven."

He found a similar indifference toward the quality of undergraduate teaching in the handling of mass classes. "Of course the sections of these introductory courses are too large," one professor told him. "I teach 350 students in Lincoln Hall Theater. *I don't even have a blackboard.* I lecture with an overhead projector in a room with poor lighting. We don't have one decent lecture hall in all of social science."

Some of the comments gathered by Mann indicated the depth of the problem:

(Full Professor) "Failure to reward faculty for teaching is the most basic of all omissions. When the decisions on promotion and salary tell you that teaching doesn't count, you can forget about improving undergraduate education."

(Associate Professor) "I'm not sure what can be done. We give research first priority, graduate students second priority, and undergraduate education third priority."

(Full Professor and Administrator) "We have many faculty who are great specialists but who are narrow in their educational perspective, and there is too much emphasis on research in many areas. Some faculty see getting excused from teaching as a real plus—status. . . . We do have some bad attitudes around here and it's too bad."

(Dean) "We use a lot of teaching assistants to teach undergraduates because the faculty wants to carry on the doctoral program. The

problem is in the department. Many of our best faculty tell me that
they will leave if they are forced to teach undergraduates."

Illinois' periodic, halfhearted reform efforts failed because none
of them dealt with the underlying values of the academic culture
or affected the sway of the academic villages over the university.
Any reform, Mann concluded, would require a fundamental reori-
entation of the university, its reward structure, or at least its
rhetoric.

"The rhetoric historically, for at least the last 25 years or so, has
clearly emphasized the importance of research, research productivity, our graduate programs, and getting grants and contracts.
Our promotion guidelines emphasized that. Teaching certainly is
mentioned. But after they talk about the importance of teaching,
they take it all back and say, but of course, research is really the
major criteria."[62]

The experience of the interviews and his own study of the
repeated failures of reform efforts lead Mann to begin entertaining
some heretical thoughts about the academic culture. "We require
the faculty to be productive," he said, "and we want them to be
productive. But the real question is the pressure we put on faculty
members to produce is not necessarily a lot of new ideas but
retelling something that's already been told either by that person
or someone else, simply because of the pressure to publish. This is
the real heresy, I guess. We've got all this proliferation of journals
and people lined up to get articles accepted. And if we were not
requiring that sort of pressure, those people who really were
interested in undergraduate teaching, who were really good at
that, if we changed the reward structure to more fully recognize
the value of that, I would say we would free up a good deal of
faculty time. . . ."[63]

But Mann knew what the reaction would be if he made such
suggestions publicly. "They would just say, you don't understand
anything about this university, you don't understand anything
about research, you're just dumb," he said. "That's basically their
answer. There's an awful lot of people who just believe in the way
things are."[64]

Mann's final report, predictably, met with a mixed reaction from the academic powers at the University of Illinois. Although Chancellor Everhart was ostensibly enthusiastic about Mann's work, Mann was nevertheless instructed to water it down. "It's toned down substantially over what the original report was," he says.[65] Even in its bowdlerized form, the report got a chilly reception. "Faculty are brought here to do research," declared Dean William Prokasy. "If they don't want to do research they can go to another institution."[66]

Publicly, University of Illinois administrators are adamant in their commitment to genuine reform. But the problems are the same as they have always been. The greatest obstacle to real change is the faculty itself, and Illinois administrators appear unwilling to challenge their power. "They are the University," says Robert Berdahl, the vice chancellor for academic affairs. "There is nothing that can be accomplished without them and there is nothing that can be accomplished against them."[67]

Professor Richard Schacht, the chairman of U of I's new Council on Undergraduate Education, takes a similarly cautious approach to reform. "We need to present changes in a way that won't frighten the professors," he says. "Academics just can't take that much change. You can't force faculty to be good teachers. No amount of beating them with a stick will do any good."

His suggestions for the kinds of encouragements that might draw professors back into the classroom reflect this attitude. If teachers put extra effort into teaching introductory courses, he suggests lowering their teaching loads "if they really work at it."[68] Thus the reward for good teaching would be *less* teaching, which, once again, reflects absolutely the attitudes of the academic culture the reforms are supposedly designed to attack.

One practical result of the Mann report was that it led to another major report, this time by a Committee on Educational Quality, which echoed many of Mann's major points and spelled out a series of possible reforms. It was chaired by Assistant Professor Steve Tozer, an untenured professor in the Department of Educational Policy Studies.

But why an *untenured* professor for chair of such a crucial committee? "Because no one else wanted it," explains Tozer. "Because they didn't have any confidence it will go anywhere."[69]

Such reaction only fueled skepticism about the administration's insistence that *this time* something would be done to change things. The cynicism of veteran academics was reflected in an interview Mann had with a senior faculty member with decades of experience in the academic culture. He bluntly labeled Mann's efforts Operation Wheelspin.

"If it makes the campus leadership feel better to go through the process of formally looking at undergraduate education, OK, but don't expect great results," he told Mann. "If it's being done for the sake of image, keep in mind that that is why you are doing it. Self-deception is the second favorite indoor sport. Every few years you have to do this sort of thing for people to learn that the more things change the more they remain the same."

Profthink

11 *The Abolition of Man: The Humanities*

A FRESHMAN composition class at Auburn University was reading the comics. Next time, they might study the newspaper's Home and Garden Section or even watch soap operas.

Their teacher, Kris Lackey, knows that some of his more traditional colleagues might assign something like E.B. White's *The Elements of Style* to a class on writing. But Lackey has written that exposing his class to such classics might overawe them and remove "the text farther and farther from the students' critical ken." So he has them read newspapers, specifically the various literary offerings in *The Atlanta Journal-Constitution*'s sports pages, its Dixie Living and Home sections, and funny pages.[1]

Perhaps even more than the critical deities at schools like Yale or Brown or the University of California at Irvine, the new face of the humanities is personified by a new variety of classroom reading material. Lackey said he was sympathetic to some of the ideas of Robert Scholes, a professor at Brown University, the author of the seminal *Textual Power* and a very hot lit crit indeed. Kris Lackey cites Scholes on "critical strength":

"In an age of manipulation," he quotes Scholes as saying, "when our students are in dire need of critical strength to resist the continuing assaults of all the media, the worst thing we can do is to foster in them an attitude of reverence before texts. . . ."[2]

Lackey uses the newspaper, specifically, to "cultivate a hardy skepticism based on the broadest assumptions of deconstruction." When his students read the paper, he has them look for "the central binary subtexts and how can they be dismantled." He gives his students a crack at an armed forces recruitment brochure, an episode of *As the World Turns*, and a college catalogue of the student's choice.

Lackey also has the students take their own flings with theory. He acknowledges that the products of such exercises might be system-ridden and heavy-handed. But, Lackey says, "better that than the studiously self-detached, self-effacing and apolitical persona so often encouraged by our own behavior as exegetes of the secular scripture."[3]

Lamentations have arisen from many quarters in recent years over the sorry state of the humanities in our universities. Since 1970, the number of English majors has dropped by 57 percent, philosophy majors declined by 42 percent, and majors in modern languages were cut in half.[4] The National Endowment for the Humanities noted with alarm that students can obtain degrees from nearly three-fourths of American universities without ever studying American literature or history, and concluded darkly that "Too many students are graduating from American colleges and universities lacking even the most rudimentary knowledge about the history, literature, art and philosophical foundations of their nation and their civilization."[5] Almost invariably, the exodus has been blamed on economics, the new social mores, the values of students and even in one notable analysis, the advent of the Walkman radio. The proposed solutions have largely been to get students back into the classrooms where the liberal arts are taught.

But perhaps the flight from the humanities had something to do with what the students found in those classes.

In fact, what passes for the study of literature in many college classrooms would be nearly unrecognizable to anyone who graduated before the new critical fads came to dominate the universities. Today, the state of the art literature classroom is a laboratory where the cutting edge is not literature or the dry, musty business of reading and understanding Great Books. It is Theory. Nor do the scholars of the humanities of the New Age digress into what the National Endowment for the Humanities calls "life's enduring fundamental questions: What is justice? What should be loved? What deserves to be defended? What is courage? What is noble? What is base? Why do civilizations flourish? Why do they decline?"[6] Who has the time to maunder on about such sentimental archaisms when the *litterateurs* have to devote themselves to such speculations as whether words mean anything at all, or only refer to other words?

The Triumph of Theory

The theory that dominates the university classroom today goes under the general rubric of "post-structuralism," an import from French literary critics who are still marveling at its prairie-fire spread through the American university. The new continental critical fashions first crept into the academic village in the late 1960s, dazzling professors of literature with an array of abstruse, intimidating, and impressive-sounding terminology like meta-texis, paralogic, non-referential, and logocentrism. The new theories were ideal for academics who (a) were bored by traditional approaches, (b) saw the new theories as a way to insinuate their political/social agendas into literary criticism, or (c) latched onto the new fads as a way to fast-track themselves into academic glory.

Originally, this strange critical hybrid from across the Atlantic was more or less limited to Yale University, but the proliferation has been breathtakingly rapid. By 1984, French writer Jacques Derrida, the godfather of deconstructionism (one of the several permutations of the movement), declared that the movement "was stronger in the United States than anywhere else."[7] In the years since, various forms of post-structuralism have not only come to dominate many of the leading literature departments but even more important, most of the academic journals in the field.

"Today it is not possible to escape from theory anywhere within the provinces of academic literary study," proclaimed Professor Murray Krieger of the University of California at Irvine.[8] His colleague, J. Hillis Miller, a former president of the Modern Language Association, has declared: "We are in the presence today of the triumph of theory."[9]

What all this means is that, where once upon a time the study of literature was dominated by particular books or poems, "texts" are now chosen arbitrarily to help elucidate whatever the theory of choice happens to be. If Chaucer happens to fit, all well and good. If not, he's out, and the same for Shakespeare, Shelley, Byron, and company.

The definition of this new theoretical movement is difficult, not only because it takes so many different forms, but because, quite simply, it strains the credulity of anyone not immersed in the academic village itself. Many of the most influential theorists argue, for example, that words do not really mean anything at all; that a poem, for example, is not about anything except itself. One of the founders of deconstructionism, Paul de Man, for example, argued that literature was little more than linguistic "noise."[10] (This is a problem for critics of the movement. After one academic wrote a scathing critique of the *avant-garde* theories, a vice president of his university called him and asked whether he had made it up—because the situation he described was so bizarre).[11]

The founders and leaders of the new movement make up an eclectic group, including such luminaries as Jacques Lacan, Michel Foucault, Roland Barthes, de Man (who spent World War II writing articles for a pro-Nazi Belgian newspaper), and Jacques Derrida. Of these, Derrida has been the most influential. Derrida's great contribution to literary studies is his slogan "There is nothing outside the text." One author summed up Derrida's deconstructionism thusly: "In sum there is no such thing as communication or knowledge that is guaranteed to be successful, there is no undistorted perception of the truth, there is no identification, as Hegel would have put it, between subject and object. Truth is not prior to error, capable of being grasped by itself; the two go hand in hand."[12]

None of this, of course, discourages Professor Derrida from writing books, articles, or papers, and it certainly has not dampened the fervor of his followers in their pursuit of academic advancement. The realization that "error and nonsense, the impossibility of determinate meaning, are built into the very essence of every code of communication," as one formulation of the new creed puts it,[13] opens infinite new vistas for the academic literaticians, especially those devoted to eras or authors that have been scratched and pawed over for centuries by determined critics who have left only scraps for the newly minted tenure-striving young junior prof to gnaw on. Theoretician Roland Barthes declares that "the birth of the reader must be at the cost of the death of the author."[14] Well, then, off with their heads, especially if that translates into full employment for literature professors, world without end.

The problem with Professor Derrida is that he is both an inspiration and a mystery to his followers. Many people, in fact, are never quite certain whether Derrida is serious in some of the things he says, or whether he is putting everyone on. In either case, he has been remarkably successful. His *magnum opus, Glas,* for example has been called an anti-book, because it bears little resemblance to anything traditionally associated with books. *Glas* is merely two columns of type; a column of quotations from Hegel's *Philosophy of the Right* juxtaposed with Genet's *Journal of a Thief.* A defender calls it "a purely speculative chain of words and associations," but critic Rene Wellek is more direct when he says of *Glas* that it is really "a series of puns."[15]

But Derrida's followers do not emulate his own odd sense of humor and apparent sense of irony. Instead, they have overlaid Derrida's "insights" with the ponderous, elephantine gracelessness that has for generations characterized the literary scholar. In *College English,* for example, the publication of the National Council of Teachers of English, Marshall W. Alcorn, Jr., a visiting assistant professor at Tulane, penned an opus titled "Rhetoric, Projection, and the Authority of the Signifier." Alcorn's prose is typical of the breed: "If we dismiss the importance of the author and think of the text as an autonomous linguistic artifact, the text still cannot exist as an objective entity, for it cannot control or deliver univocal meaning."[16]

What this seems to mean is that the author does not count and that the "text" does not mean anything. With both the author and meaning safely dead, Alcorn turns to the problem of the words themselves. But, since books are no longer books but texts, so words are no longer words but "signifiers." So what is reading? Alcorn rises to the occasion by explaining that reading is "distinct from hallucination insofar as it describes a sequential encounter with signifiers."

Alcorn clarifies his insight this way: "Signifiers in the text do not disappear, but the thing signified by the signifiers becomes a product of reading strategies." In other words, the words on the page are still there, but they don't mean anything except what the reader or, rather, the employer of "reading strategies" wants to make of them. The note accompanying Alcorn's *agon* said that he was working on a book to be called "Narcissism in the Text: Reflections on the Semiotic Transfer of Ideals."[17] We have much to look forward to.

Within the academic village, though, the cult of meaninglessness is a many-splendored thing, eliminating as it does the need for historical study of works as well as the need for teachers to be familiar with all or even any of the traditionally accepted readings. And if literature really doesn't mean anything in particular, critics are presented with what amounts to a blank slate to begin their speculations anew, because under the reign of theory, no reading is too outlandish, absurd, or bizarre—as long as it is obscure. The new term for this is "emancipated subjectivity."[18]

So one California State University professor can win points for promotion by publishing "Literary Masters and Masturbators: Sexuality, Fantasy, and Reality in *Huckleberry Finn*," in which he cites the interpretation of a passage in which Huck tries to conjure a genie from an old tin can as "remarkably suggestive of the pre-ejaculatory masturbation of latency."[19] At the University of Michigan, the English Department sponsored a "Colloquium on Critical Theory" that features "Travesties of a Travesty: Transvestism in Shakespeare, Brecht and Churchill [Caryl, not Winston]," with the alluring advertisement that "Feminist critical theory has recently introduced the concept of the reader as 'transvestite,' suggesting that the gendered subject is not fixed but produced in the process of reading."[20] And academic researchers with all their newly minted theoretical apparatus can have their way with Emily Dickinson, pulling apart the Dickinsonian texts to discover that Emily was variously a "modernist, feminist, symbolist, linguist, philosopher, crypto-politico, cultural inebriate, unrequited lover, aging adolescent, inverted astronaut, and ravished romantic. The consequence of all this truly remarkable attention is a thoroughly deconstructed Dickinson. . . ."[21]

In an age in which theory is all, not even "Beowulf" is safe. One scholar recently complained that hitherto Old English Literature "appears remarkably resistant to the influence of contemporary theory. With few exceptions, structuralism, post-structuralism . . . and deconstruction have barely grazed Anglo-Saxon studies."[22] But this oversight is already being corrected.

On campus, the Age of Theory has taken many shapes, but none quite so distinctive as at Brown University, where semiotics became the trendiest new field at the nation's trendiest school, its classes filled with students wearing black and smoking clove cigarettes and brandishing terms like post-Marxism, post-structuralism, the absent other, and the imaginary signifier.[23] Technically, of course, semiotics is the study of signs, but under the inspired guidance of guru Robert Scholes, it is a convenient catch-all for all sorts of critical arabesques. At Brown, semiotics broke off from the English Department in 1978 to form a department of its own. By then the old English Department had become remarkably crowded, teaching all manner of self-expression, including dance and theater as well as such archaisms as Milton and Donne.[24] Freed from such baggage, semiotics is the ultimate in "emancipated subjectivity."

At Brown, subjectivity is most often emancipated on film. As Brown's course brochure says, "film has been a particularly productive site for semiotic analysis both because it activates different types of signs (image, voice, music, text, etc.) and because the cinema is a social institution with significant ideological effects."[25]

There is a course in "Introduction to Cinematic Coding and Narrativity," which not only lets students watch movies but also exposes them to a vast area of contemporary theories, including psychoanalysis, linguistics, feminist theory, and ideological analysis.[26] And "Film Noir," in which the class grapples with "the inscription of subjectivity," and "Film and the Monstrous," which promises to relate German expressionism to modern slasher flicks.[27]

True to the inspiration of Professor Scholes, young Brown semioticians do not merely languish decoding inscriptions of subjectivity or linguistic ideological subtexts. They make their own "texts." One such was the 1987 production by one senior titled, "Mommy, Mommy, Where's My Brain?" The semiotician told the *Brown Daily Herald* that "he stole to finance the film and, at one point, stayed up for five days straight editing." He described it to the paper as "rocking, dated, post-modern trash."[28] Another product of the program was the film "Jupiter Shoes," described glowingly by semiotics Professor Leslie Thornton as a " '60s art happening." The movie is described as a short subject about a man whose feet are immobilized in cement.[29] The emphasis on film reflects the breadth of Scholes' vision. In fact, Scholes defines deconstruction as a latent desire to turn the whole world into a "text." At Brown, they take that very seriously.

Several times every week, students have been climbing aboard buses for a ride into the heart of Providence, Rhode Island, to spend the day shuffling about dry cleaning shops, wig stores, and City Hall. Under the tutelage of their professor, they've been looking for "signs which apparently mean Providence," (architecture, urban design, things like that) which they can then proceed to organize "into a system which can be shared and hence discussed among ourselves." The professor explains the semiotic insight into the otherness of Providence this way: "This city, like all cities, is a compaction of ideological signs, ordinarily naturalized and made familiar as part of our natural environment. We will want to make this compaction strange, to realize that Providence is a foreign place and we are strangers in it. . . ."[30]

In 1987, Brown's semioticians in effect formalized the dissolution of their lingering ties with the world of mere literature when they created a new concentration to be called "Media and Culture." When challenged to describe just what the new melange might be about, one of the semioticians allowed as how the meaning of the major "was beyond language."[31] For anyone familiar with the program, this did not come as a surprise. But its influence was already national in scope.

One scholar wrote a doctoral dissertation at the University of California at Irvine in 1985 on "Ideological Productions in the Food Service Industry." In it, he strikes every conceivable semiotic note. This cutting edge study involved four types of chain restaurants, including Denny's, Winchell's Donut Houses, the 94th Aero Squadron, and Carl's Jr. Where others might see a place to get a quick, cheap bite, the young semiotician discovered in them "a cultural artifact, a text, which can be decoded." As the author explained it: "A semiotic method is used to examine the juxtapositions, dissociations, emptyings and condensations of sign relations within the restaurant text. This is preceded by a separation of the text into components of front and back regions, entrances, doors, windows, lighting, landscaping, menus, photographic technique and other elements." Once this "text" was thoroughly pulled apart, the scholar then demonstrated how this "commercial ideology of systemization fits into a developing postmodern culture."[32]

The Cults of Illiteracy

None of this gibberish and critical doublespeak would really do much damage, of course, as long as students still had a chance to be exposed to authors like Shakespeare or Austen. Given a fair shot, the classics would more than hold their own against the new barbarians. But a central aim of the new movement in literature is the abolition of the traditional canon of literary study and, to date, its adherents have been remarkably successful.

Much of the push for dismantling the foundations of liberal education is based on political arguments: The traditional authors are too white, too male, too old, and too hard.

But the attack on the canon is also, inevitably, an attack on traditional standards of excellence and taste, even on the very *idea* of taste. Houston Baker, a professor at the University of Pennsylvania, argues that choosing between authors like Virginia Woolf and Pearl Buck is "no different from choosing between a hoagy and a pizza."

"I am one," Baker declared to a reporter for *The New York Times*, "whose career is dedicated to the day when we have a disappearance of those standards."[33] Baker has plenty of allies.

Robert Scholes, for example, has rejected the notion that students need exposure to masters like Homer, Plato, Aristotle, Dante, or Shakespeare, because he has rejected the idea that there are any "sacred texts" and has even gone so far as to suggest that the abandoned cathedrals of Western tradition could be replaced by the subway as a temple of learning.

"No text is so trivial as to be outside the bounds of humanistic study," Scholes declared. "The meanest graffito, if fully understood in its context, can be a treasure of human expressiveness."[34]

Scholes gets some unexpected support from E. D. Hirsch, Jr., who is popularly viewed as among the champions of a return to a more traditional understanding of cultural literacy. Hirsch's *Cultural Literacy*, which includes a lengthy listing of facts that an educated person should know, enjoyed a brief vogue and even made the best seller lists. His emphasis on knowing "things" was greeted with suspicion and even outrage by his colleagues. But almost from the moment the book came out, Hirsch has been pleading that all is not as it seems. Not only did *Cultural Literacy* *not* mean anything as reactionary as a core curriculum, Hirsch hastened to assure the ruffled scholastics, but it didn't even mean reading much of anything besides his own work.

To be culturally literate, Hirsch insisted, *"one does not need to know any specific literary texts,"* (Hirsch's italics). Hirsch declared that while it was perhaps desirable that someone know who Romeo and Juliet were, they certainly didn't have to go to all the bother of actually reading the play. Lest there be any misunderstanding, Hirsch insisted that "it's acceptable to take one's entire knowledge of *Romeo and Juliet* from *Cliff Notes*," not to mention television, comic books, or even graffiti.[35]

The agents of the illiteracy lobby within the academy, have thoroughly and systematically infiltrated the study of reading and writing in the modern university.

In the late 1970s, the Committee on the Undergraduate Curriculum of the College English Association handed down the sacred tablets of curricular reform, proving again that whenever literature professors get together, the resulting befuddlement and confusion of language can be immense.[36] The committee began by rejecting the idea that English literature was about any particular English literature, certainly not any specific authors, like Shakespeare, Donne, or Milton. "The undergraduate curriculum should not be defined as mastery of a body of knowledge about literature," it recommended. It elucidated that remarkable proposition with its second recommendation, which declared that "the nature of literary experience and interpretation is falsified if the work is conceived as an object." Which (apparently) is to say books are not to be regarded as having any set or objective meaning that can be taught or learned.

In its third recommendation, the committee sought to strike a note of up-to-date egalitarianism, pointing out that one of the benefits of not treating literature as an "object" was that teachers could be freed to recognize "the multiple contexts which our students actually use in their experience of reading," a phrase effulgent with fashionable and ideologically correct buzzwords.

Note, for example, that the committee does not talk about students reading but about students engaged in the "experience of reading," a Deweyesque touch that has a special meaning all its own to the literary hierarchs. Substituting "experience" for mere "learning" and "knowledge" in elementary and secondary education some decades ago marked the first great triumph of the professional educationists over the public schools. The ardor of the true believers for the transcendent value of "experience" has not been quenched by the intellectual junkyard such curricular fads

have left in their wake. The committee also hit an appropriate up-
to-date note with its reference to "multiple-contexts," which is a
nice tip of the hat to the ideal of pluralism and diversity with which
educationists have dismantled the notion of a shared body of
knowledge or common tradition that should shape the educational
curriculum. Its very vagueness is its strength. "Multiple contexts"
can mean everything from the need to recognize ethnic diversity
to a caution not to unduly burden semiliterate students with
something as thorny as Melville when comic books would do the
job just as well, and without the danger of wounding poor Johnny's
delicate self-image. But by the time the Committee of the College
English Association reached its fourth recommendation, it had
abandoned all pretense that it was doing anything more than
enshrining the latest trendy theories in the curriculum.

"It may be possible," the learned professorial congregation
declared, "to see 'resymbolization' or 're-enactment' in the
readers as the basis of the intellectual and affective experience of
reading and teaching." All of which is to say that it was less
important to teach *Hamlet* or to regard reading as trying to
learn from the authors than to evoke the right kind of emo-
tive "responses" and even "re-enactment," whatever that should
mean.

"To a large extent," crowed Professor Christopher Gould of
the University of North Carolina at Wilmington in one of the
academy's few genuine understatements, "the promise of this
ambitious agenda has been fulfilled . . ." especially among the
departments of literature that have "come gradually to view literature as a manner of response rather than a body of privileged
texts. . . ."[37] The use of the word "privileged" is yet another
crucial addition to the lexicon of the academic newspeak: the
genius of the use of the term is the economy with which it insinu-
ates the idea that Homer, Dante, and Shakespeare have been read
over the centuries not because of any inherent merit or value, but
merely as part of an elitist and therefore arbitrary imposition on
unsuspecting readers—the proletariat of literature. Breaking
down the barriers of literary privilege is thus placed on the same

level as breaking down barriers of political, social, or economic "privilege."

Glory and Riches in the Academic Villages

But the real triumph of theory, mediocrity, and inanity cannot be measured by official statements or articles in the learned journals alone. The real battlefield is the academic marketplace, and there the struggle has long since been decided. If there was any doubt that Theory is not only hot, but verily The Thing To Do in English today, it was dissolved by the goings-on at Duke, which rushed headlong into the stratosphere of the literary establishment by hiring some of the trendiest theoreticians money could buy—in the process paying out salaries of $100,000 or so for the honor of rubbing shoulders with theoretical hotshots.[38] Using money from a $200 million endowment campaign, Duke's English Department decided to take respectability by storm. The school first picked up Professor Stanley Fish from Johns Hopkins in 1985, installing him as the chair and the center around which the constellation of luminaries would be formed. Fish's credentials for the job were impeccable: His best known criticism roundly denies any notion of what he calls "textual objectivity." Fish made himself into a giant in his field by conceding that, yes, words do exist—"Fish grants that signifiers are material objects, 'marks on the page,' and that they are materially present, thus objectively present for reading," one colleague writes. But, he notes approvingly, Fish also insists that "there isn't a text that remains the same from one moment to the next."[39]

What did remain the same was Fish's determination to surround himself with like-minded theorists and to remake Duke's once proud program into the image of this Brave New World of Theory. Nor did he have any apparent doubts about the objective reality of money and the need to pay it out to attract stars like himself. He snagged Barbara Herrnstein Smith, the incoming president of the Modern Language Association, and Frank Lentricchia, the author of *After the New Criticism,* one of the seminal texts of the Faith. Perhaps his biggest steal of all was Frederic Jameson, who is certainly the best known Marxist literary scholar in the nation. Before he was hired by Duke, Jameson wrote:

"To create a Marxist culture in this country, to make Marxism an unavoidable presence in American social, cultural, and intellectual life, in short to form a Marxist intelligentsia for the struggles of the future—this seems to me the supreme mission of a Marxist pedagogy and a radical intellectual life today."[40]

Where does literary criticism fit into this? Says Jameson:

> "American Marxists have clearly recognized that the production and consumption of pleasing, exciting and 'beautiful' stories and images has a specific and very effective role in promoting acquiescence to, and even identification with, the relations of domination and subordination peculiar to the late-capitalist social order. . . . Nothing can be more satisfying for a Marxist teacher than to 'break' this fascination for students. . . ."[41]

Discussing the new face of the Duke English Department, *The Chronicle of Higher Education* reported: "Several new professors are paid in six figures, although part of that is in the form of benefits and personal research budgets for travel and supplies."

"They are the richest Marxists in the country," said one of the colleagues of Duke's new stars.[42]

Fish explained his success in the new free-agent market of literary stars thusly: "It's analogous to what's happening in the NBA. You no longer have the firm assumption that a star will play his whole career with one team." Professor Fish hired his own wife, Jane Tompkins, for the department.[43] Together they are very much the Now Couple of literary criticism.

Under Fish, Duke has abolished many of its longstanding requirements for English majors. No Duke graduate need ever touch Shakespeare, or Donne, or Marvell, to say nothing of T. S. Eliot. Even graduate students will no longer be required to familiarize themselves with the traditional works of English and American literature. Ms. Tompkins reflects the new shift from the old ways most flamboyantly. She wrote her dissertation on Melville but, according to the *Chronicle,* began concentrating on the pulp fiction of Louis L'Amour, the king of the cowboy novel.[44]

The husband-wife combos are actually the rage at Duke. Both Lentricchia's and Jameson's wives were hired to work in the department, and in 1986 the department hired Annabel Patterson from the University of Maryland along with husband Lee Patterson of Johns Hopkins. Like most of the other literary supernovas, Ms. Patterson is associated with what is euphemistically called "materialist criticism." Ms. Patterson, for example, teaches a course called "Shakespeare in His Own Time," a course in which she shares her insight that *King Lear* is really an economic critique of 17th-century England.[45]

The transformation of Duke did not pass unnoticed or unchallenged. Phillip Anderson had entered Duke as a graduate student in 1971 and received his Ph. D. from its English Department in 1975, "back in the days before it went insane," he says.[46] Anderson's frustration with the new trends in the humanities had been building for years. He found some of the new theory interesting, "rather less of it useful and, I'm afraid, very little of it finally convincing."

"If you feed *King Lear* into the meat grinder and it comes out looking like baloney and if you feed McDonald's into the meat grinder and it comes out looking like baloney, that should say something about the critical methods, that they are inflexible, insensible, and unhelpful."[47]

His contacts with the giants of the field did not reassure him. "I was in a seminar once with a distinguished deconstructionist," he recalls. "I listened for several weeks, then asked him to actually analyze a poem by Baudelaire. You've never seen a more uncomfortable man. He said he hadn't read it in many years, but it was only 36 lines long. After that the seminar more or less broke up."[48]

"It's unfortunate that professors of English should have come to this pass," Anderson says. "For years we have been the Peck's Bad Boy of academia because we believed that experiences not reducible to scientific or pseudoscientific analysis were still valuable and meaningful. As a result, most of the other fields didn't know what to make of us. In a lot of ways, we have gone from a period in which English professors were at least minor men of letters who had a sense of the literary experience as irreducible and that has intrinsic value, to people who feel desperately anxious about their status as professionals. They are concerned that unless they change their approach to literature—through theory—they will not be taken seriously by colleagues or administrators."[49]

He had followed the progress of Duke's department through its newsletters, noting the slickness and tone of cocky complacency, superficiality, and self-congratulation that increasingly dominated the communications from his alma mater. *The Chronicle of Higher Education*'s story about Fish's new team at Duke and the completeness of his transformation of the department inspired Anderson to write an 11-page open letter to his old department, in which he remarked that "it is quite clear that we are dealing with an entire department that cannot distinguish between the trivial and the important."

"I am, I suppose, intellectually conservative," Anderson said. "I do most certainly believe that the great tradition of English and American literature, and of Western literature in general, is of immense value . . . these views form the vital and dynamic principle of every class I teach, even every administrative decision I make. I *know* that the reading of Homer, Dante, Wordsworth, Shakespeare, or Yeats is of great and unique value not because of any argument, not from any theory, nor from training, but rather from deeply felt experience."

In contrast, he said, the Duke English Department was part of a trend that was turning departments once devoted to the study of literature into departments of "our personal interests at the moment." Courses that were "trivial, pretentious, vague in conception, lacking in serious intellectual stimulus, and inappropriate for an English Department," were being added, Anderson noted, even though, "given the realities of modern academic life, they have to take the place of a Shakespeare course, or a Milton course, or a course in Romantic poetry."

But the heart of Anderson's critique was his analysis of the mechanisms of the academic marketplace at work in the rarefied halls of Duke. "Where I might see merely intellectual confusion . . . ," Anderson wrote in his letter, "Mr. Fish and company see *opportunity*. If it can be plausibly or even not so plausibly argued that no real distinctions between Shakespeare and Shadwell exist, if it can be argued that no one need bother with reading widely in what used to be called the major writers of the English tradition, if it can be maintained that literary works are basically structural black boxes with only linguistic significance waiting to be 'deconstructed' by the clever critic, why what a field of opportunity for the scholarly entrepreneur! Freed from the tired old expectations that he unglamourously read, write about, and teach such dull stuff as Milton and Tennyson or, heaven forfend!, Homer and Dante, he (or she) can now turn his attention to more fashionable matters. In short he (Professors Fish, Lentricchia, Jameson, and the rest) can pursue stardom. . . . While their less enlightened colleagues at less prestigious places continue to embrace at once poetry and poverty, the 'stars' of Duke have learned that, while literature, in its seriousness, intricacy, nuance, and complexity, is a 'hard sell' in the twentieth century 'market,' the abstractions and reductions of theory, politics, and pragmatic professionalism sell like hot cakes, and at a high price too."[50]

Anderson has not, of course, been alone. One of the most widely respected figures in literary studies, Rene Wellek, has penned devastating critiques of deconstructionist theory and has warned that current theoretical fads "may spell the breakdown or even the abolition of all traditional literary scholarship and teaching."

"If literature has nothing to say about our minds and the cosmos, about love and death, about humanity in other times and other countries, literature loses its meaning. It is possible to account for the flight from literary studies in our universities. . . . The view that there is 'nothing outside of text,' that every text refers or defers only to another text, ignores that texts—political, juridical, religious, philosophical, and even imaginative and poetic—have actually shaped the lives of men and thus the course of history. Denying the self and minimizing the perceptual life of man, the theory deliberately refuses to acknowledge that the relation of mind and world is more basic than langauge. . . . In its extreme formulation, which looks for the abolition of man, denies the self, and sees language as a free-floating system of signs, the theory leads to total skepticism and ultimately to nihilism."[51]

Even a few stray university presidents have entered the fray. Frank Rhodes, the president of Cornell, threw down a gauntlet of sorts at Harvard's 350th birthday party when he declared that "Traditional liberal arts courses have lost much of their ability to exert a transforming and enriching influence on students. . . . Many of those who profess to be humanists devote their lives to areas of high abstraction, decoding texts and deconstructing poems while the larger issues of the world and humankind's place in it elude them. With notable and commendable exceptions, humanists are not demonstrably more wise, more committed, more humane than their neighbors."[52]

But neither a critic of Wellek's standing nor a university president can stand against a theoretical tide at full flood. Despite Wellek's stature, the reaction to his dissent has scarcely even been civil. At the Modern Language Association's 1983 meeting, Wellek was summarily dismissed as an "old fogey," by the keynote speaker, Professor Helen Vendler of Boston University, herself a former MLA president.[53]

And despite Rhodes' lofty perch at Cornell, he carries little weight in the groups that set the tone for literary fashions, such as the MLA or its flagship publication, the Publications of the Modern Language Association (PMLA), which bristles with examples of the New Age, from "Hermeneutics versus Erotics: Shakespeare's Sonnets and Interpretive History," ("This conspicuous ambidexterity, compounded by our declining tolerance for such deftness, has made them infamously problematic.")[54] Or "Dialogic Midwifery in Kleits' *Marquise von O* and the Hermeneutics of Telling the Untold in Kant and Plato" ("We often speak of a text 'pregnant with meaning.' But how does it give birth?")[55] Or "Literature, Psychoanalysis, and the Re-Formation of the Self: A New Direction for Reader-response Theory" ("An examination of the similarities between the experience of reading and the transference process of psychoanalysis demonstrated that, by activating the mechanisms of projection and identification, reading literature can function to re-form the self.")[56] And when the scattered tribes of English professors gather in December for their annual meeting of the MLA, the topics of the papers invariably reflect the dominance of the new sort of scholarship. Harvard Professor Susan Suleiman delivered a paper titled "Metatextual Labels and Textual Properties," indicating that even Harvard, that one-time bulwark against Theory, has succumbed to the new fashions.[57]

Perhaps the most poignant account of the intersection of professional ambition and the befogging clamminess of the new theory is told by Professor Robert Greer Cohn. He encountered one of his former students at a conference where she was presenting a paper on the French poet Mallarme. She projected a passage on an overhead projector and pronounced the meaning of the "text" to be "irrecoverable." Cohn was stunned because he had taught this very poem for years and, indeed, had written extensively on its meaning.

"I began, in the question period, to point out the perfectly obvious (even to the uninitiated) meaning in the beautiful text up there. . . . Taken aback by the audience's clear sympathy for making some sort of sense in Mallarme's work, my former student limply admitted that she had gone that route because it was the 'in' thing to do and she needed to swim with the tide in order to get a better post."[58]

"Today, 'doing' a Lacanian reading of *Ulysses* wins the young scholar many more brownie points than the ability to compare it to the *Odyssey*," Professor Marjorie Perloff says. "Joyce himself felt he had to learn Norwegian in order to read Ibsen in the original; Joyce scholars today don't read Ibsen at all, much less Thomas Aquinas or the Church fathers."[59]

There is some evidence that extended exposure to this sort of thing is more than the nerves of even a confirmed theoretician can take. Yale's Harold Bloom is himself a fairly advanced critic, but years of breathing in the rarefied air of the hothouse theoretical atmosphere of his fellow Yale critics has been a bit much even for Bloom. In an interview with a reporter for *The New York Times* in 1986, Bloom burst forth: "You cannot go anywhere without running into various covens and sects and various new orthodoxies of a self-righteous kind." There are the purple-haired semioticians, the deconstructionists, the fierce neo-Marxists, the Lacanians, the vicious feminists, and what Bloom bluntly labels the "new Stalinisms" of the modern literature department.[60]

In the Wilderness

So what is to become of reading? of literature? of the legacy of more than 20 centuries of Western civilization? In the end, the best hope may lie with the remnant huddled in their obscure schools, far enough into the wilderness to escape the notice of marauding bands of theorists who have already laid siege to or sacked all the major centers of learning.

For Phillip Anderson, Central Arkansas is as good a place as any to begin the long process of rebuilding. After leaving Duke, Anderson taught at the University of Rochester and Lafayette College before going to Central Arkansas' department, where he is now chair. There are disadvantages in working in the barrens, of course. Administrators tend to have terrible inferiority complexes and are particularly reluctant to buck the dominant trends, especially if they come with the glittering endorsement of institutions like Yale, Brown, or Harvard. Nor is even Central Arkansas far enough from the mainstream to be safe from occasional sorties of the cognoscenti. A few years ago a committee assigned to evaluate his department included a professor who had once criticized English departments for being "unashamedly departments of literature."[61]

Anderson recently presented a paper at the South Central MLA convention on the Russian poet Mikhail Lermontov's contribution to Romantic mythology. He did a quick analysis of the other papers presented at the conference and found that fully one-third of the 300 papers "were devoted to pedagogy, or composition, or critical theory—none of which, it seemed, had anything to do with literature." Of the remaining 200, no fewer than 80 were products of specifically feminist criticism. Notable by their absence were any papers about such figures as Pope, Swift, Johnson, Boswell, Dryden, Shelley, Keats, Blake, Wordsworth, Hopkins, T. S. Eliot, Hawthorne, Melville, and Poe. "I fear," Anderson says, "that experience represents another straw in the wind."[62]

But Anderson is committed to his rebuilding project in the wilderness. "There are some advantages to being in a backwater," he says. "I have found that a backwater can be, not immune, but at least buffered from the nonsense afflicting academia right now."[63]

Most of the teachers in his department are refugees from major universities, who were "disaffected with reigning orthodoxies." And his curriculum requires a heavy dosage of readings from the discarded canon. In the last 10 years, the number of majors in his department nearly tripled from 70 to more than 200, Anderson says, "oddly enough, by teaching Shakespeare, Milton, Homer, Dante, and Virgil."

But he has no illusions about the professional odds against him. Says Anderson: "It is very much easier to destroy a civilization than to create one."[64]

Sidebar:
AN ODE TO DECONSTRUCTIONISM

Farewell to Chaucer, Milton, Pope,
To cover them's beyond all hope;
It's just "not practical," you see,
To teach such stuff—when
    there's TV
The Future's ours if we can learn
Just what old books we need to burn.

Oh the sweet caress
Of Meaninglessness!
With a hey! Derri-Derri-da, da, da!

Oh Deconstruction's our high aim,
What we can't burn, we'll try to
    maim,
Prove Shakespeare empty, Yeats a
    blank,
Swift a dullard, James a rank
Impostor whose novels wait to be
Taken apart by you and me!

[Refrain]

Whereas old pedants used to find
In reading something for the mind,
We seek in books we read to show
They mean just nothing, and we go
To Works not for wisdom there,
But to prove all is empty air!

So let's sing Deconstruction's praise
That brings us in these latter days
Curricula so rare and pure—

From all taint of literature!
Hail form from substance now set
    free,
Hail method, abstraction, theory!

[Refrain]

Let English departments know their
    place
Let Shakespeare no more show his
    face,
But come pop culture, politics,
Posturing, pedagogical tricks
That lead the students in a round
Of shifting theory, jargoned sound.

[Refrain]

Lo! see the triumph of the age,
See dullness reach its final stage!
That freezing mist of empty fog,
That worship of theory as king Log,
Which long o'er K through 12 held
    sway
To college now has made its way!

Oh the sweet caress
Of Meaninglessness!
With a whoop! Derri-Derri-da, da, da!

—Phillip B. Anderson, chairman, Department of English,
University of Central Arkansas[65]

12 *The Pseudo-Scientists: The Social Sciences*

"There are four chief obstacles to grasping truth, which hinder every man, however learned, and scarcely allow anyone to win a clear title to knowledge; namely submission to faulty and unworthy authority, influence of custom, popular prejudice, and concealment of our own ignorance accompanied by the ostentatious display of our knowledge."—Roger Bacon

BY the mid-1980s, it would have been hard to name a social scientist with higher standing and more illustrious credits than Harvard's Samuel P. Huntington.

The author of a dozen books and 70 scholarly articles, Huntington had been one of the founders of the quarterly *Foreign Policy.* In 1986 he was the director of Harvard's Center for International Affairs and the newly elected president of the American Political Science Association. Twice he had been judged by his peers to be among the top 10 political scientists in the country. He had previously served as chair of Harvard's highly regarded Government Department, and he was the most cited political scientist in the country in the field of international relations.

Huntington's influence was not merely academic. He had advised the State Department, the Defense Department, and the National Security Council, where he had served a stint during the Carter administration. In the late 1960s, he had chaired a committee advising the State Department on its Vietnam policy. He was one of the three authors of a report for the Trilateral Commission. [1]

He also published a widely discussed article on Third World

dictators—bristling with charts and formulas—that said, among other things, that Ferdinand Marcos was likely to die in office—only a few months before Marcos was forced to leave the country.[2]

Huntington's eminence was such that when he was nominated for membership in the National Academy of Sciences, his election was considered a foregone conclusion.

The section of the academy that nominated Huntington for membership in the National Academy of Sciences made specific reference to his book, *Political Order in Changing Societies,*[3] noting that it was "now widely regarded as a classic."

"Huntington sets forth a highly innovative theory explaining instability in modernizing countries in terms of the imbalance between political participation and political institutionalization," his nomination explained. "He supports this theory with comparative quantitative analyses and longitudinal case studies."[4]

For a social scientist, there were few more coveted honors. Founded in 1863 to provide learned advice to the federal government, the National Academy of Sciences ranks second only to the Nobel Prize in prestige. Election to the academy would represent not only a personal triumph for Huntington, but also the apotheosis of the social sciences as a whole.

But it was not to be. Instead, the battle over the nomination would engage many of the brightest luminaries in academia and the national media, and would reopen the chasm between the hard and soft sciences that had been papered over for years.

The Rise of the Social Sciences

The social sciences' rise to respectability had not been without setbacks. The story of the relations between the soft and the hard sciences is a history of slights deeply felt and long remembered. In 1969, for example, the most notorious aspect of Harvard University's collapse in the face of the student demonstrations was the faculty's capitulation to demands to create a new Afro-American Studies program that would largely be run by students. There were many explanations for the cave-in—with fear being among the most prominent; the Harvard professoriate was no more richly endowed with backbone than their colleagues elsewhere. But another dynamic was also at work in the vote—one that left deep scars in the faculty.

Many of the votes to approve the militant-dictated Black Studies program came not from left-leaning social scientists but from the so-called "hard" scientists, who were more than happy to express their contempt for the intellectual integrity of the social sciences by sticking them with the new program.

Wrote one observer: "Natural scientists, always suspicious of social scientists, were prepared to endorse such academic experimentation precisely because they considered Black Studies to be less than a legitimate field of intellectual endeavor."5 Their vote was an expression of profound disdain, and it was felt throughout the social sciences.

The decision in 1971 to admit social scientists to the National Academy of Sciences was a watershed for the so-called "soft sciences." After years of struggle, cajoling, and lobbying, they had finally been invited into the *sanctum sanctorum* of real science. The move seemed to be a vindication for years of effort: The social sciences had labored long under the yoke of their traditional ties to the humanities with their softer, literary traditions that often made for Great Thoughts but lacked the precision, the accuracy, the certitude of real science. Over the preceding decades, the social scientists had worked furiously to adopt not only the methodologies of real science but also the language, the academic structures, and even the mannerisms of their white-coated brethren.

Traditionally, the study of political science had been based on a foundation of the great thinkers on Man and Society: Plato, Aristotle, Aquinas, Locke, Burke, Marx, and John Stuart Mill.

But the sneer by Robert A. Dahl, one of political science's new breed, that political theorizing "in the grand manner" can rarely meet the rigorous, demanding criteria for truth set out in the real sciences stung deeply. He argued that unless political science research could achieve the standard of "testability," found in such sciences as biology and physics and biochemistry, political science would be doomed to remain on par with "literary criticism."[6] This was a cruel jibe, all the more cutting for being aimed at the weak spot in the psyche of every practitioner of the social sciences.

Richard Mitchell, the author of *The Underground Grammarian,* quips that in the company of a genuine scientist, "the psychologists and sociologists and the professors of English feel like touch-football enthusiasts who have wandered by mistake into the locker room of the Pittsburgh Steelers."[7]

Like their counterparts in sociology and economics, political scientists responded eagerly to the call to scientific respectability. Specialization was virulent as scholars looking for their own niche created new subspecialties with dazzling speed. In 1967, there were only 27 widely recognized subfields in political science; by 1973, the *Biographical Dictionary of the American Political Science Association* listed more than 60.[8]

The fragmentation of the field was matched by the proliferation of new methodologies. Every field felt the need to develop its own *argot* to distinguish itself, however narrowly, from its neighbors.

By the early 1970s, not even political scientists could feel confident reading the work of political scientists outside their specialties, and sociologists and economists had drifted into linguistically sealed worlds of their own. Where the social sciences had once shared with the humanities an emphasis, if not on elegance, at least on clarity of thought, they now became fields closed off from all but specialists by the sheer numbing opacity of the terminology that increasingly hedged them around.

But not even the most blinding jargon would dazzle the groundlings as effectively as the well-placed mathematical formula. This was not a recent discovery.

The court of Catherine the Great of Russia once held a debate on theology, in which the great Swiss mathematician Euler took the part of the deity against skeptical followers of Voltaire. At a crucial point, Euler leapt toward a blackboard on which he scribbled:

$$(x+y)^2 = x^2 + 2xy + y^2 \ldots \text{ therefore God exists.}$$

His listeners were, of course, unable to refute this bold statement, so Euler was left as master of the field.[9] The lesson of the intimidating power of pseudomath was not lost on posterity.

"Hardly a year passes that fails to find a new, oft-times exotic, research method or technique added to the armarium of political inquiry," noted A. James Gregor. "Anyone who cannot negotiate Chi squares, assess randomization, statistical significance, and standard deviations is less than illiterate; he is preconscious."[10]

The average work of the new social science was crisscrossed with graphs, charts, equations, and a language as obscure as it was dense and tangled. A page of a political science essay often was indistinguishable from a study of econometrics, which tended to look like something from a physics text. The political scientists were, of course, eager to take advantage of their new status. At the University of Michigan, for example, professors in the Political Science Department have been holding joint appointments as both professors and "research scientists."

But there were problems with the new scientism. Much of the new so-called rigor of the social sciences rested on the fundamental assumption that human beings could, in fact, be measured and studied in the same way as inert phenomena.

One critic, sociologist Stanislav Andreski, attacked what he called the "wide acceptance of the dogma that nothing is worth knowing that cannot be counted, and that any information which is tabulated becomes thereby scientific—surely one of the grossest superstitions of our time, whose vogue can only stem from the fact that it enables a large number of people to make a living by indulging in easy pseudo-science."[11]

Still, the advantages were considerable. "The more mathematics has been invoked in a particular problem," wrote author Ida Hoos, "the greater the emphasis on technical aspects and the less accessible to scrutiny and understanding by persons outside the fraternal order."[12]

In practice, the new scientism of political science translated into a boom in surveys, despite the basic unreliability of such instruments and the constant temptations of lowly graduate students to generate results in the warm glow of the neighborhood tavern, rather than by ringing hundreds of doorbells in lousy weather.

The new mandarins of the social sciences tended to gloss over this fundamental (and often embarrassing) weakness at the heart of their enterprise by aggressively marrying the raw data with a new and ever more impressive nomenclature. Political scientist David Ricci discerned a troubling undertow to the changes sweeping his discipline:

"Notwithstanding formal justifications, the primary reason why political science spawns more and more new terms for describing public life has little to do with a calculated desire to transform political studies into an analogue of, say, physics. It is not at all clear, after all, that the accomplishments of the physical sciences can be duplicated in the study of society, because we cannot be sure that social phenomena are unambiguous enough to be labeled briefly and accurately, thenceforth to be studied effectively. . . . Thus the major impetus for ceaselessly creating new terminology in political science has less to do with the substance of science than with the form of organized enterprise."[13]

The summit of that organized enterprise was Harvard. Not only did its professors comprise one of the most influential departments in the nation, but they had cashed in on the new prestige in spades, shuttling between powerful jobs in Washington and jockeying for positions in the administration in between occasional stops on campus. The Harvard Government Department also reflected the "new" political science in its purest form.

The student course guide, *The Confidential Guide*, described one of the department's mainstays, its Comparative Government course, as "the epitome of the Ivory Tower in the worst sense of the term. It is frequently a fantasy-land of contrived hypotheses wandering far afield of fact. . . ."[14] Some political scientists, the guide noted, devote themselves to studying government as a quest for better lives, the clash of ideologies, the search for peace and prosperity, or the struggle to transform man's hopes and dreams into policies. "But not at Harvard. Here, Government means something entirely different. Models, towering structures of paper and ink. . . . There are abstractions of every human problem—hunger, war, poverty. . . . Nothing is messy, very little is unpleasant, and only occasionally is anything interesting or relevant at Harvard. . . ."[15]

Anatomy of an Academic Bloodbath

Even so, Samuel Huntington's election to the National Academy of Sciences would probably have been little more than a formality if it had not been for a graduate student named Ann Koblitz. The dispute that would shake the social sciences to their quantitative foundations, that was featured on the front page of *The New York Times,* in articles in *The New Republic, Science,* and *Discover,* and that would convulse the normally insouciant National Academy of Sciences, can be traced back to a single assignment in a graduate seminar on historical methodology at Boston University in 1977.

The class was assigned an article titled "The Change to Change: Modernization, Development and Politics,"[16] a paper by Huntington that summarized the major points from his *Political Order in Changing Societies* (the book later cited in his nomination to the National Academy of Sciences). One of the graduate students, 25-year-old Ann Koblitz, however, was puzzled by the article. It sought to summarize the main points of Huntington's thesis in a series of three equations relating several sociological and political concepts. Huntington's formula read:

$$\frac{\text{social mobilization}}{\text{economic development}} = \text{social frustration}$$

$$\frac{\text{social frustration}}{\text{mobility opportunities}} = \text{political participation}$$

$$\frac{\text{political participation}}{\text{political institutionalization}^{[17]}} = \text{political instability}$$

The presence of equations in an article about political science was not unusual. Actually, Huntington relied on relatively few, but the series of three equations obviously was central to his point.

But applying even elementary rules of algebra to the equations, Ann Koblitz found them absurd. If he was serious in his equations (A/B = C, C/D = E, E/F = G), then they imply:

"Social mobilization is equal to economic development times mobility opportunities times political institutionalization times political stability."[18]

When Ann Koblitz pointed out the weakness in the so-called equations, however, neither her professor nor the other graduate students were receptive: They were impressed with both the equations and the eminence of Huntington, and they were unwilling to cut themselves adrift from such anchors of their discipline by agreeing with the recalcitrant Koblitz.

"I was first amused and then indignant at this use of mathematical pseudo-methodology . . .," she recalls. "But when I brought it up, other people didn't see what I was trying to say."

"I showed my professor the algebra and he was so blocked out, he just couldn't deal with math, he couldn't deal with it. Even my advisor thought what I was saying was interesting, but he couldn't relate to it. I was a little surprised. But that's what Huntington was doing. . . . If he hadn't used equations and terms like 'correlations' and 'coefficient,' and he had just made his point clearly, people might have been willing to question it. Because it was presented in that way it was a stopper."[19]

The matter might well have been dropped there, had not Ann Koblitz brought the equation to the attention of her husband. Neal Koblitz was less willing to be impressed than his wife's classmates and professors had been. In 1977, he was a Benjamin Peirce Instructor in Mathematics at Harvard, where he had received his bachelor's degree eight years earlier. He had gone on to study algebraic geometry and number theory at Princeton where he received his doctorate in 1974. The next year he spent studying mathematics at Moscow University. Like his wife, Koblitz thought Huntington's "equations" were nonsensical, and he decided to say so publicly.

In 1981 Neal Koblitz, who was by then an associate professor at the University of Washington, published his analysis in the book *Mathematics Tomorrow,* under the title "Mathematics as Propa-

ganda," in which he accused Huntington of "mathematical quackery." Huntington's use of equations, wrote Koblitz, produced
"mystification, intimidation," as well as "an impression of precision and profundity."

"In some quarters, invoking an equation or statistic can be even
more persuasive than citing a well-known authority," Koblitz
wrote. "An argument which would be quickly disputed if stated in
plain English will often acquire some momentum if accompanied
by numbers and formulas, regardless of whether or not they are
relevant or accurate. . . . Who can argue with an equation? An
equation is always exact, indisputable. Challenging someone who
can support his claim with an equation is as pointless as arguing
with your high school math teacher."[20]

But Koblitz was still a young professor, little-known outside of
his field, and the journal in which his article appeared was not
widely read outside of his discipline, certainly not among the
increasingly rarefied circles in which Samuel Huntington was
orbiting.

But his article was read—and remembered—by a fellow mathematician named Serge Lang. Lang was already notorious as an
academic insurgent, a flamboyant controversialist with a notoriously prickly personality. Lang—who was born in Paris and
attended school there until the 10th grade—was internationally
known for his work in mathematics. Lang had a bachelor's degree
from Caltech and a doctorate from Princeton. He had taught at the
University of Chicago, Columbia, Harvard, and since 1972 was a
professor at Yale, where his reputation continued to grow as a
prolific mathematician—as both lecturer and author. By the early
1980s, he had published 28 books and more than 60 articles, and
had received the American Mathematical Society's Cole prize and
the French Academy's Prix Carriere.[21] He was also elected to the
National Academy of Sciences in 1985 and thus was given a vote on
all new members.

In March 1986, Lang received word of Samuel Huntington's
nomination to the National Academy. At first his only reaction was
to ask officials of the NAS to circulate copies of Koblitz's article on
Huntington's mathematical "quackery" to the entire membership

of the academy. The academy's officials ignored Lang's request for the mailing and informed him that if he wanted to oppose Huntington he would have to follow a carefully spelled-out legal procedure for mounting a formal challenge.[22]

That seemed, for the moment, to bring the matter to an end. Lang's time was occupied with his own research and graduate teaching. He wrote back to the officials that he had "essentially zero time or energy left for still another fight," and informed them he would not mount the challenge.[23]

Unbeknownst to Lang, however, a copy of Koblitz's article had been sent to one of Huntington's most avid boosters, Professor Julian Wolpert at Princeton. Wolpert was chairman of the section that had nominated Huntington, and he was outraged when he read Koblitz's analysis. He dashed off an angry letter to Lang with copies distributed to several people in the social science establishment in which he vociferously attacked Koblitz, who he said "merits censure for this irresponsible piece of scurrulous [sic] 'journalism' which somehow got past a peer review process of scientists." Koblitz, Wolpert charged, "has distorted severely the arguments made by Huntington and himself created a phony semblance of spurious algebra to provide a better 'strawman' to support his preconceived bias."[24]

Wolpert's letter, however, had the opposite effect he might have wished. It incensed Lang, and on April 10, 1986, Lang informed the National Academy of Sciences, simply, "I have changed my mind."[25]

A Charge of Pseudo-Science

The contrast between Lang and Huntington could not have been more sharply drawn. While Huntington was at the very apex of academic prestige, Lang was, for all his credentials in mathematics, something of an outsider, often more tolerated than accepted. His public crusades were regarded by some as intemperate and unseemly and had won him as many enemies as friends.

In the 1970s, he had waged an unrelenting and often acerbic

attack against another social scientist, Seymour Martin Lipset, who was using surveys to measure attitudes among the professoriate. Lang had excoriated Lipset's surveys as biased and poorly conceived; the fight dragged on for three years, and the correspondence that made up the artillery of the struggle was later issued by Lang in a book, called simply *The File*.[26]

In his critique of Huntington's work, Lang focused not only on the three equations analyzed by Koblitz but also on Huntington's related categorization of 26 "satisfied societies" and 36 "dissatisfied" societies and the claim in *Political Order in Changing Societies* that: "The overall correlation between frustration and instability was .50."

"What is the meaning of the two significant figures [frustration and instability]?" Lang asked.[27]

The issue was a fundamental one. Is it really possible, Lang asked, to measure things like "social frustration" or "political instability" on some sort of absolute scale? Can a single number stand for such a thing as "social frustration"? And would an "8" on the frustration scale mean the same for a Zulu tribesman as an "8" for a Belgian burgher? And if so, what are we to make of a measurement that claims—as Huntington did—that both Belgium and South Africa are "satisfied" societies with "high degrees of political instability"?[28]

Behind the impressive-sounding formulas, Lang said, Huntington was really merely saying that "the more people are frustrated, the more they are likely to act up" but had turned this triviality into "a blown up, pompous, pretentious tissue of pseudoscience by dressing such a statement in equations, correlations, tables, decimals, ratios, which make it appear scientific or precise or profound to some people."[29]

Lang undertook his campaign with his typical zeal. He mailed copies of the relevant page in Koblitz's article along with related correspondence and documentations to all members of the academy at his own expense. Some of the mailings cost Lang several thousand dollars out of pocket.[30] But Lang kept up the drumbeat. "I object to the NAS certifying as 'science' what are merely political opinions and their implementations," he declared.[31]

At first Huntington seemed to strike a detached, bemused attitude, saying, "I find it difficult to take an attack by Serge Lang very seriously."[32]

He admitted that it is "perfectly accurate," that his equations were not mathematically valid. "They were not designed to be. I don't think anybody except him has taken them to be mathematical equations. They were simply a shorthand way of summing up a complicated argument in the text."[33]

But in 1986 and again in 1987 Huntington's nomination failed to receive the required two-thirds vote of approval from the NAS membership. In 1987 he was the only one of the 62 nominees to be turned down.[34]

His defeat only seemed to escalate the fight on all fronts. Huntington's defeat was somewhat misleading, because the academy is heavily weighted to the hard sciences. Even though he failed to win the two-thirds vote, the social science establishment rallied to his cause along with a good deal of the academic establishment as a whole.

For Lang had violated some of the most sacred unwritten rules of the academic villages. Academic controversies are by no means rare. Nor was the intensity of the squabble out of line. Academic disputations often have their own special quality of brutality. But they are usually among specialists within the same field: The typical feud pits an expert in 15th-century Dutch exchange rates against a scholar specializing in 15th-century Dutch commercial routes.

Lang's sin was threefold: He had strayed from his own academic ghetto into another; he had gone public through the news media with his allegations; and most important of all, *his charges went to the very foundations of the social sciences.* Lang recognized that such scholarship was not the result of personal quirks but was really a product of the academic culture. "It is not 'dishonesty,' " he said. "It is a way of life."[35] If Samuel Huntington was guilty of pseudoscience, the entire organized enterprise might be at risk.

Within months of his apparent defeat, Huntington's supporters had brought to bear the full weight of the aroused academic village, with devastating impact. Before the academy's second

vote on Huntington, eleven political scientists signed an open
letter charging that opposition to Huntington was based "in part
on political grounds."*36

Now Huntington's supporters wheeled out their biggest gun in
the person of Herbert Simon, a Nobel laureate in economics, who
offered his own justification of Huntington's use of math. Even so,
Simon's defense is notably halfhearted. Even its title, "Some Trivial but Useful Mathematics," is hardly a ringing endorsement.37

Simon's defense is itself an example of the use of impressive
equations and portentous vocabulary, such as: "More precisely the
ordering of a set of elements by a variable associated with that
ordering is invariant under any positive strictly monotonic transformation of the variable."38

But in the end, it threw little light on the controversy.

Says Lang: "The verbiage . . . obscures the simple statement in
plain English that if one quantity increases, then so does the
other. . . ." But this was hardly a major revelation. "It takes no
special degree," Lang quipped, "no special certification, no Nobel
prize, no special knowledge, no great learning, no great intelligence, to figure out that if people get more frustrated, then they
are more likely to act up."39

Koblitz made a similar point. "Why not use plain English which
everyone can understand?" he asked. "In his entire article, Simon
fails to give any evidence that the use of mathematical jargon,
mathematical notation, theorems about 'sums modulo 2,' and so
on, will ever lead to any insight which could not have been arrived
at more quickly without all of that."40

But the main thrust of the campaign on Huntington's behalf was
to discredit Lang himself. Some leading academicians even began
discussing the possibility of censuring Lang or even removing him

---

* Lang was not, however, without some supporters inside political science's
academic village. Henry L. Bretton, distinguished professor emeritus of the
State University of New York, College at Brockport, endorsed Lang's critique of
Huntington, saying that the Harvard professor "has, of late, following a crowd,
affected jargon intended to convey a sense of scientific rigor regarding subject
matter he must know does not lend itself to that treatment. . . . (Letter to Serge
Lang, June 26, 1987)

from the NAS because of his campaign. One economist from Duke University sent Lang a letter accusing him of putting up a "smoke-screen" to cover his true motives, which he said were political. "You are a bigot!" he charged. [41]

Jeremy J. Stone, director of the Federation of American Scientists sent Huntington a "Dear Sam" letter in which he said that what he had read about Lang led him to conclude that "your main tormentor seems so ridiculous that the matter seemed minor."

"There is a very unusual, uncivilized, and paranoid quality to the campaign against you." Stone wrote. "There is a chilling effect of this campaign against you which reminds me of the political effects of the McCarthy campaigns." [42]

But his main point was to restate the creed of the closed society of the academic village. "Judging scholarship," Stone wrote, "is a very divisive business. Only political scientists can, and should, stand in judgment on the 'scholarship,' of other political scientists." [43]

Everyone else, presumably, should accept their conclusions on faith.

A pro-Huntington slant dominated most media coverage of the dispute, as well. An article in *The New Republic* titled "Bloodlust in Academia" struck a particularly derisive note. "Lang," the story said, "has a history of hounding people," and it accused him both of pursuing a political vendetta and of sloppiness in his research. Not even the crassest Washington politician has come in for the sort of abuse reserved for Lang: "Most of his references are irrelevant, some are nutty. . . ." The article included what purported to be a transcription of a telephone conversation between Lang and the story's author in which Lang acknowledged that he had not read all of Huntington's book.

The article noted with some triumph that the so-called ".50 correlation" that Lang had criticized was originally not even Huntington's—he had taken it from a 1966 study. "Huntington didn't write the study—he only cited it," the author insisted. Moreover, *The New Republic* declared, the original article had won "an award from the American Association for the Advancement of Science." [44]

The reader was left to conclude that with such an honor the original article must be beyond reproach. By association, then, Huntington was also absolved.

But that original study provided a startling look inside the world of pseudoscience.

The article in question bore the uninviting but typical title: "Aggressive Behaviors within Polities, 1948-1962: A Cross-National Study" and was published in the September 1966 edition of *The Journal of Conflict Resolution* by two researchers named Ivo and Rosalind Feierabend. They had gone far beyond anything dreamed of by Huntington in the attempt to quantify social factors. The passage cited by Huntington reads:

> "The product-moment correlation between modernity and stability is .625; the correlation between the so-called frustration index and stability is .499. [Huntington rounded it out to .50.] An eta calculated between the modernity index and the stability index, to show curvilinearity of relationship is n = .667, which is not significantly different from the Pearson r of .625."[45]

In their study the Feierabends had concluded, among other things, that Lebanon, Morocco, and South Africa should be considered among the satisfied (low frustration) societies. As absurd as that conclusion appears on its face, it was less surprising than the methodology they used to yield their "frustration index."

According to the Feierabends, the "index" was determined by assigning a coded score to six "satisfaction indices"—gross national product, caloric intake, telephones, physicians, newspapers, and radios.[46]

They then took that number and divided it by a second number created from "either the country's coded literacy or coded urbanization score, whichever was higher." The result was a ratio, which claimed to reflect the "frustration" in each of the 84 countries in their study.

The problem with this sort of thing cuts to the core of the cult of quantification with its desire to measure reality by assigning numbers to anything that moves (and many things that don't). Dividing a number that is claimed to measure newspaper reading or caloric intake by a "coded literacy score" yields another number. *But does it mean anything?* Is there any valid or meaningful mathematical or social relationship gleaned from dividing the number of physicians by "a coded urbanization score"? Any more than, say, dividing caloric intake by the number of light bulbs in a house multiplied by the earned run average of the local team's starting pitcher would yield a meaningful analysis of social satisfaction?*

This is quantification at its most outrageous: the social sciences not merely as sorcery, but as something close to voodoo. And it was *this* that was cited by one the nation's most pre-eminent political scientists.

"No doubt," Lang later noted, "one can make a correlation between any two sets of events using arbitrarily defined statistics. So what? Huntington (and Feierabend) merely pile up numbers leading to absurdities."[47]

Lang also pointed out the obvious limitations of the approach. "By measuring GNP, caloric intake, telephones, physicians, newspapers and radios, neither Feierabend nor Huntington found out the dissatisfaction among 20 million Blacks in South Africa. . . ."[48]

Huntington made an attempt to defend the glowing rating of South Africa as a "satisfied" society during his interview with *The New Republic*. "The term, 'satisfied,' " Huntington argued, "has to do with whether or not there are measurable signs that people are satisfied or not with their lot. That lot may be good, fair, or awful; what this particular term is describing is the fact that the people for some reason are not protesting it. When this study . . . was done in the early 1960s, *there had been no major riots, strikes or disturbances* [in South Africa]. . . ."[49]

Huntington's comment was remarkable in that it ignored almost two decades of protests and disruptions in South Africa before 1960, culminating in the March 21, 1960, Sharpeville Massacre in which 50 men and women were killed and scores of others wounded. Lang would later compile nearly 50 pages of clippings from *The New York Times* reporting on strikes, riots, and other disturbances in South Africa before 1960.[50]

---

* As far as I know, no one has actually tried this. But I wouldn't be surprised.

The anti-Lang campaign was a model of the way the academic village deals with dissenters. It relied essentially on an appeal to impressive authorities—Nobel laureates and academic prizes. The result was ostracism. No scholarly publication would publish any of Lang's responses over the next year. (At one low point, Lang was forced to buy a full-page ad—at his own expense—in *The Chronicle of Higher Education* to state his case.)[51] At Yale, Lang also paid a steep price for his assault on the academic Brahmins. Yale administrators were openly embarrassed by his campaign and he found himself the object of ridicule on his campus. In late 1987, an undergraduate wrote a letter to the *Yale Daily News*, complaining about the disrespect with which both students and faculty treated the mathematician. "The smirks that I received from some of my fellow students at the mention of Mr. Lang's name denote disrespect and distaste," the student wrote.[52]

The National Academy of Sciences itself amended its internal bylaws to prohibit any "remarks and criticism" about nominees from being communicated to "any person who was not a member of the Academy."[53] If the implied reaction to the Lang-Huntington dispute was not sufficiently clear, the NAS also made the gag-rule *retroactive*—applying it to past nominations as well as future ones—raising the distinct possibility that Lang himself might face expulsion unless he dropped the Huntington issue.

Meanwhile, Huntington retained his laurels. He served on a blue-ribbon panel of 13 defense experts, including Henry Kissinger and former national security advisor Zbigniew Brzezinski. In January 1988, Huntington and the others issued a lengthy report on the future of American defense policy that could influence the development of war and peace into the next century.[54]

The Failed Prophets

The moral here is obvious: Although profthink is remarkably useful in advancing academic careers and winning grants, and consulting contracts, it is almost invariably worthless outside the academy itself. The spread of junk scholarship has not, unfortunately, been limited to political science. The result is what one sociologist calls the "stunned helplessness" of academia's knowledge elite in the face of social problems.[55]

In her book *The Knowledge Elite and the Failure of Prophecy*, Australian sociologist Eva Etzione-Halevy bluntly labels social scientists "prophets who have failed."

> "Although no causality can be shown, it is nevertheless worth noting that the years in which the influence of the social scientists on policy has been growing have also been the years in which policy failures have been rife and in which a variety of formidable social problems have been multiplying. . . .[56] Yet intellectuals . . . continue to act as if nothing had happened.[57]

More than a decade earlier, Stanislav Andreski had written in his book *The Social Sciences as Sorcery:* "Most of the applications of math to the social sciences outside economics are in the nature of ritual invocations which have created their own brand of magician. . . .[58] If we look at the practical results of the proliferation of social scientists we find more analogies to the role of witch doctors in a primitive tribe than to the part played by the natural scientists and technologists."[59]

But Andreski could have included economists in his malediction. Some of the most embarrassing—and public—failures have been in economics, where profthink has turned the dismal science into a discipline focused on the construction of abstract models based on abstract assumptions rather than with economic realities.

The emphasis on abstract "model building," is captured in the story recounted by Etzione-Halevy. Three professors are stranded in a desert with an unopened can of beans among them. The physicist suggests that they use his eye glasses to focus a beam of sunlight on the can to burn a hole in it. The geologist proposes using a sharp rock to punch an opening in the can. And the economist says: "First, let's assume a can opener. . . ."[60]

And yet economists are adamant in insisting that they are practicing real science.

"The trouble with economics," wrote economist G. Barker, "is essentially that its practitioners and their theories have been elevated to a status which they cannot justify. To be an economist is, to many people, to be a combination of high priest, guru, and soothsayer; it is to possess a passkey to the secrets of the future."[61]

Another economist, H. S. Katz, is even more direct, labeling the claim of modern economics to be a science "a sham and a fraud."

> "It has all of the outer paraphernalia of science and none of its essence. It ostentatiously flaunts mathematical symbols (such as supply and demand functions) and formulae ($MV = PT$) without any real understanding of what these things are. When it fails to predict future events (an occurrence of continual embarrassment to modern economists), it does not act like the scientist, disregarding false theories in search of the truth; it acts like the Indian Medicine Man who has failed to make rain. It equivocates, rationalizes and tries to make minor adjustments."[62]

Andreski's own field, sociology, probably has been hit the hardest by the spread of profthink. In 1974, there were nearly one million students enrolled in introductory sociology courses; that year the field awarded degrees to more than 33,000 graduates. By 1981, enrollment was down by half, and the number of bachelor's degrees in sociology had dropped to 17,272.[63] Part of that has to be attributed to the growing popularity of sociobabble among the professoriate.

"We prefer to speak in tongues to ourselves about the intricacies of competing theologies, and to celebrate the mysteries of our multiple-paradigmatic discipline, rather than soiling our hands by using the discipline to discover much of value about the world," Purdue Professor Reece McGee complained in an article he co-authored with two colleagues. "Or, if we did so, we often speak of it in language so arcane as to be unintelligible, and scorn and occasionally even stone the few among us who try to speak the language of the marketplace, or do something of utility in it."[64]

Sidebar:
CLIOMETRICS, OR WHATEVER
HAPPENED TO HISTORY?

The story of Fritz Stern illustrates the pressures on budding historians.

When he was 17, Stern went to his mentor Albert Einstein for guidance: What career should he choose, medicine or history? To Einstein the choice was simple. Medicine was a science, history was not. Stern, however, chose to pursue his nonscientific historical studies and went on to great eminence in the field.[1] But the jibe by Einstein has reverberated through the nervous system of the academic village, where the scholars have been in a frenzy to retool themselves as psychohistorians, quantitative historians, social historians—anything but the outmoded old nonscientific historians of Einstein's disdain.

Perhaps because it had long been held suspended between the world of the humanities and the social sciences, history has been particularly vulnerable to the onslaught of profthink. The most pronounced shift has been away from the study of the great men and events that had traditionally been the backbone of historical study. To become more scientific, historians have replaced them with numbers and more numbers—statistics that claim to measure any historical trend. With their usual pretentiousness, the professors have labeled the new discipline "cliometrics." (Clio is the muse of history.)

The extent to which history had assumed a new face was brought home to me during a lunch with an old friend. The woman was a recently tenured professor at a distinguished university. In college I had known her as among the brightest young scholars in her department, a woman of catholic tastes and considerable intellectual breadth. But in the years since, she had become a thoroughgoing scholastic of the new breed. I was still not prepared for her prophecy.

"I think equations will eventually replace grammar," she said.[2]

Her latest work was a detailed statistical analysis of the culture of Brittany. The end product would be less literature than a data base, which was the whole point. "When people stop reading books, this will still be there," she said. (But when people stop reading books, will anyone care?)

One of the most widely touted triumphs of cliometrics was the 1974 book, A Time on the Cross, a revisionist look at Southern slavery. The book applied detailed "scientific" and statistical analyses to craft its claim that slavery was perhaps not so bad as the softer, impressionistic historians had lead us to believe. For example, the authors of the book declared that by their measurements, the average slave was whipped only 0.7 times a year. (As it turned out, the number was too low because the authors miscounted both the slaves and whipping.) But as critics pointed out, the strictly numerical model failed to take into account the fact that whipping is not only an act of punishment, it was also—and more importantly—intended as a warning to others; a violent expression of social control. In fact, slaves in the study witnessed one of their number being whipped every four and a half days.[3]

But it is just this kind of nuance that gets lost in quanto-history with its obsession with counting rather than subjective analysis.

With this new emphasis on social history and statistical analyses, one of the first major victims of the New History in the university was chronology, the idea that history was a story, a sequence of events. It is no exaggeration to say that modern history developed what almost amounted to a horror of "events." Events, like "texts," are to be deplored, because they so often have a fixed quality about them. Better to knock over the board and start over.

It should not, then, be too surprising that undergraduates in the modern university often graduate with only the vaguest notions of historical chronology nor that these graduates might pass on their ignorance of dates, facts, events, and personalities of history to their own students if they happen to be teachers themselves.

"If you want to play Trivial Pursuit and get the dates right, that's one thing," Professor Linda Grant Depauw of George Washington University said at a recent convention of historians. "If you want to be on the cutting edge, you've got to start with something quirky."[4]

Another professor took a less enthusiastic point of view. "We are in danger of bringing up a generation without historical memory," he warned.[5]

13 *Beyond the Dreams of Avarice: The Sciences*

HAVING endured the wastelands of the humanities, the vast dreary junkyards of literary theory; having successfully cut through the tangled jungles of the social sciences, the malarial, pseudomathematical, cant-infested swamps of political science, sociology, and economics; the sojourner through academia is apt to look upon the hard sciences as a shining city on a hill.

The men and women in white are, understandably, a welcome relief after the morass of junkthink and posturing that dominates the rest of the academy. And at first glance, the contrast could hardly be more striking. The scientists may speak their own incomprehensible language, but they are not playing academic dress-up; they are the real thing. They are curing cancer, developing superconductive materials, coaxing the mysteries of the universe from subatomic particles, and probing the farthest reaches of the cosmos.

Unlike their woolier colleagues, the scientific clan has rules that are rigid: hypothesis, experimentation, proof, and replication. Theories that are disproved vanish (in the humanities and social sciences they sometimes fall out of fashion but are never disproved or voluntarily surrendered), while ideas, both new and old, are constantly subjected to the searching skepticism of the scientific mind. The margin for error is slim; for humbug, nonexistent.

Clearly, the traveler through academia would conclude, this is both the sanction and justification for the academic culture. Although teaching is, or should be, at the heart of the humanities, the sciences arguably have a different hierarchy of values. Here, research, specialization, and professionalism are the essence of the discipline. Whatever distorted forms those values might have taken when transposed to the study of poetry, social relationships, or communications, they are obviously well placed in the sciences themselves.

This argument is so compelling that it is invariably used in one form or another by the defenders of higher education. When critics attack the university's obsession with research over teaching, for instance, the professoriate's response is reflexive: It is the scientist—not the literary critic, educationist, or scholar probing the esoterica of body language—who is trotted out to dazzle the peasantry. It is this work, they insist, that provides the ultimate validation—not merely for academia, but for the professoriate's perks, eccentricities, and, of course, its culture.

But if the sciences represent the academic culture in its purest form, they also reflect its corruption and failure in their starkest outlines, both in the classroom and, ironically, in that *sanctum sanctorum* of the academic enterprise, the laboratory.

Evidence of the crisis in American academic science is, unfortunately, not difficult to come upon. In 1986, the National Science Board issued an unusually alarming report, declaring that academic programs in the nation's universities for science, math, and engineering were so weak that they actually posed "a grave long-term threat," to the nation's industry, national defense, and long-term scientific and technical competitiveness.

The report made an obligatory call for more federal money, but it traced many of the problems directly to the college classroom. Laboratory instruction, it said, was often "uninspired, tedious and dull," and students were often provided with instruments and equipment that was "obsolete and inadequate." And, the report's authors charged, too often universities provided courses that "are frequently out of date in content and are poorly organized."[1]

The collapse of academia's scientific curriculum was accompanied by two related phenomena: the flight of American students from the sciences and their replacement by foreign students. Approximately 40 percent of the doctorates awarded in mathematics and computer science are now won by foreign students; in engineering the figure has reached nearly 60 percent.[2] The numbers seem certain to grow: In physics, 40 percent of the first-year graduate students in 1986 were foreign.*[3]

Here the process begins to take on a circular quality. As American students, disgusted by poor teaching and the indifference of the faculty, shun the sciences, their places are taken by foreign students. Of course, if half or more of the graduate students are foreigners, that will also mean that a large proportion of the teaching assistants—drawn from the ranks of the graduate students—will also be foreign. And there is the rub. (Especially since so much of the teaching in the sciences is done by T.A.s.)** Many of the foreign graduate students are academic stars in their disciplines but are unable to communicate in English. Even so, they are often put in front of undergraduates with a minimum of training. The results are, predictably, catastrophic.

Upon graduation, many of the foreign students return home. The result is a looming crisis in American science. The Conference Board of the Mathematical Sciences, a consortium of 14 professional societies, noting the acceleration of the trend, declared in 1987: "The prognosis for the continuing vitality of mathematics is somewhat bleak."[4]

"The people to staff universities in the 1990s are not in the pipeline right now," warned Bettye Anne Case, an associate professor of math at Florida State University. "A very scary picture is

---

* Foreign students account for 40 to 60 percent of the doctoral candidates in several crucial areas, including, biotechnology, computers, manufacturing technology, microelectronics, and robotics.

** A survey by the Mathematical Association of America found that 45 percent of the classes at "leading" math departments were taught by graduate students. One-third of those T.A.s were foreigners. (*The Chronicle of Higher Education*, October 29, 1986)

emerging: We're not producing enough young scientists to staff our universities down the road. We do not have enough Americans."[5]

What is happening in the sciences?

Again, there is little mystery. In the sciences, we can find the purest expression not merely of the academic culture, but of that culture's virulent contempt for and indifference to teaching. The teaching loads of professors in leading science departments make the five-hour-a-week loads of their counterparts in the softer sciences seem enormous. In a culture where research is everything, teaching—not to mention teaching well—is almost nothing. In some departments, given the vagaries of science funding, there are often more professors than majors; and in almost all leading departments an untoward emphasis on working with students would be regarded as clear evidence of dementia. It is not surprising then that over the years academic science has been turned into a forbidding no-man's land for undergraduates or that Harvard's professors of the natural sciences would be described as able to "bore the buzzards off a shit-wagon."*[6]

Given their villages' emphasis on specialization, the academic scientists generally make few concessions to those students who are not yet dazzled by the prospect of a life spent studying the mating habits of lower crustaceans. At the lower levels, the purpose of science courses at many institutions is less to educate or inspire than it is to weed out. "They function as gatekeepers," says Joan Straumanis, dean of the faculty at Rollins College. "In the science and mathematics sequences we sometimes content ourselves with 'discovering' the talented students and frightening off the others."[7]

The result is the increasingly rapid spiral of decline: shrinking numbers of American students who are in turn replaced by for-

---

* Another major factor in the stultification of academic science is the impact of tenure: especially in physics, many departments are "tenured-in," with no place for young scientists. By 1981, fully 60 percent of academic physisists held the rank of full professor and the median age of the faculty has been rising precipitously.

eign students who become T.A.s, who in turn manage to frustrate and discourage even more undergraduates from pursuing a career in the sciences.

Few critics, however, have pointed out that the root of the problem lies directly in the academic culture itself. Ironically, it is the obsession with research and the professors' disdain for their students that is, in effect, strangling the life out of the sciences.

Professors for Sale

But the greatest threat to the sciences might not be the failure in the classroom at all (about which the professors probably couldn't care less) but in the way that the professors have mortgaged scientific research to their self-interest.

Almost from the beginning of the modern era, the notion has been implicit in the academic culture that the professor should think of himself as an entrepreneur, a hustler in the world of grants, foundations, sabbaticals, and consulting contracts. If any one characteristic distinguished the new professor (aside from his allergy to undergraduates) it was the eagerness with which academics had, in effect, gone into business for themselves.

In the beginning was the consulting contract. The practice of what author Ronnie Dugger would later call "academic racketeering," sprang up almost immediately after World War II, in the first of academia's go-go years. One of the pioneers was the University of Texas' Norman Hackerman, who found that he could easily add 20 percent to his base pay by consulting for an oil company.[8]

Because the professors were masters of their own time, universities initially paid little attention to the faculty members who were tacking 20, 30, even 40 percent onto their salaries on the side. Some felt it necessary to impose modest restrictions, such as limiting such work to only one day of the week. But this was seldom enforced (it was, in any case, impossible to do so) and was never taken seriously by anyone involved. The petrochemical company paying a professor $40,000 for consulting was under no illusion that it was buying only one-fifth of the professor's time and knowledge, no matter what the university's official policy might say. As one early observer of academic consulting remarked, if a professor makes $10,000 for working on a Friday, "Friday will become an important day among his days."[9]

By the mid-1970s, the practice of professors-for-rent had permeated higher education at every level. Nearly half of the senior professors at Harvard reported they had outside incomes that were more than one-third of their base salaries.[10]

Many professors managed to integrate their highly active and equally lucrative consulting businesses painlessly into their academic schedules. Dugger quotes one successful consultant, who taught only advanced students:

> "Since what I'm teaching is what I'm doing, I never prepare for class—I just tell them what I'm doing, which illustrates the textbook as they read along in it. . . . The university gives me status and a steady professional income."[11]

The most conspicuous fallout from the rash of consulting contracts in academia was the way it drew the professors not only out of the classroom but off the campus altogether, often for lengthy periods of time, as they shuttled about the country servicing their diverse clientele. But even in the early days, the "racketeering" had other less obvious, but far more profound implications.

In some cases, industries hired the leading specialists in an academic field not merely for their brainpower, but also as a subtle method of co-optation. This was particularly effective for industries that were subject to government oversight. One management book, titled *The Regulation Game,* coached businessmen on the value of adding professors to their payroll:

> "Regulatory policy is increasingly made with participation of experts, especially academics. A regulated firm or industry should be prepared, whenever possible, to co-opt these experts. This is most effectively done by identifying the leading experts in each relevant field and hiring them as consultants or advisors, or giving them research grants and the like. This activity requires a modicum of finesse; it must not be too blatant, for the experts themselves

must not recognize that they have lost their objectivity and freedom of action."[12]

The authors, however, overestimated both the scruples and the squeamishness of academics. In practice, industry found that it had to employ cudgels to drive the eager professoriate off. Academics were not only willing to be co-opted but also quite amenable to upping their ante for the right price.

That included modifying or refocusing their research toward those areas of most interest to their corporate patrons. The new economics gave added force to the adage that applied research tends to drive out basic research. Basic research, once the backbone of the scientific enterprise, simply no longer paid—or to be more accurate, it no longer paid enough. (Why hunt for distant galaxies and notoriously elusive quasars when you could cash in now by helping develop new no-sag, no-run pantyhose?)

The profit-chasing, of course, did not leave the students unscathed. The newly found enthusiasms of their professors trickled down to the students whose areas of specialization were reoriented to areas with the greatest possibilities for commercial exploitation. Subtly, gradually, and fundamentally, the way that scientists were trained in American universities was being transformed.

For the most part, prudent administrators chose to simply look the other way.

But the allure of consulting contracts was destined to be overshadowed. By the 1980s, the professors had found a much, much bigger payoff.

The Feeding Frenzy of the Professors

The history of the modern professoriate could almost be divided into two eras: Before Otto and After Otto.

Otto—Professor Otto Eckstein—was a faculty member at Harvard, where he had developed a remarkably useful system of economic forecasting. Not content with purely academic applications, he turned his specialty into a business, which he was later able to sell for $100 million.[13] In doing so, he not only made himself spectacularly rich but also transformed the landscape of academia.

If Eckstein was a superstar, he was quickly followed by other role models: For several years Professor Walter Gilbert reportedly did company business out of his Harvard office; later he was able to spin the firm, Biogen, off into a company that made himself and his associates wealthy far beyond the dreams of academia.[14] And on the opposite coast, there was Herbert Boyer, who reportedly used the facilities of his school, the University of California at San Francisco, to launch Genentech, a genetic engineering firm whose stock jumped from $35 a share to $89 in the first 20 minutes it was publicly traded.[15]

A generation of ambitious young scientists thrilled to Boyer's description of the new frontiers of their discipline. "I found it just as rewarding too," Boyer said, "to see a group of investors' eyes light up over these commercial possibilities as to see a group of students' eyes light up."[16]

As early as 1981, the journal *Chemical and Engineering News* could write that "an epidemic of entrepreneurial activity . . . is running rampant on university campuses. Cool-headed scientists have turned into feverish schemers caught up in a heady delirium of corporate planning, real estate speculation for lab expansions and market watching."[17]

If the consulting contract had once been the brass ring for the professoriate, the new magic word in every faculty lounge, laboratory, and scientific conference now was *equity*. The professors had a chance to cash in directly on their expertise by either starting up their own company or by accepting shares in enterprises that could, with luck, turn handsome profits for all concerned. In 1981, an MIT scientist bragged to one science publication: "There isn't a walking biochemist who doesn't have a piece of some company in which he is a consultant."[18] And in 1982, *Science* magazine reported: "A majority of the country's leading researchers in molecular genetics and related disciplines are known to have affiliations with these new, highly competitive companies."[19]

Even the diary of American capitalism, *The Wall Street Journal,* was struck by the feeding frenzy among the academics. "Genetic-engineering conferences nowadays," the paper reported, "are crawling with venture capitalists, patent lawyers, management 'headhunters' and representatives of corporations large and small." Even *The Journal* was taken aback at the new atmosphere: "Abruptly, scientific curiosity must vie with another motive force: personal cupidity."[20]

There is, of course, nothing wrong with scientists making a profit—even a very large profit—from the fruit of their labors. Nor is there ground for objection if the professors leave their university posts to set themselves up in business, with all the risk that entails. But generally they did not leave. Therein lies the paradox of the entrepreneurial professor.

Entrepreneurial activity usually is associated with risk. But the essence of the professorial personality is aversion to risk of any kind; the professor is a direct product of a culture that rewards conformity above all traits and is designed to shelter the professors from the vicissitudes of life.

That environment shapes the strange breed of the entrepreneurial professor who wants the big payoffs, but without the risks of going after them unprotected by tenure. The entrepreneurial professor is to the genuine entrepreneur what a tank is to a sports car.

Even as they ventured out into the marketplace, the professors have tenaciously held onto their chairs, their professorships, their access to taxpayer-supported laboratories, and their graduate students. The impact of this double life on their institutions, their students, and their disciplines has been devastating.

The transformation of American science into a mad scramble for profit has shaken even some of the more hardened academics. "We are seeing a basic restructuring of the relationship between professors and their universities," the president of the University of Miami complained. "If we come to a time when our most gifted scientists spend their time capitalizing on their intellectual endowment, it will be great for profit, but it will hurt their basic research."[21]

The impact of the commercialization of science was twofold: It dramatically skewed the attention and resources of whole departments toward the immediate commercial interests of the grantors; and second, the free flow of information that had been crucial for the development of the sciences was radically curtailed.

A 1986 study by Harvard University found that faculty members taking part in research sponsored by private industry were four times as likely to say their research topics had been influenced by the possibility of commercial applications. And at half of the institutions surveyed, the professors said that the product of their research belonged to the corporate sponsor and that their results could not be published without the sponsor's consent.[22]

This new climate of proprietary secrecy hangs pall-like over the sciences that for centuries have prided themselves on their openness. But when no one knows just what microbe might be the next star on the open market or what germ could be worth millions at its first public stock offering, openness no longer makes good business sense.

"Nobody here is really talking," a participant at a professional conference of scientists told a reporter in 1981. "Even the university people are being very secretive, and that's new."[23]

"In the past, it was the most natural thing in the world for colleagues to swap ideas on the spur of the moment, to share the latest findings hot off the scintillation counter. . . . No more," said Emanuel Epstein, a microbiologist at the University of California at Davis, where his colleagues had been extremely quick to mine the commercial possibilities of some of their work. "Any UCD scientists with a promising new slant . . . will think twice before talking about it. . . ."[24]

At first blush, this transformation of the scientific culture was stunning. But in another sense it was not wholly unprecedented: In some ways it was merely an extension of the pattern repeated throughout the rise of the professoriate. This was, after all, the same professoriate that had sacrificed its teaching obligations for research; its undergraduates for its graduate students; and its institutions for its disciplines.

The professors built the entire academic structure on their

purported contributions to knowledge, the need for the free flow of information and their commitment to expanding their disciplines' horizons. As long as those values served the self-interest of the professoriate, they remained intact, even revered. But at the first hint that they might be inconvenient, they were scrapped. In their scramble for the pot of riches at the end of the commercial rainbow, the professors were also fully prepared to scrap, in turn, their research agendas, their obligations to their graduate students, and even the needs of their disciplines. The only constant was the self-interest of the professors themselves.

As early as 1946, the University of Texas' Norman Hackerman laid out the justification that would for the next four decades, serve as the centerpiece of the entrepreneurial professors' defense. "I think the faculty stays alive this way," he argued. "You do not withdraw to the ivory tower . . . if these agreements . . . keep you in the lifeline of the action, it improves the faculty."[25] His argument was not only persuasive, but almost indisputable given the tendency of American higher education to judge success on the basis of contracts, cash, and clout. Hackerman's creed was so effective, wrote author Ronnie Dugger, because it was, "a logical use of the university's own values to change its nature. Like education, ideas, too, writhe and adjust to subserve the realities of the culture they are in."[26]

The notion of tapping the ivory tower for the benefit of the private sector also had an understandable allure for both business and government leaders. Academics had learned the power of buzzwords to advance their own agenda in their battle for control of the curriculum. There, the words had been "pluralism" and "diversity." Here, the potent words were "economic development" and, best of all, "competitiveness."

Such flag-waving rhetoric also provided a rationale for the universities themselves, which were being drawn almost irresistibly to the entrepreneurial flame. By enlisting their institutions behind them, the professors made them, in effect, extraordinarily potent procurers for their deals. By 1987, according to the National Science Foundation, corporate expenditures on university research reached $670 million, up 185 percent over 1980 levels.[27]

Some schools have been more zealous than others in assuming the role of middleman. Stanford, for example, set up a nine-member Office of Technology Transfer, whose job is "to serve as matchmakers between faculty or student inventors and business investors." The director of the office, Niels J. Reimers, explains the office's value to the professors: "It allows them to concentrate more on research and teaching rather than on commercial development."[28]

Of course, academic administrators have tried to put the best face possible on their scramble for the commercial payoff, emphasizing the contribution industrial-university deals would make toward the economic vitality of their area as well as the benefits that would accrue to both researchers and students on their campus.

In 1986, however, Dennis Muniak of the Political Science Department of the University of Maryland-Baltimore County, surveyed universities that were creating massive research parks. Of the 64 goals and objectives identified by the 23 universities in his study, Muniak found only 11 related to strengthening the school's research mission. *"No one,"* he wrote, *"mentioned education."*[29]

In fact, the universities had their own motives for joining the race to the trough. The new commercial possibilities of their faculty's work raised images of vast new infusions of cash into institutions that were seldom if ever sated, and the deals provided them a way to keep their professors happy without having to give them raises. Moreover, the professors, in many cases, did not give their schools an option in the matter. The universities would either help them set up their commercial empires or the professors would leave, finding instead another university less scrupulous about its values.

As usual, Harvard was something of a pioneer. In 1974, Harvard cut a deal with Monsanto that would prove a model for dozens of similar arrangements over the next decade. The arrangement called for a $23 million grant from Monsanto to Harvard's medical school over a 12-year period. Only two professors actually received funds from the grant, M. Judah Folkman and Bert Vallee, both cancer researchers. The grant consisted of an award of $200,000 to support each professor's lab and a $12 million endowment to pay for support personnel, to equip a floor of the new medical school building, and to pay for facilities to supply research materials.[30]

In return, Harvard gave Monsanto the right to secure an exclusive worldwide license for all the inventions or discoveries made in connection with the project. That alone was a dramatic departure from Harvard's longstanding policy. Until the Monsanto deal, Harvard policy had strictly prohibited patenting any therapeutic or health discoveries for profit. Under that policy Harvard had insisted that all such breakthroughs be dedicated to the public.[31] The policy evaporated the moment Harvard accepted Monsanto's check.

Monsanto was not only one of the early leaders in university research support, but also one of the most aggressive. In 1979, five years after the first Harvard deal, Monsanto hired Howard Schneiderman, then the dean of biological sciences at the University of California, to serve as the company's senior vice president for research and development. He was immediately sent shopping for other professors, with an almost limitless budget. At Monsanto, he directs the spending of more than half a billion dollars a year in R&D.[32]

One of his first major *coups* was at Washington University, located in Monsanto's hometown of St. Louis. Monsanto's $23.5 million, five-year grant bought the company access to WU's entire School of Medicine. (The grant was later upped to $62 million.) The patents for any products developed in the course of this research are held by the university, but Monsanto gets the exclusive license to manufacture and market them.[33] Schneiderman makes no secret of the company's aims. Only 30 percent of the research grant goes to support basic research. The rest—70 percent, or nearly three out of every four dollars—goes for applied product development.[34]

Monsanto has made the most of its foothold inside Washington University. The relationship between the corporation and school grew steadily more intimate until 1986 when Monsanto scientists moved into the WU labs *en masse*. To make room for the Monsanto corporate scientists, something had to give—the students, of course. Second-year medical students at the school were ordered out of their study quarters, and both first-year and second-year students were forced to double up in both lab and study space.[35] The move eliminated any lingering doubts about the school's actual priorities.

Author Martin Kenney, in his cogent and alarming portrait of the trend, *Biotechnology: The University-Industrial Complex*, described the way the professors' cash grab was changing their relationship to their students.

> "In some cases mentors are guiding students toward commercial research and in other cases their ideas and research topics are being transferred to companies without financial compensation for the students. . . . More and more biology students are being used as workers while still being classified as students."[36]

Stories became common of professors who shamelessly exploited graduate students by holding bull sessions, asking for ideas, and then handing over those ideas to a private concern for the exclusive profit of the professor himself.

"Many graduate students are also uneasy when their advisors take equity and managerial positions in firms closely related to their research," Stanford's graduate student association complained. "Are they now working for their advisor, the professor, or their advisor, the entrepreneur?"[37]

One prominent scientist complains that the quality of doctoral dissertations has noticeably suffered because too many of them "were purely developmental product-oriented studies of little basic importance, but of considerable possible monetary value. . . .

"Regrettably, in some cases, some of the most famous faculty members in the department are rarely seen on campus. They are much too busy with other things. I hear tales of graduate students who claim that their preceptors do not even know their names because they meet them so rarely, the preceptors spending much time in the industrial facility, whether in this country or, on occasion, in Europe."[38]

Schools no longer make a secret of the fact that corporate investors are also buying access to their students. When MIT signed a 10-year, $8 million deal with Exxon to study combustion engineering, it explicitly called for the participation of MIT students in the program.[39] Carnegie Mellon's Magnetic Technology Center makes access to its student body a major selling point to potential donors. Mark Kryder, a spokesman for the center, acknowledged to *Science* magazine that he steers students toward the donor companies by actually discouraging non-donor companies from recruiting students at the school. "We're trying to preserve a benefit for our sponsors," he explains. "It's a ticklish business."[40]

Donors dictate research topics and the direction of their programs to the universities. Only a few years ago, this would have been unthinkable for an institution of higher learning to admit publicly; today many of them actually advertise their willingness to assume whatever position the patron desires.

Cornell's Biotechnology Institute, for example, explicitly offers "collaborating" corporations "a role in the guidance and development of academic biotechnology."[41]

Carnegie Mellon's Magnetic Technology Center offers a three-tiered package to potential donors. The top-of-the-line deal goes for $250,000-a-year for a minimum of three years. For that ticket, corporations can buy themselves royalty-bearing patent rights, copyrights to software, preprints of research reports, an annual conference with the center's scientists and the right to place a full-time scientist in the center itself. The $750,000 also buys the corporate investor a seat on the center's advisory board and, according to *Science* magazine, the right to "dictate three topics of research."

"In a way, they have control over the direction of research and policy issues," Mark Kryder told the publication. "We reserve a veto power, but it has never been used."[42]

By the mid-1980s, university administrators had moved to the forefront of the movement; nevertheless, its driving force remained the faculty itself. And they were prepared to go to outstanding lengths to protect their cash cows.

Academia's hierarchs have dealt with the various outrages and sellouts in a typical manner—a great deal of tut-tutting accompanied by throat clearing, culminating in inaction. A conference on the future of university-industrial deals that included most of the leading research universities in the country, for example, came to the typical academicspeak conclusion that: "Although we see no single 'right' policy, we do believe that each university should address the problem vigorously." And left it at that.[43]

There is an element of irony in all of this, albeit a somewhat tragic irony. The academy has, to date, been successful in selling the notion that the professoriate's mad dash for affluence is really a selfless contribution to the nation's economic future. Industry has increasingly found the allure of the university laboratory too seductive to resist. In the long run, however, private industry itself may be the biggest loser, because it has not yet fully realized the nature of the academic personality.

"Most academics," a 1987 report by the Economic Policy Institute concluded, "live in a world whose incentives have nothing to do with economic competitiveness. The research that will move them ahead in their professions is unlikely to be directly useful to industry."[44]

And while some companies may win a temporary edge in their fields by buying, leasing, or renting the services of professors, graduate students, and university labs, they are also aiding and abetting another trend: Information that was once freely available to anyone is now often the sole possession of a single entity. "The result," writes Martin Kenney, "is that the freely usable knowledge base is shrunk. . . ." The base of trained scientists for the future has also eroded, not merely in numbers, but also in adaptability. Will students trained to solve narrow questions of specific product design have the skills to adjust and confront a rapidly changing technological environment? Observes Kenney:

"Perhaps the cruelest irony will be experienced by U.S. industry itself. As the university is bought and parceled out, basic science in the university will increasingly suffer. The speculative, noncommercial scholar will be at a disadvantage and the intellectual commons so important for producing a trained labor force and the birthplace for new ideas will be eroded and polluted."[45]

14 *Fraud*

PROFESSOR Robert Sprague was stunned when he saw the results of an experiment involving a colleague. Two nurses were asked to evaluate, independently of one another, the severity of a movement disorder in mentally retarded patients. Sprague, a distinguished child psychologist at the University of Illinois, had been doing similar testing himself at Cambridge Hospital in Cambridge, Minnesota, and had found that nurses came up with the same evaluations only occasionally.

But in September 1983, Sprague learned that the study was showing *100 percent agreement* between the two nurses. "I almost fell out of my chair," Sprague later said. "It is impossible to obtain perfect agreement—100 percent—when raters are asked to make judgments about complex movements." On the face of it, Sprague felt that the data were fraudulent.[1]

He had worked with Professor Stephen Breuning off and on for four years; some of Breuning's work was performed under a subcontract from Sprague. But now Sprague had to face the possibility that much of Breuning's work was simply fake. This was of more than merely academic interest. Breuning's research was extraordinarily influential in the field of psychology; his studies had convinced institutions throughout the country to begin administering stimulants rather than tranquilizers to literally thousands of mentally retarded children suffering from hyperactivity or extreme aggression.[2]

Breuning had a reputation for conducting impressive, large-scale studies. One of his studies of the use of psychotropic medications on retarded patients claimed to have included about 15,000 subjects. At first, Sprague, like most of his colleagues in psychology, was impressed with both the size and the apparently definitive results Breuning had achieved. "My enthusiasm about the results impaired the critical attitude that should always be maintained in science," said Sprague.[3]

In late 1983, however, Breuning gave Sprague a copy of the annual report on research he had performed with a grant from the National Institute of Mental Health (NIMH). Sprague was shocked at the huge number of studies Breuning claimed to have made in the last year, the rigor of the methodology, and the unusual results he claimed to have obtained.

But it was in November of 1983 that Sprague came on what he believed was the smoking gun. In a paper prepared for presentation to a meeting of the American College of Neuropsychopharmacology, Breuning reported results he said he had obtained by monitoring the progress of mentally retarded patients for two years after they had left the Coldwater Regional Center in Coldwater, Michigan. Because follow-up studies over that length of time were unusual, Sprague decided to check into the matter more closely. But when he contacted Coldwater, the center's chief psychologist told him that such follow-up research was impossible. And, Sprague later said, when he challenged Breuning directly, the researcher was able to document only 24 of the 180 evaluations he had originally claimed.[4]

Reluctantly, Sprague thought he had no choice but to become a whistle-blower, and he reported his concerns. But from the beginning, he came up against a wall of indifference—the academic establishment seemed to be refusing to take his charges seriously.

At the time, Breuning was an assistant professor of child psychology at the University of Pittsburgh. After an investigation that has been described as inadequate, the university, Sprague said, announced that it had no grounds to take any action against

Breuning. Breuning subseqently resigned.[5] The National Institute of Mental Health also began an investigation, but it dragged on for years.

In an amazing twist, Sprague's school, the University of Illinois, launched an investigation into Sprague himself, as did NIMH, in the course of which he was compelled to produce hundreds of pages of documents and to appear before NIMH's investigatory panel.[6]

Meanwhile, the University of Pittsburgh went through four separate investigative committees but never made its results public. It was an example of the academic culture at its purest. "It isn't common in academia to do such investigations," a university official explained, "so we wanted to be careful both in regard to the truth and in protecting the rights of the faculty."[7]

But what about the rights of the thousands of mentally retarded children who might still be receiving treatment based on Breuning's research?

The reaction of federal officials was little better. NIMH also proceeded on the Breuning case at a glacial pace. Its final report would not be issued until May 1987, and only then after Sprague's pressure had drawn media attention to the foot-dragging on the probe.[8]

Belatedly, NIMH concluded that Breuning "knowingly, willfully, and repeatedly engaged in misleading and deceptive practices in reporting results of research." It concluded that one study, which claimed to survey 3,496 mentally retarded patients, had never been carried out.[9]

The University of Illinois completely exonerated Sprague.[10]

But the case did not end there. In March of 1987, NIMH cut off its funding of Sprague's research after more than 16 years of support, even though his work was unanimously endorsed by a panel of his peers. When it was finally renewed later in the year it was for an amount only one-tenth of what Sprague had sought, and was good for only a single year.[11] The message was clear to any other potential whistle-blowers.

The pressure to drop the matter might have deterred a scientist less adamant than Sprague, or one who did not have his strong personal motive for pursuing the matter. Sprague's wife was a diabetic, and in 1984 her kidneys failed. For the next 19 months until her death in 1986, she was placed on frequent hemodialysis to sustain her life. Later, describing why he had decided to blow the whistle and why he persisted in his fight to force an investigation even in the face of such harrowing pressure and counter-threats, Sprague wrote:

"In my case, it was because my wife's very existence depended on medication for a considerable part of her adult life. We trusted the research system that developed and delivered that medication. That trust must not be violated. But some universities and federal agencies apparently do not give this public trust a very high priority."[12]

The Code of Silence

No one knows for sure how widespread outright fraud is in academia. Part of the reason is that no one wants to find out. In the social sciences, attempts to reproduce the research claims of a professor are almost unheard of; in the sciences, attempts to ensure the integrity of research are crippled by academia's unwillingness to police itself or to take action against faculty members who falsify data, fabricate research, and defraud the public.

The atmosphere is shaped by the adamant refusal of the scientific establishment to even admit that fraud might be a serious problem.

But the evidence is not reassuring.

At the School of Medicine at the University of California, San Diego, Dr. Robert Slutsky had, over six years, flooded academic medicine with his research on heart disease. In all, he produced 161 papers for scholarly journals. During one particularly prolific spell, he was turning out papers on patient and animal studies at the rate of *one every ten days*.[13]

But an investigation concluded that apparently some of those experiments never happened. After an investigation by a 10-member panel of doctors from the university's medical school, 55 of his papers were found to be "questionable," and 13 were declared to be outright fraudulent.[14]

"He did it again and again, and he got into a vicious circle," Dr. Paul Freedman, the medical school's associate dean for academic affairs, told *The New York Times*.[15]

In 1981, another heart researcher's work, this time at Harvard, came under scrutiny. Dr. John Darsee had claimed that two drugs he had tested on dogs had shown significant results in limiting the damage from heart attacks. But when other laboratories were unable to reproduce his results, Darsee was unable to substantiate his research. This was because, investigators from the National Institutes of Health, Harvard, and Emory University concluded, he had fabricated much of it.[16] Darsee was forced to resign his post at Harvard and was later stripped of his medical license by New York State authorities.[17]

But Darsee's work had already been widely disseminated. Darsee's data (much of it now known to be fake) had appeared in 109 articles published in scholarly journals, many of them co-authored with prominent scientists at both Harvard and Emory University. Most or all of these articles were later withdrawn.

In August 1986, Dr. Charles Glueck of the University of Cincinnati College of Medicine published results of his research which claimed that drug therapy and a low-cholesterol diet were both safe and effective in treating children considered to be facing a high risk of heart disease. But officials of the National Institutes of Health later found that he had fudged some of the data on which his conclusions rested and accused him of "serious scientific misconduct."[19]

Faced with such cases, the American Medical Association was troubled enough to ask: "What do we really know about editorial peer review in science?" It answered: "Not much."[20] But its mood of introspection was not matched by the research establishment itself.

Despite the troubling implications of such cases for the entire system of scientific checks and balances, officials of the federal government's National Institutes of Health have stated publicly that they doubted that misconduct of any kind occurs in more than one-tenth of 1 percent of all research supported by NIH money. [21] Perhaps the most remarkable instance of outright denial was the statement by Daniel Koshland, the editor of the magazine *Science*, that "99.9999 percent of [scientific] reports are accurate and truthful. . . ." He provided no evidence to substantiate his statement that fraud occurred in only one in every one million papers. [22] But his statement was perhaps not meant to be taken literally. It can best be read as a kind of shorthand for the science establishment's reluctance, even aversion, to probe too deeply into what could well be a cancer eating at its own vitals.

That attitude has already had a profound impact on the willingness of academics to speak out on possible cases of fraud. One survey found that one-third of the scientists and social scientists at a leading university suspected that one of their colleagues was guilty of fraud. But fewer than half of those with suspicions ever took any action. Part of that resulted from fear of possible retaliation against themselves. Some were perhaps reluctant because they knew that little would actually come of any investigation. In the survey, only 30 percent thought that one of their colleagues who was caught falsifying research data would actually be fired by their institutions. [23]

The combination of indifference, denial, and cynicism within the academy has meant that most academics have been conditioned simply to look the other way. So, for years, the only evidence of scientific fraud was anecdotal. By that measurement, the cases of fraud were relatively infrequent and widely scattered.

But two NIH scientists, Walter Stewart and Ned Feder, were piqued by the question, and in 1983 they set out to research the researchers. Feder, who was then in his mid-50s, was a graduate of Harvard College and Harvard Medical School; Stewart, then in his late 30s, was also a Harvard graduate but had never obtained his doctorate. The two had worked together for years at the NIH, and Stewart had established a bright reputation in scientific circles with a well-regarded paper on so-called "Lucifer dyes" that made it possible for researchers to actually see the branching patterns of nerve cells. [24]

Stewart had become interested in the subject of fraud in 1971, when he had investigated a series of research papers that described a chemical called "scotophobin," which the authors claimed was found in the brains of rats that had been trained to avoid the dark—contrary to the behavior of normal rats. The scotophobin researchers had gone so far as to claim that if they injected this substance into normal rats, they would also become afraid-of-the-dark rats. Because it promised to be a major break-through in what was known as the "chemical transfer of learning," the studies had enjoyed a brief celebrity.

But Stewart concluded that scotophobin did not exist, and his investigation proved, he says, the entire scheme to be an elaborate fraud.[25]

In 1983, Stewart and Feder chose a wider target. The fraud by Harvard's John Darsee was appalling enough, but it also raised other questions as well. How, for example, could Darsee have published more than 100 papers without his misconduct having been detected once by either his colleagues or peer reviewers? How was it that not one of the dozens of scientists who had allowed their name to appear on Darsee's articles had not thought to question the young researcher's work?

For their study, Stewart and Feder decided to focus on the 47 researchers who had co-authored papers with Darsee. They set aside the actually fraudulent data in the papers.

Even on the surface, their findings were explosive: They con-cluded that more than half of the scientists in their study had engaged in "questionable practices." In the papers they examined, they found an average of 12 errors apiece, with a high of 39 errors.[26] Some of these were minor, the result of carelessness or haste. But they also found "some fairly serious misconduct," including the publication by scientists of statements which "they knew or should have known" were false.[27] "About one-fourth of our sample had, according to our analysis, engaged at least once in the more serious type of misconduct," the two men later told a congressional subcommittee.[28] Their findings raised provocative questions about whether some of the co-authors had even both-ered to read the articles to which they appended their names. In one instance, a paper described research on heart disease in which one of the subjects was supposedly a 17-year-old male who was listed as the father of four children ranging in age from 4 to 8. The eight-year-old would have to have been born when the father was 8 or 9 years old himself.[29]

As the two men wrote, scientific self-regulation had failed spectacularly.[30]

Even so, Stewart and Feder were careful to limit their conclusions. They readily acknowledged that their sample may not have been typical of the work of scientists as a whole. But their findings were another straw in the wind; at minimum they were a strong warning that beneath the placid surface of the sciences, massive fissures were opening in the foundations of science. For obvious reasons, this was not a message that was greeted with any enthusiasm in the academy. But neither man expected the protracted and bitter three-year fight that would result from their attempts to publish their results.

Some publications flatly rejected their article. Eventually, the magazine *Nature* accepted it, only to be immediately bombarded with threats of libel suits by some of the scientists involved in the study. Unwilling to engage in what promised to be an endless war of attrition with the litigious scientists, *Nature* quickly backed off from publishing the article, and Stewart and Feder were forced to take the highly unorthodox route of attempting to circumvent the entire academic publishing system.[31]

Shut out of the scientific journals, they took their case before a congressional subcommittee, where they complained of the chilling effect of the threats and outlined the scope of the problem they sought to address. Their charges won widespread publicity. In January 1987, *Nature* finally published a toned-down and carefully expurgated version of the original paper, an editor's column that sought to separate the publication from the findings, and an accompanying rebuttal by one of the scientists who had hired the lawyers to prevent its publication in the first place.*[32]

The resistance to publishing Stewart and Feder's findings was a product of the academic culture's self-imposed code of silence on

---

* The rebuttal said that the Stewart and Feder article contained errors and unfairly assigned "guilt by association" to the Darsee co-authors.

questions of misconduct. "Criticism of theories and research methods is widely accepted as essential to the quest for scientific truth," Boyce Rensberger, a writer for the *The Washington Post*, noted. "Criticism of the more subjective aspects of professional misconduct, often based on ethical grounds, however, is another matter."[33]

Stewart and Feder had also made themselves outcasts because they fingered the academic culture itself in the spread of scientific junk and fraud. The intensive pressure to publish, they argued, made sloppiness and even misconduct almost inevitable. To bolster their case, they obtained a copy of a memorandum written by the director of research at a leading biomedical research institution in which he informed two junior scientists working under him that he expected them to publish four research articles a year. "There is no demand that these be literary masterpieces in first line publications," the research director wrote. "Journeyman works for publication in second, third, or fourth line archival publications will be quite satisfactory."

"The research director treated the production of fourth-rate work as acceptable," Stewart and Feder wrote. "Surprising as it may seem, demands like this are common, though rarely in written form. Under such pressures, many scientists will do work that is hasty, sloppy and fourth rate."[34]

The pressures on ambitious scientists to maximize their rates of publication and citation (with all of the goodies that flow to the most productive academics) had also led to the nigh-on universal practice of co-authoring. Academics believe instinctively that there is safety in numbers. This translates into research papers garlanded with four, five, and even more scientists listed as the "authors." In practice, the names of scientists are often added as purely honorific distinctions; they do little work on the research described and may not even have read the article that they were supposed to have co-written. But the promiscuity with which such bylines are handed out cannot obscure the fact that the practice is misleading.

"Honorary authorships falsify assignment of responsibility for published research and increase the likelihood that inaccurate data will be published," insisted Stewart and Feder. "The honorary author is in a poor position to judge the validity of the work, yet he often lends a prestige that may lull other coauthors, the reviewers or the readers into uncritical and inappropriate acceptance."[35]

They had identified one of academic science's dirtiest little secrets. "If people do not agree on the solutions, at least they agree on the cause," Tabitha Powledge, editor of *The Scientist* commented.

"The simple decent impulse to acknowledge the help of a colleague has been transmuted into a desperate grab at any smidgen of credit that will help advance a career in these competitive times. Livelihoods and lives depend on the size of a [curriculum vita]. It is not hard to get scientists to agree in principle that what matters is quality of work. But that's lip service. In practice, what mostly counts is quantity, and everyone knows it. The publish-or-perish mentality is central not only to the co-author problem, but to other problems that reduce the utility of the scientific literature. These include outright fraud, but also much more frequent difficulties that range from honest error to endemic unintelligibility."[36]

But to the pressure to publish for reasons of academic advancement was now added another element: money.

From 1980 to 1985, Dr. Louis G. Keith, a professor of obstetrics at Northwestern University, worked as a paid consultant for the A. H. Robins Company, the maker of the Dalkon Shield birth control device. In that five-year period, Keith reportedly was paid $277,000 for consulting and for acting as an expert witness for the company in lawsuits brought by women who claimed they had been seriously injured—some said they were made sterile—by the use of the device.

In March 1983, he played a central role in one trial, in which he testified that he had personally overseen experiments that indicated the Dalkon Shield was safe. Partly as a result of his testimony, the plaintiff in the case, a Tampa woman named Linda Harre, lost her suit in the trial court. But only eight months later in a deposition in a separate but related case, Keith admitted that he had never conducted any experiments himself and had not overseen any experiments. On the basis of that admission, the U.S. Court of Appeals in 1985 ordered a new trial for Mrs. Harre and bluntly accused Keith of perjury.

Despite the court's blistering condemnation of Keith, he remained on the faculty at Northwestern's Medical School; the school took no public action against him. On March 3, 1988, Professor Keith was indicted by a federal grand jury on eight counts of perjury and one count of obstruction of justice.[37]

But such dramatic action is still the exception. Too often, it is the whistle-blower himself who ends up being penalized. The NIH, for example, has been far more determined in its actions against Stewart and Feder than it has been in investigating some of the instances of fraud the two men have uncovered. After having worked in a spacious laboratory in the National Institutes of Health, they have since been summarily relocated into a tiny, windowless room in the basement. The NIH has also subjected the pair to periodic, petty harassment.[38]

The experience of the two men in investigating scientific fraud has convinced them of two things: Fraud is endemic in science, far more widespread than ever officially acknowledged; and because of the overwhelming odds against whistle-blowers and critics, fraud, fabrication, and even theft are often, in Stewart's words, "a sure thing."

"The one thing they can count on is that no matter what happens, apart from a miracle, nothing will happen," Stewart said. "What for a politician would be an unacceptable chance, is a matter of everyday practice, I guess."[39]

Stewart's pessimistic assessment seems borne out by the experiences of the few academic whistler-blowers who have spoken out.

Wrote one whistle-blower, "Although I am embarrassed to say this," he wrote in *The Scientist*, "I cannot recommend that junior scientists who discover scientific misconduct blow the whistle. That is, unless they want to experience immense personal suffering and a possible end to their scientific careers."

Sidebar:
THE FATE OF CRITICS

As critics of academia quickly learn, there is a paradox at the heart of the academic culture. Although the professors insist on absolute freedom for themselves, they accord no such tolerance to anyone who challenges their own privileges and status.

"The only thing that we can't criticize or investigate is ourselves," notes David Berkman, himself a dissident academic.[1] When national figures such as Secretary of Education William J. Bennett critique the pretensions of the universities, they are accused of being ignorant, racist, elitist, and hostile to higher learning. Robert Isoue, the president of York College, quickly discovered the limits of academia's tolerance of dissent when he broke ranks to chide his fellow academics for their avoidance of teaching and to declare that as a result of academia's distorted priorities, "students are getting ripped off."

"The mere mention of Isoue's name," noted *The Chronicle of Higher Education,* "draws groans from his colleagues. . . ."[2]

When students rebel against the vagaries of the professoriate, the university faculty and administration often respond with arrogance and hostility verging on hysteria.

The case of *The Dartmouth Review* is illustrative. Published by conservative students at Dartmouth College in New Hampshire, *The Review* is a controversial, irreverent newspaper that has vigorously championed quality teaching, traditional educational values, and high academic standards. Unfortunately, its spirited young editors have also been given to a certain amount of sophomoric excess, including an incident in which some of them tore down a shanty town erected by anti-apartheid protestors on the Dartmouth campus. Subtlety is not their forte. *The*

Review's staffers sometimes find themselves writing excruciatingly close to the far-edges of good taste and, on occasion, have crossed over.

But it is not necessary to unconditionally endorse *The Review*'s tactics to recognize the full-flowering hypocrisy of Dartmouth College's treatment of the youthful muckrakers.

The Review's cardinal sin was its frontal assault on Dartmouth's academic pretensions. Taking note of the $18,000-a-year Ivy League school's *au courant* low-calorie curriculum, the paper administered E. D. Hirsch's basic cultural literacy test to 349 Dartmouth students. Only half could identify Charles de Gaulle as the leader of the French government-in-exile in World War II or name any three of the liberties protected by the First Amendment.[3] This was provocative enough. But the paper went further by publishing trenchant critiques of the teaching styles of some of Dartmouth's celebrated faculty.

In January of 1983, Laura Ingraham, then a Dartmouth sophomore, was assigned by the paper to sit in on a music class taught by Professor William Cole. In her subsequent article, she said that while Cole was a competent musician, his classroom demeanor was characterized by a sloppy handling of the subject matter, politically charged rambles, and occasional racial asides. Much of her article was composed of direct quotes from Cole.

Her report was published in *The Review* on a Thursday. Two days later, early on Saturday morning, Ingraham's dorm roommate was awakened by a loud banging on the door. According to Ingraham, Cole stood outside of her dorm room shouting that he was going to have her thrown out of Dartmouth if she didn't come to his class to apologize to him. "I was in New York, but he woke up the entire dormitory," Ingraham says. "It was really unprofessional behavior." But it only marked the beginning of a bizarre chain of events involving *The Review* and Cole.

Cole announced that he was suspending his class indefinitely until Ingraham apologized and then made attendance at the class optional, thus, says Ingraham, "illustrating Professor Cole's dedication to learning."[4] Cole also filed a libel suit against *The Review*. (He dropped it two years later.)

Cole was reprimanded by his dean for pounding on Ingraham's door,[5] but otherwise Dartmouth stood loyally behind its faculty member. One of his colleagues was even quoted in print as saying that if Ingraham ever showed up in one of his classes he would have "busted her kneecaps."[6] The refusal of Dartmouth officials to take any effective action did little to defuse the increasingly tense atmosphere.

In the summer of 1985, another editor of *The Review*, Debbie Stone, was walking across the campus with a classmate and an alumnus when Professor Cole reportedly began shouting at her. According to Stone, he pointed at her and yelled: "I'm going to fucking blow you up!" When she reported the incident to the local police, they told Stone to change her walking patterns and to avoid walking alone on campus. "My parents were definitely concerned," she says. But when she reported the incident to Dartmouth authorities, Cole denied her allegations and college officials decided to take no action. Instead, she says, they told her not to file any further complaints about the incident or tell anyone else about it.[7]

The Review editors were not, however, deterred. In February of 1988, the paper again published a critique of Cole's teaching style. Like the 1983 piece, the article was largely based on a transcript from one of Cole's classes—an indictment of Cole using Cole's own words. The story said that Cole's class "does not meet Dartmouth standards," and labelled it one of the school's "most academically deficient courses." Following standard journalistic practice, the paper's staffers made several efforts to get a response from Cole. When they reached him by phone, however, he hung up.[8] On the advice of counsel, the paper's editor also wrote to Cole to solicit his point of view.[9] Finally, four

Review staffers went to Cole's classroom to get his comments. Specifically, they wanted to present Cole with the paper's written policy, giving him the right to submit a response of up to 1,500 words "as long as it contained no obscenities."[10]

According to the students, Cole reacted angrily, shouting obscenities and racial epithets. Somehow in the exchange, the student photographer's flash device was broken.[11] The students say that Cole not only broke the camera, but also threatened them.[12]

What followed was a combination of academic farce and tragedy. The incident took a genuinely Kafkaesque quality when Dartmouth President James Freedman moved to discipline, not Cole, *but the four student journalists*. The school's Afro-American Society called rallies to attack *The Review* as racist (Cole is black). Freedman addressed one of the rallies, saying: "I feel dreadful about the attack on Professor Cole."[13] It was in this climate that the school's disciplinary committee met in private and refused to hear the students' countercharges against Cole for assault and damage to property. In April of 1988, three of the student journalists were suspended and a fourth was put on probation for allegedly "harassing" Cole, violating his privacy, and disorderly conduct.[14]

President Freedman waxed Orwellian in explaining the sanctions against the student reporters. *The Review* staffers, he said, should not be protected by First Amendment free press rights, because they were merely "ideological provocateurs posing as journalists." The administration stepped up its attack on the student paper by issuing a news release that labelled the newspaper "sexist, racist and homophobic."[15] (Notes one former editor: "It's interesting to note that *The Review* has more blacks on its staff than Dartmouth has tenured black professors." In addition, two of the paper's seven editors have been women.)[16]

But even Dartmouth College's full-court smear campaign against the student paper and the racial and political overtones of the case cannot obscure the fundamental issues at stake.

"We suspect," *The Wall Street Journal* commented aptly, *"the students' true crime was presuming to assess scholarship at their college."*[17]

In other words, they had dared to attack the academic culture. The treatment of the four students—contrasted with the school's indulgence of Cole's conduct—was an obvious travesty of justice. But it is an example of the academic culture in its purest, most distilled form. The virulence of that culture's reaction to its Dartmouth critics indicates how close they came to the heart of the culture itself. And it provides a clue to the shape that any sort of meaningful reform must take.

15 *Storming the Ivory Tower*

What, then, can be done to save our universities?

We must recognize that reform will not be easy, that the system fails *because it is set up to fail,* and that the professoriate—a profession run amok and without responsibility or accountability to students, society, or learning—will guard its prerogatives ferociously.

But the universities must be saved, and they will be saved, only when they are forced to break away from the academic culture itself.

The key elements of this secession will entail:

- **Puncturing the Research Myth.** At best, only one academic in ten produces original research of any value, so it is ludicrous to continue to pretend that every professor in every institution is capable of being a researcher. Similarly, the notion that research is essential for good teaching is a discredited fiction, but it continues to distort the priorities of the university. Forcing every faculty member to conform to the same model is not only absurd but mindlessly wasteful of the resources of higher education. The demand that *everyone* produce published research has merely bloated the university libraries and has contributed massively to the spread of spurious new cults,

257

methodologies, and bizarre scholastic mutations to justify all this cutting-edge stuff. The elimination of the blanket requirement would in effect cut off the life support systems to the centers of profthink. Dozens of the more outlandish sects would collapse since they are sustained not by any intellectual substance but merely by the demands of academic careerism.

As many as three-fourths of the journals would also be vaporized. Unread, unreadable, and unused except to bulk up academic resumes, the vast majority of the learned journals could disappear tomorrow without the slightest diminution in the world's collective knowledge. Each individual school can strike a small blow by simply dropping the subscriptions they have and spending the money saved on something more valuable, like teaching.

- **Abolishing tenure.** Tenure corrupts, enervates, and dulls higher education. It is, moreover, the academic culture's ultimate control mechanism to weed out the idiosyncratic, the creative, the nonconformist. The replacement of lifetime tenure with fixed-term renewable contracts would, at one stroke, restore accountability, while potentially freeing the vast untapped energies of the academy that have been locked in the petrified grip of a tenured professoriate.

- **Requiring teachers to teach.** No proposal generates more fear and loathing among the professoriate than the occasional suggestion that professors actually be *required* to spend a certain number of hours a week in the presence of students. But putting professors back into the classroom would be a major first step toward the regeneration of the academy. State legislatures should require all professors (in state universities) to teach at least three courses a semester—or nine hours a week (actually seven and a half, but let's not quibble). Such legislation would be both moderate and reasonable, except to the most myopic academics. The three course limit would immediately cut class size, reduce the universities' costs, eliminate the need for thousands of teaching assistants and would still allow professors ample time for research. But a uniform minimum teaching load would also send a clear and unambiguous message about the revived—and even paramount—importance of teaching in the new university.

Of course, it is one of the central dogmas of the academic culture that good teaching is impossible without a heavy research emphasis. The success of the outstanding liberal arts colleges, however, gives the lie to the teaching/research myth. Schools like Carleton or Alverno, where the focus is solidly on teaching, or St. John's College, where the curriculum is centered on the Great Books, where seminars are focused on ideas, and where undergraduates are trained in clarity of thought and expression, provide a dramatic counterpoint to the drivel that passes for learning at some of the nation's most prestigious universities.

For many professors at larger universities, the return to the classroom would be a form of radical shock therapy. Forcing them to actually communicate with someone other than a fellow specialist would also force them to make a stab at clarity. The refusal of the professoriate to deal with undergraduates is a kind of shorthand for their refusal to deal with the world as a whole or to address real problems. Some of those long lost in the outer reaches of esoterica may find the return traumatic; many will no doubt have a tough time adapting. Some might never make it. But the return of the teacher-professor could also mark the beginning of an academic renaissance, for both students and professors.

But once in the classroom, universities also need to ensure quality teaching. That means a quality control program with some teeth. A good first step would be the creation of teacher-review panels made up of students and professors from other departments, and even other schools, to visit classrooms and monitor performance. In research, such peer review is taken for granted. There is no reason why it cannot be extended to teaching as well.

- **Insisting on truth-in-advertising.** Schools that brag about the quality of their faculty should be required—by trustees and state legislators—to make those faculty members available to students by insisting that university administrators openly disclose the workloads of their faculty and spell out on a course by course basis in the school's catalog, the degree of the professors' reliance on teaching assistants.

- **Restoring the curriculum and the canon.** Without apology, the undergraduate curriculum should be centered on the intellectual tradition of Western civilization. Quite simply, there are certain books and certain authors that every college graduate should read if he is to be considered truly educated. Whether it is in the form of general education or a core curriculum, its designers should not hesitate to insist on a prescribed curriculum for underclassmen that would ensure that all students are exposed to the basic classics of Western thought.

Change, when it comes, is likely to emanate from below, rather than above. And it is likely to come from small institutions in the hinterlands, voices crying in the wilderness, rather than from one of the bulwarks of the academic establishment. The battle will no doubt be fought one school at a time, perhaps even one department at a time. The shock troops will be:

- Trustees, who must realize that they are not merely ornamental fixtures of the university. Much of what is happening in higher education is possible only because of the wholesale abdication of responsibility by trustees, who, either through neglect or timidity or lack of purpose, allowed the very values they were sworn to uphold to be undermined. They acquiesced in a *coup d'etat* by the professoriate almost without a struggle. Many are perhaps so deluded as to imagine they still actually control the university; others are so beaten down by the doublespeak of academic administrators or the recalcitrance and arrogance of the faculty that they have simply given in to defeatism, or what Ronnie Dugger called "surrender with a shrug." It is time for them to return to the trenches. Their first task should be the selection of a new sort of administrator whose agenda is more profound than merely placating the faculty or seeking a consensus on everything from the planting schedules of azaleas on campus to the shape of the curriculum. Trustees should seek out presidents willing to challenge the powers of the professors and the tyranny of the academic culture; and then back them.

- Legislators, who should demand accountability for the tax dollars they send down the maw of their states' universities. The lawmakers who have annually increased university budgets only to find that fewer classes are taught, the teaching loads of professors are cut, and the undergraduate program is allowed to go to seed, have been played for fools. The wise among them should recognize this before their constituents do. Despite the opposition it will provoke, they should not hesitate to insist on minimum teaching loads and to guarantee the free flow of scientific information generated by public facilities. Although many legislators have been reluctant to take on their universities, they are in a unique position to assault academic privilege from a vigorously populist perspective—and they can arm that populism with a heavy financial punch.

Every governor has the opportunity to do what Secretary Bennett has done—focus public attention and outrage on the way his state's public universities are being held hostage by the professors. Every legislature has a chance to restore accountability and ensure genuine access to learning. The politics of the situation alone should make such leadership attractive because it is increasingly obvious that the burdens of the failure of academia tend to fall not on the elites, but on the large middle class and on students at the lower end of the economic spectrum for whom a college education is the only hope for upward advancement. To a large extent, the middle class is stuck in the academic gulags created by the professors' culture. It constitutes a potentially irresistible political force for reform.

- Congress, foundations, and research grantors, all of which have been sugar daddies of the academic culture. Their lavishness encouraged and funded the professoriate's flight from teaching and succeeded in institutionalizing the academic villages. Even modest changes in the allocation of the billions of dollars in federal spending would send tremors throughout the academic culture. Why not, for instance, begin emphasizing specific endowments and awards for undergraduate teaching? Why can't the grantors tie their gifts to specific reforms in undergraduate instruction? And why shouldn't they withhold their largess if the professors refuse to make such concessions?

• Students, who are under no obligation to tolerate the arrogance or the abject neglect of the professoriate. Because they might see actual professors only in their last two years of their university education, students are at a disadvantage. By the time they are onto the scam, they are conveniently hustled off into the world. But most of them know lousy teaching when they see it, and nowhere is it written that they need suffer in silence in a classroom taught by an utterly incomprehensible teaching assistant. The student press in particular should rediscover the university campus. If the average student publication devoted half as much space to what is happening in its school's own classrooms as to U.S. foreign policy, the pressure for reform would grow by tenfold. For starters, every campus ought to have its own version of Harvard's *Confidential Guide*, a no-holds-barred, uncensored, student-run critique of the classroom performance of the faculty. And if alumni are looking for a place to help out, they could not do better than to fund it.

• Parents, who can assure themselves of the attention of university administrators by threatening to take their tuition money elsewhere.

A new age in academia will dawn the day a full professor is asked (by a parent, donor, trustee, etc.) to sit in his office and explain why his teaching assistants don't speak English and why his schedule of sabbaticals and leaves is so generous when he is hardly in the classroom anyway.

But parents must remember that there *are* alternatives to the academic culture. Despite the cost of some of the excellent liberal arts colleges, they offer an education that is worth far more than

than what passes for an education at many major state universities. Parents choosing a school for their child must recognize that the widely published rankings of the "hottest" or the most prestigious schools have no bearing whatsoever on the quality of education their sons or daughters can expect. Those rankings are made up or heavily influenced by professors and they reflect their values and priorities alone.

The savvy parent will ignore them and will instead employ a battery of pointed questions: How many actual professors will my son or daughter have in his or her introductory courses? How big will those courses be? How many papers will he or she have to write? Will they be graded by professors or graduate students? How many courses do tenured professors teach? Are professors available for counseling? (*Really.*) What are the requirements of the curriculum? What books will he or she be expected to have read by the time of graduation? What is he or she expected to know when he or she graduates? How much of my tuition money goes to subsidize research?

Unfortunately, even the best-armed parent and the feistiest student is at a terrible disadvantage in any face-off with the academic establishment. Arrayed against them is the solid phalanx of the academic villages and all their *apparatchiks:* the Modern Language Association, the American Political Science Association, the American Sociological Association, the American Association of University Professors, and so on virtually *ad infinitum.* All of them have, at bottom, the same goal: the defense of the values and mores of the academic culture against all comers.

What is desperately needed is a national association or union for parents and students that will serve as a counterweight to the institutional power of the professors. Ideally, it would be an academic version of groups like the Consumers Union. It would be non-partisan, non-ideological, non-sectarian, and would have as its specific mission the role of watchdog and advocate for quality in American higher education. Such a national organization would recognize that although reform will be local, the issues are essentially the same everywhere; whether the fight is being waged in Vermont or Berkeley, the enemy is the same academic culture.

By being a clearinghouse of information, the academic consumers union would be an invaluable asset to parents mounting an otherwise quixotic assault on the Ivory Tower. Such an association could publish periodic newsletters rating the performance of various schools from a consumer—i.e., parent and student—perspective and provide information and updates on the reform movement. By doing so, it would endeavor to focus the attention of the media on many of the concerns raised in this book.

But, at bottom, the union should be action-oriented. It should provide moral, financial, and public relations support—in short, organizational muscle—to any group of local students and parents working to restore academic standards in their schools.

And finally,

- The Professors, among whose number are those few hardy souls who have kept the spirit of genuine intellectual commitment alive, however muffled and clandestine it may be. Although the villains of this book have been the professors, they have also been, in a sense, the heroes. Teachers like Fred Gottheil at the University of Illinois and Phillip Anderson of the University of Central Arkansas, continue to wage lonely rear-guard actions against the dominant trends of the academic culture. There is no shortage of men and women committed not only to teaching but also to the traditions of taste, reason, and a common intellectual discourse that were once taken for granted, but which are now fugitives from the academy.

These renegade professors know that every genuine idea, every article written in lucid, clear prose, employing logic, reason, insight, and wit is a subversive act within the academic culture—a shot fired across the bow of the obscurantists, sorcerers, and witch doctors of profthink.

These true scholars—and their students—keep the tiny flame of learning alive on their campuses and within their disciplines. They will inevitably form the core of a reborn higher learning. In the meantime, they should keep the candle in the window lighted.

Help is on the way.

Notes

Chapter 1: The Indictment

1. Cited in Mitchell, Richard, *The Graves of Academe*, New York, Simon & Schuster, p. 69

2. Mencken, H. L., *Prejudices: A Selection*, New York, Vintage Books, 1958, p. 149

3. Andreski, Stanislav, *Social Sciences as Sorcery*, New York, St. Martin's Press, 1972, p. 16

4. *NLRB v. Yeshiva University*, 100 S. Ct. 856 (1980)

Chapter 2: The Rise of the Professors

1. Sykes, Jay G., "The Sorcerers and the 7½ Hour Week," *Milwaukee Magazine*, October 1985 (Author's note: I am also indebted to my father for the Shakespeare anecdote that opens this chapter.)

2. O'Toole, Simon, *Confessions of an American Scholar*, Minneapolis, University of Minnesota Press, 1971, p. 10

3. Jarrell, Randall, *Pictures from an Institution*, New York, Alfred A. Knopf, 1954, p. 10

4. Finn, Chester, "Higher Education on Trial: An Indictment," *Current*, October 1984

5. Von Humboldt, Wilhelm, "On the Organization of Institutions of Higher Learning in Berlin," printed in *The Great Ideas Today 1969*, Chicago, Encyclopaedia Britannica, 1969

6. Rudolph, Frederick, *The American College and University*, New York, Vintage Books, 1965, p. 403

7. Ibid., p. 409

8. Ibid., pp. 395–397

9. Babbitt, Irving, *Literature and the American College*, Boston, Houghton Mifflin, 1908, p. 152

10. Rudolph, Frederick, *op. cit.*, p. 402

11. Von Humboldt, Wilhelm, *op. cit.*

12. Flexner, Abraham, *Universities: American, English, German*, excerpted in *American Higher Education, A Documentary History Vol. II*, Chicago, University of Chicago Press, 1961, pp. 905–921, ed. by Hofstadter, Richard and Smith, Wilson.

13. Hutchins, Robert Maynard, *No Friendly Voice*, Chicago, University of Chicago Press, 1936, p. 28

14. Bonner, Thomas N., "The Unintended Revolution in Higher Education Since 1940," *Change*, September/October 1986

15. Ibid.

16. Ibid.

17. Ibid.

18. Ibid.

19. Barzun, Jacques, *The American University*, New York, Harper & Row, 1968, p. 146

20. Quoted by Hal Draper in "The Mind of Clark Kerr," *Revolution at Berkeley*, New York, Dell Publishing, 1965, p. 63

21. Arrowsmith, William, "The Shame of the Graduate Schools," *Harper's*, March 1966

22. Caplow, Theodore and McGee, Reece, *The Academic Marketplace*, New York, Basic Books, 1958, p. 206

23. Caplow and McGee, *op. cit.*, p. 85

24. Jencks, Christopher and Riesman, David, *The Academic Revolution*, Chicago, University of Chicago Press, 1977, p. 14

25. Dugger, Ronnie, *Our Invaded Universities*, New York, W. W. Norton Company, 1974, p. 175

26. Ibid.

27. Lynn, Kenneth S., "Son of 'Gen Ed,'" *Commentary*, September 1978

28. Keller, Phyllis, *Getting at the Core*, Cambridge, Harvard University Press, 1982, pp. 19–21

29. Rau, William and Baker, Paul, "The Organized Contradictions of Academic Sociology," unpublished manuscript, 1987, p. 6

30. Caplow and McGee, *op. cit.*, p. 221

31. Quoted in Dugger, *op. cit.*, p. 174

32. Fussell, Paul, "Schools for Snobbery," *The New Republic*, October 4, 1982

33. Chase, Alston, "Skipping Through College: Reflections on the Decline of Liberal Arts Education," *The Atlantic*, September 1978

34. Weiss, John, "The University as Corporation," *New University Thought*, Summer 1965

35. Kerr, Clark, *The Uses of the University*, Cambridge, Harvard University Press, 1964

36. Ibid.

37. Ibid.

38. Dugger, Ronnie, *op. cit.*, p. 178

39. Kerr, Clark, *op. cit.*

Sidebar: What Is a University For?

1. Source: Center for Statistics, U.S. Department of Education, *The Chronicle of Higher Education*, March 19, 1986

2. Interview with author, September 10, 1987

Chapter 3: The Flight from Teaching

1. Sykes, Jay G., "The Sorcerers and the 7½ Hour Week," *Milwaukee Magazine*, October 1985

2. Gardner, John W., "The Flight from Teaching," in *Learning and the Professors*, ed. by Ohmer, Milton and Shoben, E.J., Jr., Athens, Ohio University Press, 1968

3. Orlans, H., "Federal Expenditures and the Quality of Education," *Science*, December 27, 1963

4. Dugger, Ronnie, *Our Invaded Universities*, New York, W. W. Norton & Company, 1974, p. 173

5. Gardner, *op. cit.*

6. Dugger, *op. cit.*, pp. 170–171

7. Ibid., p. 170

8. *Science*, June 18, 1965

9. Report by the Legislative Audit Bureau to State Representative David Travis, April 8, 1986

10. Ibid.

11. Ibid.

12. Report to Members of the Joint Finance Committee on the 1987–89 Biennial Budget of the University of Wisconsin System—Funding for Instruction by the Legislative Fiscal Bureau, May 13, 1987

13. Interview with author

14. *The Milwaukee Journal*, January 24, 1988

15. Ibid.

16. *Wisconsin State Journal*, December 1, 1986

17. *Milwaukee Sentinel*, October 21, 1986

18. Letter from Michael V. Fox, *Badger Herald*, September 16, 1987

19. *Isthmus* (Madison, Wisconsin), July 25, 1986

20. Sykes, Jay G., *op. cit.*

21. Ibid.

22. State of Wisconsin, Staff Detail, 1986–87 Budget for the University of Wisconsin

23. University of Wisconsin Course Catalog, Spring 1986–87

24. University of Illinois Course Catalog, Fall 1987

25. University of Michigan Faculty Salaries and Class Schedule, Fall Term 1987

26. Mann, Lawrence R., "Challenges and Opportunities: Observations on Undergraduate Education at the University of Illinois at Urbana Champaign," Fall 1985

27. Ibid.

28. Ibid.

29. Ibid.

30. Association of American Colleges, "Integrity in the College Curriculum: A Report to the Academic Community," February 1985

31. *The Confidential Guide 1981–82*, Cambridge, Harvard Crimson, Inc., 1981

32. Bennett, James, *The New Journal*, April 17, 1987

33. *Yale Undergraduate Course Critique*, Spring 1987

34. *The Confidential Guide 1985–86*, p. 121

35. *The Confidential Guide 1985–86*, p. 61

36. Bennett, James, *op. cit.*

37. *Yale Daily News*, April 22, 1987

38. *Yale Undergraduate Course Critique*, Spring 1987

39. *Brown Daily Herald*, February 4, 1987

40. *The Confidential Guide 1987–88*, p. 158

41. *Brown Daily Herald*, February 4, 1987

42. Sanders, Dennis, *Rutgers* [Alumni Magazine], May/June 1987

43. *The Chronicle of Higher Education*, October 29, 1986

44. Ibid.

45. Bowen, Howard and Schuster, Jack, *American Professors*, New York, Oxford University Press

46. *Time*, January 12, 1987

47. Flynn, John, "The Part-Time Problem: Four Voices," *Academe*, January/February 1986

48. Flynn, Elizabeth A., ibid.

49. Chell, Cara, "Memoirs and Confessions of a Part-time Lecturer," *College English*, January 1982

50. Maitland, Christine, "Tales of a Freeway Flyer," *Change*, January/February 1987

51. Interview with author

52. *Yale Daily News*, April 23, 1987

53. Heinzelman, Kurt, "The English Lecturers at Austin: Our New MIA's," *Academe*, January/February 1986

54. Ibid.

55. Ibid.

56. Ibid.

Sidebar: The Mass Class

1. Author's notes, "Teaching Workshop. Teaching Sociology in Large Classes," American Sociological Association Annual Convention, August 18, 1987, Chicago, Illinois

2. Ibid.

3. Sutch, Richard, "In Defense of the Large Lecture Class," *Teaching at Berkeley*, Spring 1985

Chapter 4: The Crucifixion of Teaching

1. *The Harvard Crimson*, 1987 Commencement Issue

2. *The Harvard Crimson*, April 29, 1987

3. *The Confidential Guide 1985–86*, p. 133

4. Manderly, Evan J., "Learning by Decree," *Harvard Independent*, Spring Registration Issue, 1987

5. *The New York Times*, October 5, 1986

6. Ibid.

7. *The Confidential Guide 1985–86*, p. 129

8. Ibid.

9. *The Confidential Guide 1980–81*, p. 124

10. *The Confidential Guide 1982–83*, p. 119

11. *The Harvard Crimson*, April 29, 1987

12. *The Harvard Crimson*, March 12, 1987

13. *Yale Daily News*, April 23, 1987

14. Ibid.

15. Ibid.

16. Ibid.

17. The Holmes Group, "Tomorrow's Teachers: A Report of the Holmes Group," text reprinted in *The Chronicle of Higher Education*, April 9, 1986

18. Author's notes from seminar on academic litigation at convention of American Political Science Association, September 4, 1987

19. Mann, Lawrence, "Challenges and Opportunities: Observations on Undergraduate Education at the University of Illinois at Urbana-Champaign," Fall 1985, p. 52

20. McGee, Reece, "Lies We Live By," *Teaching Sociology*, July 1985

21. Interview with author, September 9, 1987

22. Barol, Bill, "The Threat to College Teaching," *Newsweek on Campus*, October 1983

23. Avis, Harry, "The Satisfying Switch from Research to Teaching," *The Chronicle of Higher Education*, June 18, 1986

24. *Brown Daily Herald*, November 15, 1985

25. Rau, William and Baker, Paul, "The Organized Contradictions of Academic Sociology: An Agenda for Change for the 21st Century," unpublished manuscript, pp. 11–12

26. Jencks, C., and Riesman, D., *The Academic Revolution*, New York, Doubleday, 1968

27. McGee, Reece, *op. cit.*

28. Sykes, Jay G., "The Sorcerers and the 7½ Hour Week," *Milwaukee Magazine*, October 1985

29. *Yale Undergraduate Course Critique*, Spring 1987 (Economics 251b)

30. *The Confidential Guide 1982–83*, p. 96

31. Interview with author, November 1987

32. *Course Evaluation Guide 1986–87*, Committee on Undergraduate Education (known as the CUE Guide) pp. 68–69

33. *Yale Undergraduate Course Critique*, Spring 1987

34. *The Confidential Guide 1982–83*, p. 96

35. *The Confidential Guide 1984–85*, p. 117

36. *The Confidential Guide 1980–81*, p. 151

37. Ibid., p. 149

38. *The Confidential Guide 1981–82*, p. 33

39. *Course Evaluation Guide*, Committee on Undergraduate Education, 1986–87, p. 38

40. Ibid., p. 62

41. Ibid., p. 76

42. Ibid., p. 95

43. *The Critical Review 1983–84*, The Undergraduate Council of Students, pp. 79–80

44. Arrowsmith, William, "The Future of Teaching," in *Improving College Teaching*, Washington, D.C., American Council on Education, 1967, pp. 58–59

45. Interview with author, August 19, 1987

46. Interview with author, November 1987

47. Author's notes from meeting of department chairman, American Sociological Association, Chicago, August 17, 1987

Sidebar: An Endangered Species

1. Interview with author, September 10, 1987

Sidebar: The Stars

1. Associated Press, *The Milwaukee Journal*, October 29, 1986

2. *The New York Times*, November 16, 1986

3. *The New York Times*, November 17, 1986

4. *The Chronicle of Higher Education*, November 19, 1986

5. Berkman, David, "A Maverick's View of UWM," *The Milwaukee Journal, Wisconsin Magazine*, April 26, 1987

6. Hutchins, Robert Maynard, *The Higher Learning in America*, New Haven, Yale University Press, 1936, pp. 27–28

7. "Tracking the Faculty Stars," *Newsweek on Campus*, September 1987

8. *The Confidential Guide*, 1986–87, p. 79

9. "Tracking the Faculty Stars," *op. cit.*

Sidebar: The Seminar

1. Barzun, Jacques, *The American University*, New York, Harper & Row, 1968, p. 67

2. Dugger, Ronnie, *Our Invaded Universities*, New York, W. W. Norton Company, 1974, p. 170

3. Van den Berghe, Pierre, *Academic Gamesmanship*, New York, Abelard/Schumann, p. 81

4. Interview with author, January 1988

Sidebar: Audio-Visual Pedagogy

1. Davis, Sam, "Keeping Students in the Dark," *Teaching at Berkeley*, Spring 1984

2. Interview with author, November 1987

Chapter 5: Dare to be Stupid

1. Association of American Colleges, "Integrity in the College Curriculum: A Report to the Academic Community," February 1985

2. *Daily Illini*, January 22, 1986

3. Jonathan Yardley, *The Washington Post*, January 28, 1985

4. *Bulletin of Auburn University, 1987–88*

5. *Kent State Undergraduate Catalog, 1987–88*

6. *University of Illinois Catalog, 1987–88*

7. *University of Massachusetts at Amherst, 1987–88 Undergraduate Catalog*

8. Shuger, Scott, "My Semester in PE 402," *Ann Arbor Observer*, September 1987

9. "In this Course, 'Dare to Be Stupid' Can Be the Route to Intellectual Growth," *The Chronicle of Higher Education*, January 6, 1985

10. Association of American Colleges, *op. cit.*

11. Ibid.

12. Ravitch, Diane, "Decline and Fall of Teaching History," *The New York Times*, November 17, 1985

13. *The Chronicle of Higher Education*, January 22, 1985

14. Ravitch, Diane, *op. cit.*

15. "For College Students, Lack of Interest Breeds Ignorance of Foreign Affairs: ETS," *Phi Delta Kappan*, June 1981

16. Bennett, William, Text of Speech at Harvard University Anniversary Celebration, reprinted in *The Chronicle of Higher Education*, October 15, 1986

17. Rau, William and Baker, Paul, "The Organized Contradiction of Academic Sociology," unpublished manuscript, 1987, p. 14

18. Engel, Peter, "Harvard's Soft Core," *The Washington Monthly*, January 1980

19. *The Washington Post*, August 25, 1986

20. Rau and Baker, *op. cit.*, p. 16

21. Berkman, David, "Student Quality Fall Affects J-Schools," *Journalism Educator*, Winter 1985

22. Richardson, Richard C., "How Are Students Learning," *Change*, May/June 1985

23. Interview with author, November 1987

24. *The Harvard Crimson*, 1978 Commencement Issue

25. Lamont, Lansing, *Campus Shock*, New York, E. P. Dutton, 1981, p. 63

26. Ibid.

27. Rau and Baker, *op. cit.*, p. 15

28. "Higher Education for Democracy: A Report of the Presidential Commission on Higher Education," excerpted in *American Higher Education, A Documentary History*, ed. by Hoftsadter, Richard and Smith, Wilson, Chicago, University of Chicago Press, 1961, pp. 970–990

29. Ibid., pp. 998–999

30. *Atlanta Constitution*, February 3, 1986

31. Keller, Phyllis, *Getting at the Core*, Cambridge, Harvard University Press, 1982, p. 143

32. Gittell, Marilyn, "Reaching the Hard to Reach," *Change*, September-October 1985

33. *The New York Times*, December 21, 1983, and *The Chronicle of Higher Education*, June 22, 1983

34. *Brown Daily Herald*, April 13, 1985

35. *The Chronicle of Higher Education*, June 22, 1983

36. Weiss, Philip, "Good Times vs. Great Books," *The New Republic*, June 9, 1986

37. *Brown Daily Herald,* September 19, 1985

38. *The Chronicle of Higher Education,* June 22, 1983

39. Massey, Walter, "The Brown Curriculum," March 10, 1978

40. *College Hill Journal,* June 1979

41. Sledd, James, "A Basic Incompetence in the Defining of Basic Competencies," *English Journal,* November 1986

42. Simon, John, "Pressure from Below," *Esquire,* June 20, 1978

43. Mitchell, Richard, *The Graves of Academe,* New York, Simon and Schuster, 1981 p. 35

44. "Teacher Education in Massachusetts (The Public Sector), A Report for the Board of Regents of the Commonwealth of Massachusetts," May 21, 1986

45. *Daily Illini,* February 7, 1986

46. *The New York Times,* August 27, 1986

Sidebar: Great Guts

1. Gutmacher, Glenn, "Some Advice from a True 'Gutmaster,'" *Yale Daily News,* January 20, 1987

2. *The New York Times,* March 18, 1986

3. *The Confidential Guide 1984–85,* p. 153

4. *The Confidential Guide 1985–86,* p. 15

5. Ibid., p. 93

6. *The Confidential Guide 1984–85,* p. 55

7. *The Confidential Guide 1987–88,* p. 49

8. *The Confidential Guide 1987–88,* p. 151

9. Ibid., p. 152

Chapter 6: Through the Looking Glass

1. Bok, Derek, *Higher Learning,* Cambridge, Harvard University Press, 1986, p. 77

2. Finn, Chester, "Higher Education on Trial: An Indictment," *Current,* October 1984

3. Isoue, Robert, "How Colleges Can Cut Costs," *The Wall Street Journal,* January 27, 1987

4. Finn, Chester, *op. cit.*

5. Rosovsky, Henry, "Our Universities Are the World's Best," *The New Republic,* July 13 & 20, 1987

6. "Evolution of the Potholder: From Technology to Popular Art," *Journal of Popular Culture,* Summer 1985

7. "Women's Shopping: A Sociological Approach," (thesis), State University of New York, from Dissertations, Humanities and Social Sciences, May 1987

8. "Smithsonian Institution Awards $1 Million in Fellowships to 101 Researchers," *The Chronicle of Higher Education,* October 15, 1986

9. "What Does Girls' Cheerleading Communicate?" *Journal of Popular Culture,* Fall 1986

10. "Submerged Sensuality: Technology and Perceptions of Bathing," *Journal of Social History,* Summer 1986

11. Cited by Sykes, Jay G. in "The Sorcerers and the 7½ Hour Week," *Milwaukee Magazine,* October 1985

12. "The Influence of Contextual Variables on Interpersonal Spacing," *Journal of Nonverbal Behavior,* Winter 1986

13. "Intimacy in Conversational Style As a Function of the Degree of Closeness Between Members of a Dyad," *Journal of Personality and Social Psychology,* September 1985

14. *The Chronicle of Higher Education,* October 7, 1987

15. Sykes, Jay G., *op. cit.*

16. "In The Mick of Time: Reflections on Disney's Ageless Mouse," *Journal of Popular Culture,* Fall 1986

17. "Pigeons and Children: What Are the Differences?" *The Psychology Record,* Winter 1987

18. *Dissertations Abstracts International 1972*

19. Armstrong, J. Scott, "Barriers to Scientific Contributions: The Author's Formula," *The Behavioral and Brain Sciences,* 1982, p. 197

20. Barzun, Jacques, *The American University,* New York, Harper & Row, 1968, p. 221

21. Schuster, Jack and Bowen, Howard, *American Professors,* New York, Oxford University Press, p. 179

22. Interview with author, September 10, 1987

23. Ibid.

Chapter 7: Profspeak

1. Berkman, David, "Gable *Almost* Had It Right: It's 'REFEREED SCHOLARS' Teaching Amateurs to Be Amateurs," unpublished manuscript

2. Ricci, David, *The Tragedy of Political Science*, New Haven, Yale University Press, 1984, pp. 224–225

3. Andreski, Stanislav, *Social Sciences as Sorcery*, New York, St. Martin's Press, 1972, pp. 82–83

4. Ibid., p. 67

5. Ibid., p. 63

6. Ibid., p. 68

7. "Analyzing Utterances As The Observational Unit," *Human Communication Research*, Winter 1985

8. "Articulating the People's Politics: Manhood and Right-Wing Populism in The A-Team," *Communication*, 1987, Vol. 9

9. Cited in Sykes, Jay G., "The Sorcerers and the 7½ Hour Week," *Milwaukee Magazine*, October 1985

10. "Multiple Modeling of Propensity to Adopt Residential Energy Conservation Retrofits," *Social Science Research*, June 1987

11. "The dialectic of the feminine: Melodrama and commodity in the Ferraro Pepsi commercial," *Communication Journal*, 1987, Vol. 9

12. Mitchell, Richard, *The Graves of Academe*, New York, Little Brown, 1981, pp. 52–54

13. Nisbet, Robert, "Sociology as an Art Form," in *Sociology on Trial*, Englewood Cliffs, N.J., Prentice-Hall, Inc., 1963, p. 159

14. Barzun, Jacques, "Doing Research—Should the Sport Be Regulated," *Columbia*, February 1987

15. Cahn, Steven M., "The Authority of the Teacher," *Academe*, May/June 1982

Chapter 8: The Weird World of the Academic Journals

1. Mahoney, Michael J., "Scientific Publication and Knowledge Politics," *Journal of Social Behavior and Personality*, 1987, Vol. 2, No. 2 (Part 1)

2. "The Case for Book Burning," *The New Republic*, September 14 & 21, 1987, and Barzun, Jacques, "Doing Research—Should the Sport Be Regulated?" *Columbia*, February 1987

3. Interview with author, January 1988

4. Price, D. J. S., *Little Science, Big Science*, New York, Columbia University Press, 1963, pp. 62–63

5. Mahoney, Michael J., *op. cit.*

6. Bracey, Gerald, "The Time Has Come to Abolish Research Journals: Too Many Are Writing Too Much About Too Little," *The Chronicle of Higher*

Education March 25, 1987 (Bracey's original manuscript was entitled, "Should Publishing Perish?" For simplicity's sake, all citations are from the original, unedited manuscript. Some of them do not appear in *The Chronicle* version.)

7. Ibid.

8. Mahoney, Michael, *op. cit.*

9. Bracey, Gerald, *op. cit.*

10. "Scholars Fault Journals and College Libraries in Survey by Council of Learned Societies," *The Chronicle of Higher Education*, August 6, 1986

11. Leonard, Douglas, "The Art of Walt Whitman's French in 'Song of Myself,'" *Walt Whitman Quarterly Review*, Spring 1986

12. Kuttner, Robert, "The Poverty of Economics," *The Atlantic Monthly*, February 1985

13. Oshinsky, David, "What's Wrong with the History Journals?" *Change*, March 1973

14. Lewis, Lionel S., *Scaling the Ivory Tower: Merit and Its Limits in Academic Careers*, Baltimore, Maryland, Johns Hopkins Press, 1975 p. 41

15. Ibid., pp. 41–42

16. Wiener, Jon, "The Footnote Fetish," *Telos 31* (1977)

17. Mahoney, Michael J., "Participatory Epistemology and Psychology of Science," Paper presented at the Psychology of Science Conference, April 18, 1986, Memphis State University

18. Ziman, John, *Public Knowledge: The Social Dimension of Science*, Cambridge, England, Cambridge University Press, 1968, p. 111

19. Mahoney, Michael J., "Scientific Publication and Knowledge Politics," *op. cit.*

20. Mahoney, Michael J., "Publication Prejudices: An Experimental Study of Confirmatory Bias in the Peer Review System," *Cognitive Therapy and Research, 1*, 1977

21. Mahoney, Michael J., "Scientific Publication and Knowledge Politics," *op. cit.*

22. Peters, Douglas and Ceci, Stephen, "Peer Review Practices of Psychological Journals: The Fate of Published Articles, Submitted Again," *The Behavioral and Brain Sciences*, 1985

23. Mahoney, Michael J., "Scientific Publication and Knowledge Politics," *op. cit.*

24. Starr, Paul, *The Social Transformation of American Medicine*, New York, Basic Books, 1982

25. *The New York Times*, April 21, 1985, and April 28, 1985

26. Andreski, Stanislav, *Social Sciences as Sorcery*, New York, St. Martin's Press, 1972, p. 110

27. *The Harvard Crimson*, March 22, 1985

28. *The New York Times*, April 21, 1985

29. *The New York Times*, April 28, 1985

30. *The Harvard Crimson*, April 8, 1985, and *The New York Times*, April 21, 1985

31. *The Harvard Crimson*, April 8, 1985

32. Ibid.

Sidebar: Bookscam

1. Arnold, Kenneth, "University Presses Could Still Become the Cultural Force for Change and Enlightenment They Were Meant to Be," *The Chronicle of Higher Education*, July 29, 1987

2. *The Chronicle of Higher Education*, July 29, 1987

3. "How to Publish," The Edwin Mellen Press, New York

4. Veliotes, Nicholas A., president, Association of American Publishers, Letter to University Presidents, March 4, 1987

Chapter 9: Academic License

1. "Free Speech Incident Leads to Tenure Denial and Divides Faculty Opinion at Northwestern," *The Chronicle of Higher Education*, February 18, 1987

2. *Daily Northwestern*, April 15, 1985

3. Ibid.

4. *Daily Northwestern*, April 16, 1985

5. Ibid.

6. Letter from Thomas Jefferson to William Roscoe, December 27, 1820

7. Rudolph, Frederick, *The American College and University*, New York, Vintage Books, 1965, p. 414

8. Ollmann, Bertell, "Academic Freedom in America Today: A Marxist View," in *Regulating the Intellectuals; Perspectives on Academic Freedom in the 1980s*, ed. by Kaplan, Craig and Schrecker, Ellen

9. Rudolph, Frederick, *op. cit.*, p. 414

10. Rudolph, *op. cit.*, p. 411

11. Ibid., p. 412

12. Nisbet, Robert, "The Future of Tenure," *Change,* April 1973

13. *The Chronicle of Higher Education,* January 13, 1988

14. *The Chronicle of Higher Education,* January 8, 1986

15. Rudolph, Frederick *op. cit.,* p. 413

16. *The Confidential Guide,* 1987–88, p. 34

17. "A Skirmish Involving a Pacifist," *The New York Times,* November 17, 1986

18. Minority Report of the Council for Special Curricula On the Current Status of the Peace and Conflict Studies Program, Academic Senate, August 21, 1986

19. Ehrlich, Robert, "Accuracy in Academia: The Chief Thing to Fear Is Our Own Hysterical Reaction," *The Chronicle of Higher Education,* May 21, 1986

20. Epstein, Joseph, "A Case of Academic Freedom," *Commentary,* September 1986, pp. 37–47

21. *Daily Northwestern,* May 28, 1987

22. Epstein, Joseph, *op. cit.*

23. Ibid.

24. Ibid.

25. "Marxist Northwestern professor finds open protest leads to closed door," *Chicago Tribune,* April 26, 1987

26. Epstein, *op. cit.*

27. *Daily Northwestern,* March 4, 1987

28. Epstein, Joseph, *op. cit.*

29. Epstein, Joseph, *op. cit.*

30. *The Chronicle of Higher Education,* February 18, 1987

31. Foley, Barbara, *Telling the Truth,* Cornell University Press, 1985

32. Ibid.

33. *The Chronicle of Higher Education,* February 18, 1987

34. *Daily Northwestern,* September 19, 1986

35. *The Chronicle of Higher Education,* February 18, 1987

36. *Daily Northwestern,* September 19, 1986

37. *The Chronicle of Higher Education,* February 18, 1987

38. Ibid.

39. "Professor's Ouster Stirs Academic Freedom Issue," *The New York Times,* April 5, 1987

40. Ibid.

41. *Daily Northwestern*, October 28, 1986

42. *Daily Northwestern*, January 16, 1987

43. *Daily Northwestern*, January 21, 1987

44. "Northwestern U. Upholds Denial of Tenure to Faculty Member Who Disrupted Speech," *The Chronicle of Higher Education*, March 4, 1987

45. *The Chicago Tribune*, April 26, 1987

46. Ibid.

47. *Daily Northwestern*, March 4, 1987

48. *Daily Northwestern*, May 28, 1987

49. Ibid.

50. Ibid.

Sidebar: Hands Off the "Hands on" Professor

1. *The Chronicle of Higher Education*, February 12, 1986

2. Abbott, Isabel, "Sexual Harassment: A Fact of Campus Life Too Long Ignored or Tolerated," *Change*, September 1984

3. Parker, Eric, "Extracurricular Harassment," *Isthmus*, November 21–27, 1986

4. Ibid.

5. Sykes, Jay G., "The Sorcerers and the 7½ Hour Week," *Milwaukee Magazine*, October 1985

Chapter 10: The Deformation

1. Dugger, Ronnie, *op. cit.*, p. 173

2. Quoted in Dugger, Ronnie, *op. cit.*, p. 178

3. *Education at Berkeley*, University of California Academic Senate, 1966

4. Ibid.

5. Ibid.

6. "Academic Planning for 1986–90," Report of the Committee on Academic Planning, Office of the Academic Senate, June 17, 1986, p. 45

7. Ibid., p. 28

8. "Lower Division Education in the University of California," University of California Task Force Report, June 1986, p. 10

9. "Academic Planning for 1986–90," *op. cit.*, p. 44

10. "Lower Division Education in the University of California," *op. cit.*, p. 11

11. "Academic Planning for 1986–90," *op. cit.*, p. 45
12. "Lower Division Education in the University of California," *op. cit.*, p. 13
13. Ibid., p. 19
14. *The Los Angeles Times*, October 1, 1984
15. Ibid.
16. *Education at Berkeley, op. cit.*
17. Cited in *Academics in Retreat*, by Fashing, Joseph, and Deutsch, Steven, Albuquerque, University of New Mexico Press, 1971, p. 17
18. *Daily Californian*, January 5, 1987
19. "Academic Planning for 1986–90," *op. cit.*, p. 5
20. "Teaching at Berkeley," Council on Educational Development, Spring 1983
21. Loftus, David J., *The Unofficial Book of Harvard Trivia*, Boston, Quinlan Press, 1985, p. 37
22. Ibid., p. 36
23. Ibid., p. 34
24. Engel, Peter, "Harvard's Soft Core," *The Washington Monthly*, January 1980
25. *The Confidential Guide 1987–88*, p. 11
26. Keller, Phyllis, *Getting at the Core*, Cambridge, Harvard University Press, 1982, p. 3
27. Ibid.
28. Ibid.
29. Committee on the Objectives of a General Education in a Free Society, *General Education in a Free Society: Report of the Harvard Committee*, Cambridge, Harvard University Press, 1945
30. Lynn, Kenneth, "Son of 'Gen Ed,'" *Commentary,* September 1978
31. Ibid.
32. Keller, Phyllis, *op. cit.*, p. 16
33. Ibid., p. 18
34. Lynn, Kenneth, *op. cit.*
35. Keller, Phyllis, *op. cit.*, p. 18
36. Keller, Phyllis, *op. cit.*, p. 39
37. Keller, Phyllis, *op. cit.*, p. 29
38. Bok, Derek, *Higher Learning*, Cambridge, Harvard University Press, 1986, p. 36
39. Ibid.

40. Hutchins, Robert Maynard, *The Higher Learning in America*, New Haven, Yale University Press, 1936, p. 70

41. Hutchins, Robert Maynard, *No Friendly Voice*, Chicago, University of Chicago Press, 1936, p. 38

42. Keller, Phyllis, *op. cit.*, pp. 34–35

43. Keller, Phyllis, *op. cit.*, p. 38

44. Ibid., p. 135

45. Engel, Peter, *op. cit.*

46. Harvard Courses of Instruction, 1986–87, Faculty of Arts and Sciences, p. 1

47. Keller, Phyllis, *op. cit.*, pp. 79–80

48. Engel, Peter, *op. cit.*

49. Ibid.

50. *Time*, September 8, 1986

51. Levin, Harry, "Core, Canon, Curriculum," *College English*, April 1981

52. Engel, Peter, *op. cit.*

53. Engel, Peter, *op. cit.*

54. Text of speech reprinted in *The Chronicle of Higher Education*, October 15, 1986

55. *The Confidential Guide 1987–88*, p. 11

56. Rowe, Gary, *The Harvard Crimson*, December 1986

57. Mann, Lawrence, "Challenges and Opportunities: Observations on Undergraduate Education at the University of Illinois at Urbana-Champaign," Fall 1985, p. 34

58. Report of the All-University Committee on Undergraduate Education (Hilton Committee), 1962

59. Mann, Lawrence, *op. cit.*, p. 53

60. Mann, Lawrence, *op. cit.*, p. 4

61. Interview with author, September 10, 1987

62. Ibid.

63. Ibid.

64. Ibid.

65. Ibid.

66. *Daily Illini*, February 10, 1986

67. Interview with author, September 9, 1987

68. Ibid.

69. Ibid.

Chapter 11: The Abolition of Man

1. Lackey, Kris, "Amongst the Awful Subtexts: Scholes, The *Daily Planet*, and Freshman Composition," *College Composition and Communication*, February 1987

2. Lackey, Kris, *op. cit.*

3. Lackey, Kris, *op. cit.*

4. Bennett, William J., *To Reclaim a Legacy*, Washington, D.C., National Endowment for the Humanities, November 1984, p. 2

5. Ibid.

6. Ibid., p. 3

7. Winkler, Karen J., "Post-Structuralism: An Often-Abstruse French Import Profoundly Affects Research in the United States," *The Chronicle of Higher Education*, November 25, 1987

8. Krieger, Murray, "Theory, Criticism, and the Literary Text," *Academe*, March-April 1984

9. Winkler, Karen, *op. cit.*

10. Ibid.

11. Interview with author

12. Nehemas, Alexander, "Truth and Consequences: How to Understand Jacques Derrida," *The New Republic*, October 5, 1987

13. Ibid.

14. Cited in Alcorn, Marshall, Jr., "Rhetoric, Projection, and the Authority of the Signifier," *College English*, February 1987

15. Wellek, Rene, "Destroying Literary Studies," *The New Criterion*, December 1983

16. Alcorn, Marshall, Jr., *op. cit.*

17. Ibid.

18. Kramer, Hilton, "The MLA Centennial Follies," *The New Criterion*, February 1984

19. "Literary Masters and Masturbators: Sexuality, Fantasy, and Reality in *Huckleberry Finn*," *Literature and Psychology*, No. 2, 1978

20. Poster in Classics Department of University of Michigan, September 1987

21. Loving, Jerome, "Dickinson's Deconstruction in the Eighties," *ESQ, A Journal of the American Renaissance*, 3rd Quarter 1986

22. Frantzen, Allen and Venegoni, Charles, "The Desire for Origins: An Archeology of Anglo-Saxon Studies," *Style*, Summer 1986

23. *The Brown Daily Herald*, January 30, 1986

24. Ibid.

25. Brown Course Announcement, 1987–88

26. Ibid.

27. Brown Catalogue of the University for the Years 1985–87

28. *The Brown Daily Herald*, February 6, 1987

29. Ibid.

30. Brown Course Announcement, 1987–88

31. *The Harvard Crimson*, March 7, 1987

32. "Ideological Productions in the Food Service Industry," *Dissertation Abstracts International*, April 1986, 3171–A

33. *The New York Times*, January 6, 1988

34. Scholes, Robert, "Aiming a Canon at the Curriculum," *Salmagundi*, Fall 1986

35. Hirsch, E. D., Jr., " 'Cultural Literacy' Does Not Mean 'Canon,' " *Salmagundi*, Fall 1986

36. Gould, Christopher, "Literature in the Basic Writing Course," *College English*, September 1987

37. Ibid.

38. Heller, Scott, "A Constellation of Recently Hired Professors Illuminates the English Department at Duke," *The Chronicle of Higher Education*, May 27, 1987

39. Alcorn, Marshall, Jr., *op. cit.*

40. Quoted in Balch, Stephen and London, Herbert, "The Tenured Left," *Commentary*, October 1986

41. Jameson, Frederic and Kavanagh, James, "The Weakest Link: Marxism in Literary Studies," *The Left Academy II*, ed. Ollman, Bertell, New York, Praeger, 1984

42. Heller, Scott, *op. cit.*

43. Ibid.

44. Ibid.

45. Ibid.

46. Interview with author, November 1987

47. Ibid.

48. Ibid.

49. Ibid.

50. Anderson, Philip, "Astrophobe and Stellae: An Open Letter to the Duke English Department," unpublished

51. Wellek, Rene, *op. cit.*

52. Rhodes, Frank H. T., ". . . Or What's a College For?" Source: Cornell University

53. Kramer, Hilton, *op. cit.*

54. Rosmarin, Adena, "Hermeneutics versus Erotics: Shakespeare's Sonnets and Interpretive History," *PMLA*, January 1985

55. Smith, John H., "Dialogic Midwifery in Kleist's *Marquise von O* and the Hermeneutics of Telling the Untold in Kant and Plato," *PMLA*, March 1985

56. Alcorn, Marshall W., Jr., and Bracher, Mark, "Literature, Psychoanalysis, and the Re-Formation of the Self: A New Direction for Reader-Response Theory," *PMLA*, May 1985

57. Kramer, Hilton, *op. cit.*

58. Cohn, Robert Greer, "Derrida at Yale," *The New Criterion*, May 1986

59. Perloff, Marjorie, "An Intellectual Impasse," *Salmagundi*, Fall 1986

60. Campbell, Colin, "The Tyranny of the Yale Critics," *The New York Times Magazine*, February 9, 1986

61. Interview with author

62. Anderson, Philip, Letter to author, November 3, 1987

63. Interview with author

64. Ibid.

Sidebar: An Ode to Deconstructionism

1. This poem first appeared in *The Chronicle of Higher Education*, October 14, 1987. Reprinted with permission of Philip Anderson

Chapter 12: The Pseudo-scientists

1. Various sources: *The New York Times*, *The Chronicle of Higher Education*, *The Harvard Crimson*, and *Science*

2. Huntington, Samuel P., and Betts, Richard K., "Dead Dictators and Rioting Mobs," *International Security*, Winter 1985–86

3. Huntington, Samuel, *Political Order in Changing Societies*, New Haven, Yale University Press, 1968

4. Recommendation of Class V, National Academy Of Sciences, 1986, cited by Serge Lang in April 10, 1986, letter to NAS membership

5. Cited in Lipset, Seymour Martin and Riesman, David, *Education and Politics at Harvard*, New York, McGraw-Hill, 1975, pp. 222–3

6. Dahl, Robert, "Political Theory: Truth and Consequences," *World Politics*, (October 1958)

7. Mitchell, Richard, *The Graves of Academe*, New York, Simon & Schuster, 1981, p. 43

8. Ricci, David, *The Tragedy of Political Science*, New Haven, Yale University Press, 1984, p. 222

9. Andreski, Stanislav, *Social Sciences as Sorcery*, New York, St. Martin's Press, 1972, pp. 126–7

10. Gregor, A. James, *An Introduction to Metapolitics*, New York, Free Press, 1971, p. 3

11. Andreski, Stanislav, *op. cit.*, p. 111

12. Hoos, Ida, *Systems Analysis in Public Policy: A Critique*, Berkeley, University of California Press, 1983, p. 37

13. Ricci, David, *op. cit.*, p. 224

14. *The Confidential Guide, 1986–87*, p. 90

15. *The Confidential Guide, 1981–82*, p. 115

16. Huntington, Samuel, "The Change to Change," *Comparative Politics*, April 1971

17. Huntington, Samuel, *op. cit.*, p. 55

18. Koblitz, Neal, "Mathematics as Propaganda," *Mathematics Tomorrow*, 1981

19. Interview with author, November 1987

20. Koblitz, Neal, *op. cit.*

21. Lang, Serge, *The Beauty of Doing Mathematics*, New York, Springer-Verlag, 1985

22. Crawford, Bryce, Home Secretary, NAS, Letter to Serge Lang, March 17, 1986

23. Lang, Serge, Letter to Bryce Crawford, Home Secretary of NAS, March 26, 1986

24. Wolpert, Julian, Letter to Serge Lang, March 26, 1986

25. Lang, Serge, Letter to NAS Members, April 10, 1986

26. Lang, Serge, *The File*, New York, Springer-Verlag, 1981

27. Lang, Serge, "A Recent Non-Election to the National Academy of Sciences," unpublished manuscript, August 17, 1987

28. Huntington, Samuel, *op. cit.*

29. Lang, Serge, "A Recent Non-Election," *op. cit.*

30. Interview with author, December 1987

31. Lang, Serge, "On a Recent Non-Election," *op. cit.*

32. *The Chronicle of Higher Education*, April 1, 1987

33. Marshall, Eliot, "Academy Membership Fight Goes Public," *Science*, December 5, 1986

34. *The New York Times*, April 29, 1987

35. Interview with author, December 1987

36. *The New York Times*, April 29, 1987

37. Simon, Herbert, "Some Trivial but Useful Mathematics," unpublished manuscript

38. Ibid.

39. Lang, Serge, "On a Recent Non-election," *op. cit.*

40. Koblitz, Neal, "A Tale of Three Equations; Or the Emperors Have No Clothes," manuscript, August 1987

41. Interview with author, February 1988

42. Stone, Jeremy, Letter to Samuel Huntington, August 10, 1987

43. Ibid.

44. Zakaria, Fareed, "Blood Lust in Academia," *The New Republic*, July 27, 1987

45. Feierabend, Ivo and Rosalind, "Aggressive Behaviors within Polities, 1948–1962: A Cross-National Study," *The Journal of Conflict Resolution*, September 1966

46. Ibid.

47. Lang, Serge, "On a Recent Non-Election," *op. cit.*

48. Ibid.

49. Zakaria, Fareed, *op. cit.*

50. Lang, Serge, "A Journalist and Some Political Scientists (so-called) Meet Reality," manuscript, August 7, 1987

51. *The Chronicle of Higher Education*, February 3, 1988

52. *Yale Daily News*, December 16, 1987

53. Press, Frank, president of the NAS, letter to members of the National Academy of Sciences, March 8, 1988

54. "Evening in America," *The New Republic*, February 1, 1988

55. Etzione-Halevy, Eva, *The Knowledge Elite and the Failure of Prophecy*, London, George Allen & Unwin, 1985, p. 5

56. Ibid., p. 44

57. Ibid., p. 67

58. Andreski, Stanislav, *op. cit.*, p. 129

59. Ibid., pp. 24–25

60. Etzione-Halevy, Eva, *op. cit.*, p. 80

61. Barker, G., "The Poverty of Economics," *The Age*, November 20, 1982

62. Katz, H. S., *The Paper Aristocracy*, New York, Books in Focus, 1976, p. 62

63. McGee, Reece and Vaughan, Charlotte and Baker, Paul, "Introductory Instruction for a Discipline in Decline," *Teaching Sociology*, October 1985

64. Ibid.

Sidebar: Cliometrics

1. *The New York Times*, October 6, 1987

2. Interview with author, November 1987

3. Haskell, Thomas L., *New York Review of Books*, October 2, 1985

4. *The New York Times*, January 9, 1988

5. Quoted in Ravitch, Diane, "Decline and Fall of Teaching History," *The New York Times*, November 17, 1985

Chapter 13: Beyond the Dreams of Avarice

1. *The New York Times*, March 28, 1986

2. *The New York Times*, July 19, 1987

3. *The Chronicle of Higher Education*, October 29, 1986

4. *The Chronicle of Higher Education*, July 15, 1987

5. Ibid.

6. *The Confidential Guide*, 1981–82, pp. 14–15

7. Testimony at a hearing of the House Subcommittee on Science, Research, and Technology, printed in *The Chronicle of Higher Education*, April 1, 1987

8. Dugger, Ronnie, *Our Invaded Universities*, New York, W. W. Norton, 1974, pp. 160–161

9. Ibid., p. 163

10. Ibid., p. 165

11. Ibid., p. 166

12. Cited by Noble, David F. and Pfund, Nancy, "Business Goes Back to College," *The Nation*, September 20, 1980

13. Kenney, Martin, *Biotechnology: The University-Industrial Complex*, New Haven, Yale University Press, 1986, p. 93

14. Ibid., p. 92

15. *The Wall Street Journal*, August 27, 1985

16. *The Wall Street Journal*, November 24, 1980

17. Fox, Jeffrey, "Can Academia Adapt to Biotechnology's Lure," *Chemical and Engineering News*, October 12, 1981

18. Rosenberg, R., "Patent or Perish," *Genetic Engineering News*, January/February 1981

19. Culliton, Barbara, "The Academic-Industrial Complex," *Science*, May 28, 1982

20. *The Wall Street Journal*, May 4, 1981

21. *The Wall Street Journal*, August 27, 1985

22. *The Chronicle of Higher Education*, July 29, 1987

23. *The Wall Street Journal*, May 4, 1981

24. Cited in Kenney, Martin, *op cit.*, pp. 109–110

25. Dugger, Ronnie, *op. cit.*, p. 161

26. Ibid., pp. 161–162

27. *The New York Times*, December 14, 1987

28. *The Chronicle of Higher Education*, July 29, 1987

29. Muniak, Dennis, "State Governments, Public Universities, and the Promotion of High Technology: A Lost Opportunity for Strategic Development Planning," paper prepared for delivery at the American Political Science Association, Chicago, September 3–6, 1987

30. Kenney, Martin, *op. cit.*, pp. 58–59

31. Ibid., p. 58

32. *Business Week*, June 23, 1986

33. Kenney, Martin, *op. cit.*, p. 67

34. *Business Week*, June 23, 1986

35. *St. Louis Post-Dispatch*, January 8, 1986

36. Kenney, Martin, *op. cit.*, p. 131

37. Ibid., p. 121

38. Stettin, D., Jr., "Recombinant Molecules: Anxieties and Hazards," in *Proceedings of the 1981 Battelle International Conference on Genetic Engineering*, Vol. 1, held in Rosslyn, Virginia, June 6–10, 1981

39. Fox, Jeffrey, *op. cit.*

40. Biddle, Wayne, "Corporations on Campus," *Science*, July 24, 1987

41. Kenney, Martin, *op. cit.*, p. 112

42. Biddle, Wayne, *op. cit.*

43. Parajo Dunes Biotechnology Conference Statement, reprinted in *Tech Talk*, April 7, 1982

44. *The Chronicle of Higher Education*, November 18, 1987

45. Kenney, Martin, *op. cit.*, p. 246

Chapter 14: Fraud

1. Sprague, Robert L., "I Trusted the Research System," *The Scientist*, December 14, 1987

2. Greenberg, Daniel, "Publish or Perish—Or Fake It," *U.S. News & World Report*, June 8, 1987, and *The Chronicle of Higher Education*, June 3, 1987

3. Sprague, Robert L., *op. cit.*

4. Ibid.

5. Greenberg, Daniel, *op. cit.*

6. Sprague, Robert, *op. cit.*

7. *The Chronicle of Higher Education*, June 3, 1987

8. Sprague, Robert, *op. cit.*

9. *The Chronicle of Higher Education*, June 3, 1987

10. Greenberg, Daniel, *op. cit.* and *The Chronicle of Higher Education*, June 3, 1987

11. Sprague, Robert, *op. cit.*

12. Ibid.

13. Greenberg, Daniel, *op. cit.*

14. Ibid.

15. *The New York Times*, October 10, 1986

16. "Tempests in a Test Tube," *Newsweek*, February 2, 1987

17. *The Boston Globe*, January 15, 1987

18. *The Chronicle of Higher Education*, December 3, 1986

19. *The New York Times*, July 18, 1987

20. *The New York Times*, July 21, 1987

21. Stewart, Walter and Feder, Ned, "We Must Deal Realistically with Fraud and Error," *The Scientist*, December 14, 1987

22. Koshland, Daniel E., Jr., "Fraud in Science," *Science*, January 9, 1987

23. *The Chronicle of Higher Education*, September 9, 1987

24. Culliton, Barbara, "Integrity of Research Papers Questioned," *Science*, January 23, 1987

25. Stewart, Walter, Sworn affidavit, on file in the United States District Court for the Western District of Wisconsin

26. Stewart, Walter and Feder, Ned, "The Integrity of the Scientific Literature," *Nature*, January 15, 1987

27. Culliton, Barbara, *op. cit.*

28. Stewart, Walter and Feder Ned, Statement for the Subcommittee on Civil and Consititutional Rights of the Committee on the Judiciary, U.S. House of Representatives, February 26, 1986

29. Stewart, Walter and Feder, Ned, *Nature, op. cit.*

30. Stewart, Walter and Feder, Ned, *The Boston Globe*, November 30, 1986

31. Stewart, Walter and Feder, Ned, Congressional Statement, *op. cit.*

32. "Fraud, Libel and the Literature," *Nature*, January 15, 1987

33. Rensberger, Boyce, "Fraud, Laxity in Research Are Detailed," *The Washington Post*, January 27, 1987

34. Stewart, Walter and Feder, Ned, *The Boston Globe, op. cit.*

35. Stewart, Walter and Feder, Ned, *Nature, op. cit.*

36. Powledge, Tabitha, "Stewart-Feder (Finally) in Print," *The Scientist*, February 9, 1987

37. *The New York Times*, March 4, 1988

38. Greenberg, Daniel, "Want a Career in Science? Don't Blow the Whistle," *The Washington Post*, May 18, 1986 and Stewart, Walter, Interview with author, September 1987

39. Interview with author, September 1987

Sidebar: **The Fate of Critics**

1. Interview with author, May 1987

2. *The Chronicle of Higher Education*, October 14, 1987

3. "Dartmouth Teaches . . . Censorship," *The Wall Street Journal*, March 8, 1988

4. Interview with author, June 24, 1988

5. Raspberry, William, "The Beautification of Dartmouth, Phase II," *The Washington Post*, March 7, 1988

6. Interview with Laura Ingraham, June 24, 1988

7. Interview with author, June 24, 1988

8. "Blackmail," *National Review,* April 1, 1988

9. "Dartmouth Teaches . . . Censorship," op. cit.

10. "Four college journalists suspended for harassment," *Editor & Publisher,* March 19, 1988

11. "Blackmail," op. cit.

12. "Dartmouth Teaches . . . Censorship," op. cit.

13. Ibid.

14. Ibid.

15. "The Joys of Hypocrisy," *The Wall Street Journal,* April 4, 1988

16. Interview with Debbie Stone, June 24, 1988

17. "The Joys of Hypocrisy," op. cit.

Index